KT-150-963

KNOWING THE SCORE

KNOWING THE SCORE

My Family and Our Tennis Story

Judy Murray

With Alexandra Heminsley

Chatto & Windus

LONDON

1 3 5 7 9 10 8 6 4 2

Chatto & Windus, an imprint of Vintage,
20 Vauxhall Bridge Road,
London SW1V 2SA

Chatto & Windus is part of the Penguin Random House group of companies
whose addresses can be found at global.penguinrandomhouse.com.

Penguin
Random House
UK

Copyright © GETSET2PLAY LIMITED 2017

GETSET2PLAY LIMITED has asserted its right to be identified as the author of this
Work in accordance with the Copyright, Designs and Patents Act 1988

First published by Chatto & Windus in 2017

www.vintage-books.co.uk

A CIP catalogue record for this book is available from the British Library

Hardback ISBN 9781784741792
Trade paperback ISBN 9781784741808

Typeset in 12/17.25 pt Minion Pro by Jouve (UK), Milton Keynes
Printed and bound in Great Britain by Clays Ltd, St Ives PLC

Penguin Random House is committed to a sustainable future for
our business, our readers and our planet. This book is made from
Forest Stewardship Council® certified paper.

To my mum and dad for instilling in me good values,
a love of sport, and a sense of community

Contents

CONTENTS

Illustrations

Unless otherwise stated, all pictures come from the author's family collection.

First picture section

1: As a baby with my mother, Dunblane, 1960.
2: With my father learning to ski in Aviemore, aged six; climbing a tree on a family walk; and sledging with my mother and brothers.
3: Aged fourteen with various tennis trophies; Scottish Grass Court Championships final, 1981.
4: Jamie aged fifteen months and Andy only a few days old; Jamie in the garden aged eighteen months old; family photograph.
5: The boys playing football; and with their toddler wheels.
6: As Scottish National Coach; at Gleneagles coaching in the Virginia Wade tennis clinic, 1989; LTA coach of the year Award, 2001; the Dunblane Primary School team in 1994, Jamie and Andy are in the middle of the front row.

7: Andy and Abbie, his puppy, in 1997; Jamie, aged twelve, playing in the Orange Bowl Championships in 1998; Jamie and Tom Burn winning the British Under 18 Doubles Championship in 2003.

8: Andy the Junior US Open champion, in 2004 (Getty Images).

Second picture section

1: Jamie and Jelena Jankovic win mixed doubles at Wimbledon in 2007 (Getty Images).

2: Andy loses to Roger Federer in the 2012 Wimbledon final; Andy beats Federer at the London Olympics, held at Wimbledon, to win gold; the Adidas photobooth at the Olympics; Andy wins the US Open 2012 (all Getty Images).

3: Watching the 2013 Wimbledon final; Andy beats Novak Djokovic in the 2013 Wimbledon Men's Singles Final (Getty Images).

4: Me and Leon Smith, GB Fed Cup and Davis Cup captains, running a kid's training session in Scotland in 2015; the Fed Cup team in 2013: Anne Keothavong, Laura Robson, Johanna Konta and Elena Baltacha (Getty Images).

5: Fed Cup team 2015: Anna Smith, Johanna Konta, Heather Watson and Jocelyn Rae; Jamie and Andy playing doubles in the winning 2015 GB Davis Cup team (both Getty Images).

6: The Tennis on the Road van; a Miss-Hits gathering.

7: Jamie and Bruno Soares win the Australian Open 2016; watching the boys claim their number 1 spots in singles and doubles in December 2016 at the ATP Master's Final (both Getty Images).

8: The Murray family is presented with the Outstanding Contribution to Sport award at the Sports Industry Awards, 2016 (Getty Images).

Acknowledgements

To Alex Heminsley for persuading me I had a story to share and then writing it for me.

To Juliet and her girl gang at Chatto for believing in that story and for letting me into their fun, booky world.

To Sarah, Caroline, Jan, Elizabeth and Raffaella at IMG/WME for guiding me through this new experience and for always having my back.

To Laura, Val and El my oldest friends who have managed to keep me sane through all the years of tennis madness.

To Leon Smith, my third son (not literally), who played such a crucial role in Jamie and Andy's formative years.

And finally to my boys, for continuing to inspire me with their capacity to work hard and achieve ridiculous levels of success against all the odds. But mostly for staying grounded and humble in spite of everything.

Introduction

I t was the day I put the tennis balls into the tumble dryer that I realised I thought about tennis a little bit differently. I had started coaching some local kids in Dunblane, and it was – to put it mildly – a shoestring operation. Tennis balls are expensive, and I had barely any money. I wasn't working as my boys were just toddlers, and when I was coaching I didn't charge; I just asked the parents of the kids I was teaching to wheel Jamie and Andy round the duck pond near the tennis courts in their buggy. Those tennis balls were precious, and they were getting trashed.

The town had just four courts, all outdoors, and it was almost always either freezing cold, blowing a gale, or pouring with rain. When artificial grass gets wet, it behaves like a carpet: it becomes totally sodden. Even when it stopped raining the sun was rarely strong enough to dry the court out properly, so the rainwater would be absorbed by the tennis balls, the balls would get heavier and heavier, and before long the kids could barely hit them. And to make matters worse, the balls began to stink. I knew if I couldn't find a solution to freezing cold tennis with pungent soggy balls, the children of Dunblane would just find another sport and there would be even less tennis in my home town.

At first, I tried putting the balls on the radiators at home, but that made the entire house smell of damp. Then I tried the tumble dryer. Results were mixed the first time: the sand that had come off the court with the rainwater clogged up the machine, and the rubber seals around the felt of the balls started to heat up, bubble and lift off. There was also the noise: twenty tennis balls rattling around a tumble dryer does not help a rowdy toddler take a lunchtime nap. Finally, I realised that if I put the tennis balls into an old cloth bag that had come with a pair of boots a while back, the plan would work. The fabric kept most of the sand at bay, and the bag kept the balls closer together in the machine. The balls lived on, and so did tennis in Dunblane.

Tricks like these ended up becoming something of a speciality: adapting to get as much tennis played regardless of the facilities – and the weather – making the best of what we had to hand, prioritising having fun with the kids over having the best kit. And I didn't mind a bit. As I pressed 'power' on the dryer that first time and quietly congratulated myself on nailing the art of tennis-ball maintenance, I truly believed, in that moment, that anything was possible – the sky was the limit! It's just that when you tell yourself that, you don't actually expect that feeling to last . . . let alone come true.

1

The power of parents, or how I learned to love competition

In which I learn about the game in the simplest yet most effective way possible – by witnessing my parents' enthusiasm for tennis . . . particularly winning tennis.

Tennis didn't start with the coaching, the boys or the tumble dryer; it had always been there. My mum and dad were big players, and had been very involved at that very same Dunblane Tennis Club since we moved to the town when I was about five. There were four blaes courts – an early, less luxurious version of clay – and a cute little wooden pavilion at the club. It seemed enormous then, but now it doesn't even exist, replaced by the slicker facilities at the new and improved Dunblanc Sports Club.

My earliest memories are that they – and by default we, my brothers and I – were almost always down at the tennis club. My mum and her best friend ran the kids coaching sessions on Saturday mornings, and they both played competitively for the adult team, too. At first, I hated having to spend so much time down there, but only because I was too small to play. Aged five, I was too short and too slight to wield an adult racket, and children's ones were years away from being invented, let alone making it to Dunblane. And the courts seemed enormous, a bigger space than I ever could have covered, and that shale surface was agony to fall on and made your trainers dirty.

So I'd hang around, looking after my two younger brothers and longing to be allowed a piece of the action. I was supposed to be keeping an eye on the boys, but they preferred kicking balls around, feeding the ducks or climbing trees. What I was really doing was watching the adults and the older kids from my spot on the grass, peering eternally through the green diamond mesh of the fencing. Everyone seemed to be having a blast, regardless of the cold or the rain. The frustration was immense – to see the fun but not be able to take part. Frankly, it was agony. A pain only mildly alleviated by playing badminton over the washing line with my brothers when we got home.

At home, the tennis theme continued. My mum, especially, was a huge fan. During Wimbledon fortnight we couldn't watch anything else on the TV, and to be honest we barely got fed. It was just Wimbledon on the telly all day long, punctuated by cold food – a bit of salad or something from the back of the fridge perhaps. At first, it was a real shock to the system as my mum is a great cook, but after a few years we accepted it as standard procedure. Dad would always be home from work bang on 6 p.m. to catch as much of the tennis as possible. They'd discuss the day's play as if nothing else mattered, and we just rolled with it. It was Wimbledon.

We didn't care, though; it was intoxicating to see Mum and Dad so excited about something to the point where normal rules fizzled away, and in the end we started to absorb the excitement, too. There wasn't anything else to watch, so over time the rules and the scoring system started to make sense, the patterns began to slot together as the match took shape and we caught Wimbledon fever along with them. My mum, ever the armchair tactician, would explain the various shots to me, pointing out how one player was beating another and why, and talking about what she would do in that situation. Many years later I would realise she had no idea what she was talking about! And as the finals rolled round, there was no question of us doing anything else. Wimbledon would be on, my mum would be gasping, clapping and commentating, and the channel wouldn't be changed until someone was lifting the trophy.

Eventually, early one summer, the day came. I was allowed to have a shot. My mum gently showed me how to swing the racket – her way too big and way too heavy racket – but I had been watching for so long I was like a coiled spring ready to go. My dad chipped in with the teaching, too, and before long I was given the chance to have a first racket of my own. I was at home, half-heartedly playing in the garden with my brothers when my dad came home with two rackets to choose from. He sat me on the sofa and showed them both to me carefully, showcasing them like an expert holding precious artefacts in a museum. I'd like to think he had painstakingly whittled down a multitude of choices available to just these two, and selected them especially for me, but I knew the reality: one was from the sports shop in the next village and the other was from Woolworths. These were the only two junior rackets in town.

I can remember them both so clearly, it was as if I were choosing my first pet. The one from the sports shop was a Junior Dunlop Maxply. The Maxply was quite a famous racket at the time, and this was the junior version, slightly lighter and a little shorter, although not a mini size. It must have cost my dad about £11! And the

Woolworths' one, well, it was a pale imitation. It had cheap, two-tone flecked strings and felt flimsy even to me, a ten-year-old. I knew it cost only about a quid, and I knew that my dad would have loved me to choose it. I did *think* about it, and I even felt really guilty about wanting the Dunlop, but . . . not quite guilty enough. I wanted the proper one. I wanted to play. I told the truth. The Dunlop Maxply was mine and I cherished it like a beloved toy.

Once I had a racket to call my own, there was no stopping me. I didn't have anyone to play with at home as my brothers were still too little, so I would spend hours hitting the wall on the side of our house. It was hard to find a space with no windows, so I made do with the strip of brick – covered in harling – between the metal door of our garage and the building's edge. It was a tiny narrow strip though, as the huge square door took up most of the space. This meant that every good shot knocked the little stone chips off the wall and every duff shot brought a deafening clang as the metal reverberated against the tennis ball, shortly followed by the front door opening and my mum running out to yell, 'Stop hitting the ruddy door!' She just wanted the occasional bit of peace and quiet – but the end result was a good one: I got pretty accurate, pretty fast.

It was at that wall that I started to forge my own little space in family life. If I was practising, I didn't have to look after my brothers; I could do my own thing. And if I got better I could play with Mum and Dad, and eventually the other kids at the tennis club.

Back then there weren't really any official tennis coaches in Scotland. There were no indoor courts in the whole country, so no one could coach for a living as it could only ever be a seasonal thing – it was mad to think you could get a full-time job out of it! In the winter we'd go indoors and play badminton, then as summer came round again the activity in the clubs was entirely driven by volunteers. Sure, there were people who would help you to learn and there were always adults around who wanted to share the game – but as for coaches, no way.

This meant that I learned the game through a combination of semi-enforced Wimbledon-watching, my mum and dad teaching me, and trying to avoid that garage door. And in time, I got quite good. My dad was the better player, and he was the one I was most like in character. He has a huge love of strategy, a real sense of mischief and is a fierce competitor and a bad loser. He loved to plan ahead in a game – to work out his opponent's strategy and what they would struggle to return. And then he loved to try and trick them with his flashy shots. He thinks he invented topspin – he honestly believes he was playing that shot before Björn Borg was – and he loved a slice or a drop shot when you were least expecting it. He liked to make it hard for his opponent, even if that opponent was his pre-teen daughter.

Learning from someone with a wicked sense of competitiveness taught me well and taught me fast. He was completely unashamed about wanting to make winning as hard as possible for me, and that in turn gave me the freedom to be completely unashamed about wanting to beat him back. Ambition was – and still is – nothing to apologise for.

Thirst to win aside, he was far from a pushy father – a sense of mischief and fun ran through every activity, whether it was tennis with me, football in the garden with my brothers or family French cricket on a rare sunny summer's day. We were all treated the same, all considered as free as each other to have a go at everything. There was no question that I should sit out just because I was a girl. All three of us found it frustrating playing any sport with him as he always seemed to win, and *genuinely* didn't want to get beaten by his kids. It was only years later, as adults, that we realised he had been making up the rules of whatever game we were playing on any given day . . . to his benefit! Hilarious now, but it certainly was perplexing back then.

His sense of competitiveness wasn't entirely unexpected though. He had been a professional football player before I was born, in so far as you could be a 'professional' player in the early 1950s. Payment was £1 per game, which the teams had to queue up outside the manager's office after matches to collect, and all training and playing took place outside normal working hours as the players still worked their regular 9 to 5 jobs. Still, there wasn't much need for excessive training as the ground was twenty-five miles from my dad's house back then – a distance he cycled every time. Car ownership for families like ours was rare, so his bike was his daily transport.

There was no money, and no potential for big money in sport in those days, so his experience then was radically different from that of the boys now. It was enthusiasm and camaraderie that drove teams, rather than the lust for big cash you see in some parents' eyes these days when they realise they may have a talented child on their hands. My sons adore hearing about the pure love of the game that the players had back then; it's gold dust to them when Dad starts to tell tales of the old days at Christmas or family events. He played for a number of Scottish clubs, including Hibernian, but it may as well have been a different world. Apart from the thirst to win, that is . . .

My mum was the total opposite – an excellent sofa strategist and a woman with a warmth that she couldn't contain on the tennis court, the sort of player who will say 'Good shot!' to her opponent without hesitation. My dad made no secret of thinking this was clearly a bad idea, and I agreed. I learned never to compliment an opponent while playing. Why would you want them to know what you found difficult? It would only encourage them to do it again. Mum didn't seem to care a jot if she lost, she'd simply enjoyed a lovely afternoon's tennis. I couldn't understand that mentality at all.

Dad could make tennis hard for me. He had so much variety in his game that he could change the pace, spin, height, depth and direction of his shots without a second thought. Even when I was still learning the basics, I grasped that if I tried hard enough to copy him I could make it tough for him, too. I learned the shape of the shots. I practised the shots against the wall and, before too long, I could return a sneaky lob, I could make him run, I could hit with back spin and I could – occasionally – win a point. And that, well *that* opened the doors to a whole new world of fun.

I played my first competition when I was eleven, about a year after getting that starter racket. It was just a local thing, organised via the Dunblane Tennis Club, but before long I went to what was called a 'district sift', which I suppose would be called a 'talent ID day' now. The clubs in the local area sent their best juniors up to a central venue to see a national coach (part-time of course) who would assess them. A couple of other Dunblane kids and I turned up and were given a numbered piece of card and two safety pins, to attach it to our sleeve.

It was the first time I'd felt genuinely nervous playing tennis. In one short year I had gone from longing to play to being a pretty good player, and now I was bundled in with a gang of kids from all over the district, hoping desperately that I'd catch this coach's eye. And I did! Within a few months I was sent to a 'national sift' up at the Inverclyde National Sports Centre. This was another change of pace. It was an entire weekend away from my parents, staying in what seemed like impossibly glamorous and grown-up accommodation on site. I was sharing a room with a couple of other girls, and of course we were totally overexcited by the whole experience. With almost admirable inevitability we stayed up talking, playing pranks and having midnight feasts and woke up bleary-eyed.

Adrenalin got me through: it was nothing but playing my favourite sport with kids I had never met before, with a ticker tape of drama and anticipation constantly running as we all hoped it would be *us* who would impress, *us* who would be picked. That weekend there was barely a trace of my mother in me; I was all my father's daughter.

It was thrilling when I was selected for the national squad, even though that constituted little more than the odd training weekend through the winter at Inverclyde, in a hall that doubled up for both badminton and cricket. The glamour! I was so young, only just thirteen, but I remember being totally fearless. I would head off on the train to Glasgow, change stations by walking across the city with my racket bag and carry on the journey to Largs, then walk up to the sports centre. A four-hour shift! After a winter of being able to play (albeit infrequently) for the first time, I was soon travelling all over the country to take part in matches and tournaments.

The following summer I was a pro at all this travelling: I would be put on the train to London by my mum, meet an elderly aunt at King's Cross (who had come all the way from Woodford by tube to pick me up), and stay overnight with her before heading to the other side of London the next morning for a tournament at the Queen's Club in Kensington. I had seen nearly all of London by the time I got there, and read several books. I can't imagine letting a child do that now, but it was the most relaxed of adventures back then. I had not a shred of nerves and no idea of the potential dangers. It was just one of the things about being in Scotland at that time: if you were even slightly good at something, especially a summer sport like tennis, you would outgrow the opportunities at home pretty quickly, making travel an inevitability. Having to travel was a sign of doing well and it was still that way twenty-odd years later when Jamie and Andy reached a similar stage.

The travel was exciting, and it all felt so terribly grown up, but it was the competing that I really lived for. And competing was mostly what we did – there was barely anything in the way of training. There weren't really any formal coaches, and nothing as grand as individual lessons or a fitness programme to follow: we learned to play the game by playing the game. I became a pretty good athlete – thanks to my sporty genes – and a pretty good competitor simply because I wanted to win. I worked out how to make things difficult for my opponent. I would evaluate what they could or couldn't do, and use that to my advantage. It was satisfying to try and get the measure of someone, but devastating to have them do the same to you. Whenever I lost, I'd sulk, but I'd always learn from it.

My greatest asset was having parents who were happy to play with me, apparently endlessly. And as I got better I was invited to play on the Dunblane ladies' team, alongside adults, even while I was still a junior. It didn't matter that they were perhaps not top-drawer players – they were adults with a level of experience and maturity that couldn't help but rub off on me. I was playing doubles, too, so I was having to learn how to communicate, how not to let an adult partner down by having a tantrum if things didn't go our way, how to make the space work with two people on the court, and understanding the value of being part of a team. The adults at

Dunblane were always happy to play with us kids in a way that I don't see happening so much in clubs today. Kids get talent-spotted, slotted into squads and programmed how to hit the ball but not given enough opportunities to learn how to play the game. There's too much coaching and not enough free play. We were bundled in with a mix of ages, abilities and sizes and just had to work it all out as we went along. Tennis is a thinking sport, and you need to learn to solve all sorts of problems on court. The more variety you have in competition, the better.

I played in competitions nearly every week between April and August, my poor mum picking me up from school to drive me to Glasgow or Edinburgh. With the obliviousness of youth, I had no idea what a grind this must have been for her. She had to find someone to look after my brothers, take me to the match, drive me home, say a brief 'hi' to my dad (who had assumed the brother duties after work), grab something to eat and put me to bed. I didn't even let her watch me play. She made me nervous. Seriously nervous. So she became quite adept at hiding behind trees, clubhouses or newspapers. Tennis parenting is the sort of chore you never realise is so mind-numbing until you're a parent yourself doing it for your own kids. Back then, I was only interested in playing the matches.

Well, playing the matches and David Cassidy. These were now my twin passions. With a bit of Donny Osmond and Andy and David Williams, too. Now, they were gorgeous. If I wasn't playing tennis, I was busying myself with my little jotters, doodling their names and obsessively monitoring how they were doing in the charts every week. I would lie in bed with my transistor radio under the covers, listening to Radio Luxembourg and scribbling down all the chart positions, ready to discuss at school the next day. It was the only thing I cared about as much as tennis, and perhaps the only stage in my life when I really thought about music until I took part in *Strictly Come Dancing*.

From the age of ten I was at an all girls' school in Crieff, a forty-minute bus ride north of Dunblane. The sporting opportunities there were great, and being part of a team and representing my school was my first experience of sport being a form of self-expression. When your body is changing, you're growing up and life all around you is opening up, there is a huge sense of satisfaction and belonging from being part of a group who are all aiming for the same goal rather than being caught up in personal teenage worries. There was a social aspect to being on the tennis team, and a consistency in the routine of match days and scoreboards, all of which meant feeling as if I fitted in somewhere. I belonged, I was part of something bigger than myself.

I remember one summer when I was thirteen watching Evonne Goolagong on TV (the Australian player who won Wimbledon twice, for the first time in 1971 when she was only nineteen), and thinking: She's still a teenager, maybe I could be as good as her one day. But I had no idea what I would need to achieve in the next six years to get there. I thought maybe I needed to get a bit fitter? A bit faster? But I was clueless as to how to do that. I vaguely felt that something called 'hill training' might be involved, so I would run up the farm road behind our house with the dog from time to time. It was barely a slope but it was better than nothing. And that was the extent of it; there simply wasn't anyone to tell me about interval training, or sprints, or anything specific that might improve my fitness. And, as I grew older, there was a second factor that started to creep into the lack of direction in my game: girls were clearly second-class citizens on the national training weekends.

The sessions at Inverclyde National Sports Centre were about every six or eight weeks, and the vast majority of the kids taking part were boys. There were very few girls involved, and after a few months it dawned on me that we were given significantly less attention. The centre had two wooden courts, and one air hall, which was basically a sort of rubber court with a bubble over it. It was quite a new-fangled thing at the time, with the added space-age effect of an airtight door which trapped you inside.

The weekend sessions were great fun the first couple of times, but after a while we realised that the coach would always send us girls to the air hall. He would pack us off with some instructions on what we might practise, then come back a couple of hours later to check on us. We would try and explain what we'd been up to, only to be met with little more than 'Sounds great, time for a break then'. At one point we actually set up a competition to see who could guess the exact number of words he would bother to say to the girls' group over an entire training weekend. I don't think he ever reached more than about fifty, and the all-time low was three: 'Girls. Air hall.' Every session we spent playing games and doing drills without guidance; he was on court with the boys, actively watching, coaching and paying rapt attention.

This treatment was frustrating, because we could tell that we weren't being valued equally, but by this point the girls on the team were solid friends. We weren't going to complain too loudly because tennis was our social life and we didn't want access to it taken away. We were learning valuable life skills as we travelled – largely unaccompanied – up and down the country to play: how to find our B&B or youth hostel, the right time to have a decent breakfast if you were playing a big game later that day, or simply how to get yourself from A to B with the right money in a world without mobile phones, credit cards, ATMs or the internet. We knew that these were great opportunities and we didn't want to waste them.

I left school aged sixteen in the summer of 1976 and up until then I had fully intended to try to pursue tennis as a career. Perhaps it was naivety, but I had managed to spin out that young teen phase of thinking 'anything is possible' without restrictions for quite a while. The whole 'I want to be an astronaut! Or a pop star!' stage had manifested itself in pro tennis for me. But there was a massive stumbling block: there was simply no infrastructure in Scotland. I couldn't, for the life of me, see how I could do this. I had no idea how much it would cost, what it would take and, crucially, I saw no template for it in anyone like me, anywhere near me. Back then Dunblane was a town with a population of only three to four thousand; there just weren't that many people who had taken huge risks and pursued dreams on that sort of scale.

As I approached the end of high school, I had two options: I had an unconditional offer to study French and German at Edinburgh University the following year, and I was offered a tennis scholarship at a US university which would have covered virtually all costs. This was highly unusual back then. It was an incredible opportunity but I backed out of it at almost the last minute. On the one hand I badly wanted to go, but on the other it felt too far away. This was forty years ago, there was no way to research what it might be like or find someone who had done it before me. There was no Skyping a friendly face on the current scholarship to hear how they were getting along. The leap was just too big for me, and too far into the unknown and I turned it down with a heavy heart.

As the dream of becoming a professional player via a US scholarship faded, I set my heart on becoming a PE teacher as a sort of back-up. It seemed more manageable, more realistic, less far from home. My parents had seemed to think that was a natural progression too, but then I encountered *one of those* teachers. You know the one – the teacher who just doesn't get you, and squanders what enthusiasm you had for doing something. Anyone who has come across one of these will remember them: they are the very opposite of the inspiring teachers who open up a world of possibility to their students. This teacher told me in no uncertain terms that the entire teaching profession was in a terrible mess and that there were no jobs to be had and, being the student, I believed her.

In the end I decided to go to Edinburgh University, deferring it for a year to see how far I could get with playing tennis off my own bat. I was so dejected to have let the opportunity in America go, but it really was as simple as it being too daunting for me. And if I couldn't be a PE teacher, maybe another year of playing would be an adequate consolation prize for these disappointments.

It all began with great excitement when I headed to the British Junior Championships, which were played on the clay courts at Wimbledon, and got through to the quarter-final of the singles and the semi-final of the mixed doubles. Not long after that the Lawn Tennis Association (LTA) announced a full-time squad of girls to be based at Queen's Club. They selected the top six girls. I was ranked number 8. I just missed out. It was the difference between getting everything I'd dreamed of, and nothing at all.

So I had to go it alone.

There was no indoor circuit at that time, which meant that if you wanted to carry on playing tennis as autumn approached you had to go abroad. That is how I found myself in Barcelona's Club de Campo the following spring, playing Björn Borg's then fiancée. Most of my tennis adventures up to this point had felt like a series of gleeful treats and expeditions, but this was now beyond the realm of my wildest dreams. I was in sunny southern Europe, playing none other than Mariana Simionescu, who was engaged to the man himself!

In those days it was customary for any match winner to offer their opponent a drink in the club bar after the match. It was a really old-school tradition, but still very charming, and I was at an age where even being in a bar or restaurant of a venue like that felt like playing at being a grown up. Mariana beat me quite easily and came up to ask if I would like a drink. I was parched, so I said that yes, I would actually.

'Do you mind if we pop to the changing rooms first?' she replied. I said that was fine, and followed her to the changing rooms where she sat down, dropped her bag beside her on the bench and rooted around in it for a pack of cigarettes. She immediately lit up. I didn't really know what to say. I was naive enough to think that surely sportswomen wouldn't smoke. Perhaps I looked as shocked as I felt, because she looked back, saying, 'Sorry, it's just that Björn doesn't let me smoke, so I have to do it in secret.'

I was numb, barely able to compute how I was in this, the most adult situation of my life. I was a child really, completely unused to being confided in or spoken to as an adult. A couple of days later I was queueing at the club's buffet for something to eat and realised that I was in front of the Polish player Wojtek Fibak, the world number 5. There he was, just behind me! I had never dared to imagine that I might be rubbing shoulders with these stars one day, but apparently this was my life now. But not for long.

Because it was only a couple of days later that I blew it.

I had taken the bus into Barcelona to go to the poste restante, where I could change some traveller's cheques and mail some postcards.

It was hot and very busy on the bus so I had to stand, and I was jostled a lot as people fought to get on and off at the various stops. I didn't think anything of it though, and happily waited for my stop.

It was only once I got off the bus that I saw that the toggle which fastened my bag was twisted in the wrong position. And the bag itself was open. I can clearly remember peering into the bag and thinking, my purse is gone, that can't be right, before somehow believing that if I closed the bag and looked again, things would rectify themselves.

So I closed the bag, fixed the toggle, then opened it again to look for my purse. This time it would be there. But it wasn't. I sat on the dusty edge of the pavement and emptied every single thing out of the bag. Still, it wasn't there. There was my comb, my map and my hanky. All of the boring, annoying things that I only carried with me to make my mum happy. But no passport, no ticket home and absolutely no money at all.

After staring around me in shock for a couple of minutes, letting the severity of the situation sink in, I had the wit to go and find a passing policeman. He spoke no English but managed to find me someone who did, who in turn took me to the police station to call the British Embassy.

I didn't cry – I very rarely do, and usually it's when I'm happy – instead I went into a sort of automated 'I have a problem there must be a solution' mode. Perhaps the years of travel for tennis had toughened me up more than I realised, like the time I arrived at King's Cross, aged thirteen, to find my aunt wasn't there to meet me and then the following day got lost on the tube en route to the Queen's Club and so on.

But apparently I wasn't tough enough. When I eventually got home, my parents actually weren't cross. And we all know that it feels worse when your parents are merely disappointed. In fact, I think they were mostly worried. Because later that weekend my dad sat me down and said, 'Look, this is too dangerous. You can't be doing all this on your own and we can't come with you. So it has to stop.'

I was bitterly disappointed, but deep down I didn't disagree with him. In a way, I was quite relieved that he had made the decision for me. I had slowly begun to understand that I just wasn't cut out for this life, the life of a professional sportswoman: travelling alone internationally, communicating in such a spectrum of different languages, coaching myself and doing all of the organisation and scheduling needed for such a complicated life. I was a good enough player in Scotland, but I wasn't good enough – or tough enough – for the global circuit.

There are times when you just need your parents to parent you, and this was certainly one of them. I was in that horrible adolescent situation when you know what you want, but you just don't want to be the one to have to say it out loud. You want an adult to take that weight for you. In hindsight, my dad having the guts to stand up and make a difficult decision for me helped me later with the boys when it was my turn to do the active parenting. It gave me the confidence to step in when I saw them making a wrong decision or when they were simply too young to be entrusted with a decision so important.

But it didn't stop the hurt over the end of my short-lived tennis career. What could? Instead, I headed to university with my tail between my legs and forgot about the idea of tennis as a profession for many, many years.

2

To be a coach, or how I found a way of getting out of the house

In which I learn that sport is never just about winning, but about building communities, taking chances and changing lives. That, and how to kid kids into training when they think they're on a bit of a jolly.

Being a pro player may have been benched as a career, but tennis remained a huge part of my life, so with my dad's encouragement I decided to try and make the best of my time and skills by taking my first coaching qualification.

It was a local course spread over three weekends. It gave me some useful information on what tennis students needed to know. But, as I quickly learned, it left me woefully unprepared for actually organising or managing a class. I passed the course, but I still had no idea how to communicate ideas or even to get things going in a teaching environment. At heart, I was still just a player.

The reason I had taken the course was to make a bit of pocket money while I was at university, so not long after finishing it

I applied for and was given a role teaching my first group. I had eight kids, aged eleven to twelve, and as they filed onto the court, I felt my heart lurch, my nerves turn to ice and my body just . . . freeze.

The children themselves picked up on this immediately. Half of the class eyed me with enormous discomfort, well aware that they were on a court with someone out of their depth, and the other half were just happy to have a teacher who wasn't in control, and busied themselves doing their own thing for a while. It took several minutes before my heart rate returned to normal and I had the common sense to look across to the adjacent court and see what the other coach was doing. Once I had worked out that I could just copy him, I got through the rest of the lesson, but it wasn't exactly enjoyable, and as time moved on and university began to take up all of my time, I was glad that I was too busy playing my own tennis to take up coaching in any sort of serious way. Clearly it wasn't for me, I told myself. For nearly ten years.

While I was studying I remained a member of the Scottish national squad, taking part in tennis tournaments all over the country throughout the summer, as well as the annual international matches against England, Wales and Ireland. I also represented GB in the World Student Games in my final year. Friendships I'd had since school were strengthened, and I made new friends, too, turning tennis into an emotional support network as much as it was a sport. It was a huge part of my life. I even kept it up when, for reasons I now cannot fathom, I elected to work in the fashion industry after graduation. I had never had a huge interest in fashion and perhaps it was a summer fad that got a bit out of hand, but within weeks of graduating with a 2:1 in 1981, I had a job as a trainee manager at Miss Selfridge. Initially I worked in Glasgow at the concession within Lewis's department store. After a while I was transferred down to Peterborough to be an assistant manager, but a few months later I was bored. I had got the hang of the job, it wasn't really challenging me in any way, and so I concluded that it wasn't worth living so far from all of my friends and I came home to Glasgow.

Before long, a friend who worked as a sales rep for Wrigley told me about a role they had seen going, and the resulting job at Cavenham Confectionery suited me to a T. They had all sorts of 1980s sweet brands, the most famous of which was probably Chewits. I got a decent car with the job, and it was structured around lots of incentives and bonuses, so I was constantly challenged and on the move. I spent a couple of years careering around Scotland in that car, selling sweets to shops, supermarkets and wholesalers before being promoted to National Accounts Manager, handling the likes of Woolworths and John Menzies. That's where I met the boys' dad. Will was a regional manager for the newsagents R.S. McColl. We set up home together and then in 1986 had Jamie. I had always known that I wanted to have a family while I was young enough to be active, and I certainly was that. I carried on playing sport through both pregnancies, a bit further than I had imagined I would be able to. I can remember playing a squash match when I was six months pregnant with Jamie and it felt great to be well and moving around, but at the end of the match my opponent confessed to me: 'That was awful, I felt so terrible – I hated having to make you run like that.' I hadn't minded one bit! My doctor had told me to do what I felt comfortable with, not what anyone else might feel comfortable with – and I hadn't even considered that she might feel awkward.

I was still Scottish number 1 when I had Jamie, as well as captain of the North of Scotland ladies' team, so after I had him my goal was to stop breastfeeding in time to be able to go to County Week – a five-day doubles team competition, played on grass courts in mid-July. I was young and fit enough so getting back into shape wasn't too much of a worry for me, but I did want to have done my best with the feeding before I headed off for a week.

His had been a long and challenging birth and that week of tennis with my friends was really something to look forward to. The tournament had been my annual highlight for many years, as it meant seeing my best, oldest friends regardless of where our various careers had taken us. Before social media or smartphones, and if you didn't have the time or money to spend hours making phone calls, you could only really have a proper catch-up with people when you saw them in person. Tennis was the thread keeping our gang of pals all together and County Week was the time we all reconvened. It was wonderful to see all my friends again, as well as to spend a week looking after myself and myself alone – every shower I took that week, without having to worry about what the baby was up to, felt like a treat. And not a pureed vegetable in sight.

I went back to work for a bit not long afterwards, but while I was pregnant with Andy we decided to move from Glasgow back to Dunblane, to be close to my family. We moved the day that Andy was due, and he was kind enough to hang on until we had got ourselves over the threshold of our new home before making an appearance.

Having spent nine years living away from Dunblane, I soon realised that I no longer had any good friends my age in the town. The following few years were a challenging time. Having given up my job, I no longer had a car, and even my brothers had now moved out of town, which left me with hardly anyone I knew nearby, apart from my parents. With two very small children so close in age and no means of transport, I found myself quite lonely, and quite trapped, pretty quickly.

We were at home a lot, with me coming up with ever more inventive ways to keep two infants occupied. The solitude, the isolation caused by not having my own means of getting around, and the desire for some adult company made me ache for my friends. Will was a sales manager, too, so he was often on the road which meant the isolation didn't have quite the same impact on him, but I used to daydream about the days when I had been close to my mates, in a city, near to a thriving tennis club.

In those days, the most adult company I would get was at the Toy Box, the toyshop my mum and her best friend Elsie used to run on Dunblane High Street. My dad had bought the shop as an empty unit around the time I headed to university, and my mum and Elsie had decided that the Dunblane community needed a toyshop. They didn't have any major altruistic or commercial aims with this; it was simply a case of us having enjoyed taking our pocket money to the High Street on a Saturday morning and carefully choosing a treat. They wanted to keep that going, and so they did. It was a gorgeous shop, and everyone in the town loved it, but it would not be a lie to say that my mum, while she might have the warmest heart, was probably the worst businesswoman of all time.

If someone came into the shop looking for, say, Scrabble, and she didn't have it in stock, she wouldn't answer with, 'Ooh, I'll order one in for you.' She would get in her car, drive to Stirling, buy it in Woolworths and then call the customer back an hour or two later.

'We've got one in for you now!' she would say, as if she were business mind of the year.

She didn't care that she was making no money and nor did we really. We had always been a community-focused family. My dad was the local optician so he knew everybody, too, and even if I was missing pals my own age, it made a positive difference having the social hub that the shop provided. After a while, Elsie was ready to retire but my mum was far from ready to give it up, still determined that 'Dunblane must have a toyshop', so I said I would help her.

It was great fun working with my mum, as she has such fabulous people skills, and she thrived on the idea of serving the community. Dunblane High Street was a challenge as it didn't have a huge foot-fall, and the shop was never really profitable, but I tried to help Mum change some things around like bringing in some children's clothes and greetings cards that have higher mark-ups than toys. We even changed the name to Torags, to let people know it was no longer *just* toys that we were selling. Helping out at the shop lasted for years, but it was still never quite *my* project. For a while in the late eighties I worked – again, inexplicably – in fashion, selling high-end lingerie on commission to shops across Scotland. It got me out of the house and away from smelly nappies once in a while and, crucially, sane and earning. But what really changed everything was a fleeting favour that I offered almost off the cuff, which went on to alter the course of my life and indeed the whole family's.

One summer, when the boys were still tiny, the central district's jun-ior tennis tournament was held nearby at Stirling University Courts. In my capacity as former Scottish number 1, I was asked if I would head down and present the prizes. I was honoured – I had loved that tournament as a child – so thought I would dust off my dormant coaching skills and offer to give the winner and runner-up of the boys' and the girls' Under 12s tournament an hour of free coaching.

I had done very little coaching since that one class at university. I hadn't done anything formally organised for years and years, and it had certainly never been a source of proper income. So I didn't really think anything of it when I offered; it just seemed like a nice thing to do. Perhaps I fancied an hour of hitting balls, perhaps I fancied the exercise or the time away from the kids or perhaps it was all that time with my community-minded mum that had been rubbing off on me.

The first session that I took with these four kids, two of whom were brother and sister, went really well. My mum looked after my boys for me for the hour, and it was great to be out on the tennis court having fun. I really did feel as if I was helping their game by sharing my skills. I was still pretty fit, and I got a good run around showing the kids what they needed to be doing. It was a real release, physically and emotionally.

When their own mums came to pick them up, they asked me if I would take them for another lesson. I was happy to, but explained that I couldn't rely on my mum for childcare again, so they would have to look after my boys during the session. One of the mums agreed without hesitation, so the next time we met, I had Jamie and Andy in the double buggy all ready to go, and she happily wheeled them up to the park across the road, round the duck pond to feed the ducks and let them have a little play in the fresh air while I got to work on the tennis court. By the time they were back, my hour's coaching was nearly over. It was from these tiny seeds that a Dunblane tennis community grew, one that exceeded my wildest expectations.

After a couple more sessions with my original pupils, word began to spread that I had started giving lessons, and the parents of some of the older children at the club asked me if I would coach them, too. As long as my boys were taken care of, I was happy to do it. I wasn't even asking for formal payment at first. I set up some evening and weekend squads and after a few years we had our first success when Dunblane High School won the Scottish schools boys tennis championship. We weren't superstars, but four of the sixteen-year-olds from the club were really solid little players by now and they

did well. I was so proud of them, even if on Finals' Day I was sting-
ing at my first experience of being sidelined as a female coach. I had
been training them after school for months, organising and super-
vising every match, fully invested in every inch of their progress as
they progressed through each stage of the tournament.

Then, as Finals' Day approached and we were making plans to
head to Edinburgh for the match I was told that, no, I would not be
accompanying the team. That privilege would be going to their head
PE teacher, the chap who knew next to nothing about tennis and
had done less than nothing to support them all of this time. It wasn't
the first occasion on which I would encounter someone steaming in
to take the glory after others had been putting in the hard work for
months, but I was adamant that it wouldn't deter me. I went along
anyway, travelling separately and cheering their every shot. I surprised myself by how emotional I was when I saw them win – my
first little triumph, with these lovely local kids, coming out of
nowhere!

This small success galvanised us and boosted our confidence
and I committed to coaching regularly at the tennis club, on a
largely voluntary basis. There was no one else teaching there so
there were no toes for me to step on with my lack of experience and
ramshackle tumble-dried tennis balls. I started where my mum and
her friends left off nearly fifteen years before, and the community
just seemed to go with it. I was working with older kids to begin
with, and in time we developed quite a big pool of boys and girls,
which meant that I started to be able to use them to play with some
of the younger kids – to help build their confidence, to teach them
how to keep score while actually playing the game rather than me
explaining over and over again.

Mindful of my years of boredom and frustration before I was old enough to play properly, we introduced a system that meant no child should ever be left hanging around without being included in something. We would have football in the park, swingball in the driveway, there was table tennis in the clubhouse, coordination training on the squash courts and others helping to run the café. Every one of them had a part, which meant that all of them had the chance to be involved in endless play in the club environment.

We don't get that many sunny days in Scotland, and just like I did, these kids were growing up playing tennis in relatively poor conditions. Our attitude was usually: 'Eh, just pop on a waterproof and let's do it anyway. A little rain never hurt anybody.' But I still tried to keep things diverse so that we didn't lose the attention of swathes of kids. The more we had who were regularly turning up, the more we could do – because by now I had realised that it wasn't just me who thought that most of the fun came from playing the game and being part of a team who wanted to win. In order to hold competitions, we needed enough kids to play. Finally, we were getting there.

Just as we reached a point where we had enough kids to hold some decent competitions, I was now faced with the reality of actually arranging them. Setting up a tennis tournament is hard enough. There's a lot more to it than booking courts and collecting entry forms. You need to understand scheduling, refereeing, budgeting and the art of communication. This is why I am for ever grateful to one of my first ever mentors: Dorothy Dick.

Dorothy was the first in a considerable line-up of women who have appeared in my life, told me that the ability to do something was absolutely within my grasp, helped me to believe that I could reach that next goal, the one I hadn't dared to reach for . . . and changed the course of things for ever. She was no great woman of authority, she was a maths teacher from Falkirk who had three tennis-playing kids and an eye for detail. But she was a passionate tennis parent, and someone who saw the game as a way to help a community gel in the same way that I did – and still do.

She was running the Central District's local tournament, sorting out the regional squads, the schedules, the travel, the payments, the coaches, the venues – the lot. And she took it upon herself to teach me how to do the same. She was fabulous at understanding the logistics and explaining them to me in turn. She asked me if I would like to take on some of the district coaching. At that time Scotland was divided into nine districts of a few counties each, and ours was called Central, as it was slap bang in the middle of the country. It was one of the smallest districts though, with only eighteen clubs in it at the time. As I was enjoying what I was doing, I accepted the offer. I had even started to charge money to cover childcare costs by now, as the duck-pond plan could not last for ever . . .

These coaching sessions were nearly all on a Sunday evening during the winter months when the weather was at its worst. As there were no indoor courts we often ended up in school halls, on those horrible polished, lino-like surfaces which made the balls move like lightning, and where the baseline and tramlines were up against the walls. It just wasn't representative of playing on a regular court, and it terrified some of the kids, so in time I left the balls in the tumble dryer that little bit longer, until they had sort of . . . fluffed up. This in turn slowed them down, and saved us from several trips to A & E.

I loved planning my lessons as the classes got bigger, and absolutely maxing out the time and space we had. As my confidence in my organisational skills and creativity grew, I became more and more determined to make every single second count. I became a bit of an expert in working with big numbers in small spaces. You can divide the space up into stations and have some of them doing drills, some of them working on technique or coordination skills, some of them doing a bit of fitness, some hitting against the wall and if you're imaginative enough you can con all of them into thinking that they're just playing a big game.

I used to rip up strips of newspaper, scrunch them into little balls, and put them into an old supermarket bag, chucking in a few sweets along the way. Then I'd tie it to the end of my tennis racket and hold it up so that the younger kids had to hit it at full stretch – *voilà*! They don't know they're learning the movements for good serving; they think they are whacking a home-made *piñata*. Kids don't want to 'go to a lesson' or listen to a biomechanical breakdown of strokes, they want to play games, especially ones that reward them with sweets at the end.

I see too much coaching these days that is just organised activity – it's not actual teaching, properly thought out. To get kids to learn and keep their attention you have to put them in a game situation to ensure that they're having fun. The coach has to make sure every exercise or activity is there for a reason. There is more to teaching a sport like tennis than simply fostering the ability to hit the ball well. It's a game, with a strategy – and that's where the fun lies. Too often I see young kids on programmes that demand multiple hours of practice a week, and there is little sense of fun in any of those sessions, just 'work' that needs to be got through without them really grasping the point of the practice. For children, that will never last. Of course, the best way of all to distract them from practice is to turn it into a competition – which I soon learned myself when I saw this in action. Making drills and exercises competitive keeps

31

players engaged, makes them think and is as close as you can get to simulating the emotional experience of playing a match.

With Dorothy's help, I started to run local tournaments for different age groups, and then to organise matches between clubs and against other districts. Coaches or parents from other areas would bring the kids to Dunblane and we started to travel, too. I was mindful that no child felt left out even if they were knocked out in an early stage, so I tried to make sure that the clubhouse (or my car) was always well stocked with table tennis, dominoes, playing cards, draughts, or all sorts of quizzes. Parents whose kids had outgrown board games at home would donate them to us, and whenever we made a bit of money with our tournament cafés, we'd spend the proceeds on more kit for the club: new balls, bats and games whenever we could. At one point we even managed to buy a ball machine so kids could practice on their own. The kids enjoyed it, I was enjoying it, and the parents were happy too, so as the months rolled by, things grew and grew.

After a year or so I realised that I couldn't do it all myself, so I started to rope in other parents and some of the older kids to help. I was always happy to do the tennis coaching, but soon we had so many teams that I needed help with updating the fixture list, the club noticeboard, transportation and so on. It was the early 1990s, we had no email or convenient Facebook pages to let everyone know dates and times and I was spending hours at the kitchen table with home-made spreadsheets, making phone calls, arranging collections and drop-offs for children all around the area. As a club, we developed a really great parent workforce. It made sense to use them as much as we could – after all, who wants to make things happen for their kids more than anything? Parents. So they were usually more than happy to help. As things evolved we started taking the players all over the country and beyond – soon we were heading off down south to play English counties and staying over with other families. In time, we even headed to Wales, whose national coach was my friend Ellinore, my doubles partner at the GB National Under 14 Championships at Eastbourne back in the early 1970s, who I was always delighted to see. A qualified PE teacher and an experienced coach in her own right, she was another female face in the male-dominated tennis world who was both a valued confidante and source of support.

Organising and implementing all of this meant getting to know so many more parents than I might otherwise have done, and consequently I made friends and settled into the Dunblane community in a way that had seemed so out of reach that first year. And the boys grew up in an environment where children were having fun. We had a good bunch of players back then. They were all learning the game fast and improving all the time. If we were away at a tournament and they weren't playing a match, I would get them scouting: I'd give them a piece of paper with a blank court template on it and they'd have to tick where winning balls were scored from, put a cross where the player was standing when they made a mistake, or mark ones and twos where first and second serves landed. Then they'd feed back their observations to their pals after the match. It kept them engaged, kept them learning and encouraged a sense of team spirit, of working together. This was a step ahead of just wearing young kids out with a racket and ball, both technically and emotionally, and left me committed to match analysis for life.

The whole set-up with these competitions was fantastic, character-building stuff: travelling as part of a team, having sleepovers. Each of the wider lessons around scouting, overnight stays or supporting your team-mates taught the players just as much as forty-five minutes focusing on their backhand might. They would start to understand, as I had years before, that staying up all night talking or having midnight feasts meant they might not play very well the next morning. But tell a kid that and they won't believe you. It's one of those things they have to find out for themselves.

3

The power of play, or how to do a lot with very little

In which I learn how much can be done with very little, as long as you have enthusiasm, imagination and a role model. From home-made pinãtas *to bedroom wrestling bouts, the whole family discovers that if you want to play, you can find a way.*

While I was making this first foray into more structured coaching and club organisation, Jamie and Andy left their toddler years behind. They had developed great hand-eye and foot-eye coordination skills at a young age, simply by playing all sorts of home-made games around the house using pretty much anything we had lying around. Part of this compendium of fun was born out of my love of all things sporty, and partly out of necessity. The weather isn't so good in Scotland and I had to invent things to tire out two active little boys without spending a fortune. Naturally, as they spent so much time down at the clubhouse surrounded by children playing tennis, they wanted to play almost as soon as they could walk.

Their first 'game' of tennis was bumping balloons across the sofa, swiftly followed by kitchen table tennis using biscuit tin lids as bats and cereal boxes for the net. Then they graduated to swingball in the back garden with their tiny rackets before making their first court from chalk lines, two chairs and a piece of rope in the driveway. There was never any shortage of kids to entertain them at the club, and before long they were comfortable on the proper courts and had moved on from sponge balls to grown-up tennis balls. You could now buy kid's rackets (so much shorter than the junior sized one I had played at eleven) but pressureless balls and small courts hadn't been invented yet. They'd use both hands to hit the ball initially, and stand as close to the net as they dared.

Things moved up a notch when Andy was almost six years old and barely as tall as the net was high. After a spirited afternoon of playing tennis down on the bottom courts at Dunblane with my mum and me – an afternoon I thought he was enjoying, by the way – he threw his (ridiculously big) racket to the ground and let out a huge sigh.

'What's wrong?' I asked.

'I'm bored of playing with you and Gran,' he said, looking at us. 'I want to play a proper match.'

Once I'd got over my momentary fury that my precocious five-year-old had decided that I was not his perfect practice partner, it dawned on me that while watching the rest of us he had not only worked out what needed to be done on the court, but how to keep score and play a proper game. And now he was desperate to start playing properly himself.

If he had played against Jamie they would have just ended up fighting. They were always playing their own made-up games, or having kickabouts together, but if they had practised formally together, they'd have lasted ten minutes before it ended in dispute:

'Don't hit it so hard', 'Stop making me run', and so on. Mercifully they had a supply of parents and grandparents who were happy to play with them, so we could usually implement a bit of 'divide and conquer' for informal playtime. But where proper matches were concerned, the youngest league at the time was for fourteen and under, and the youngest age allowed in the competition was twelve. Oh God, I thought, I can't wait six years before he can start competing. We'll all go mad.

So I called up five or six of the coaches I had met on my travels across Scotland and asked, 'Do you fancy coming down to Dunblane if we put together a little Under 10s competition? Just a fun thing . . . lots of little mini matches, we'll get the older kids to keep score and have a picnic afterwards? And water bombs? And swingball?'

I was pretty determined to persuade them.

And persuade them I did. A whole load of them, coaches, parents, kids, the lot, came down and we had a great day, our first ever Under 10s competition. It wasn't an official tournament, just a fun event, but fun it certainly was. At the end of the day, the other coaches agreed that it had been a great success and decided to take on setting up a return event at their club. And so it started. In time, these events became official Under 10s competitions, but they began as just a good way to allow the smaller kids to play the game.

I didn't realise it at the time, but there was an extraordinary little crop of talented young players taking part in that inaugural event. Elena Baltacha, the future British number 1 was there, aged nine. It was her first proper competition, and she was already a standout. She made the final which was umpired by one of the older club juniors. Play stopped at one stage and both players plus the umpire were stood on court with their hands up for help – I assumed they'd had some kind of dispute with the score, as they usually did at that age.

'What's wrong, girls?' I asked, looking around.

'We've run out of balls,' explained the young girl from Aberdeen whom Elena was playing. 'They're all stuck in the fence and none of us can reach them.'

I looked across. They weren't wrong. Elena had this unbelievable service action already and was so strong that the balls had been repeatedly served into the back fence – without bouncing first – and were lodged too high for small arms to reach. It was no surprise that she went on to make top 50 in the world.

Jamie and Andy were playing competitively for the first time as well, and so were Jamie Baker and Colin Fleming. All of these kids went on to play in the Davis Cup – the World Cup of tennis – and yet that day I think I was probably more worried about the parking and whether we had enough sausages for the hot dogs. When you run a big junior tournament like this you get all of the mums and dads and grannies and granddads coming along, too, so if you have thirty kids you've got at least sixty adults in attendance who want toasties, hot dogs, jumbo ketchup, chocolate biscuits, paper towels and plenty of tea and coffee all day. Of course, this was a great opportunity for us to make a little bit of money for the club to keep the whole programme of activities going. So on tournament mornings I'd be up at the crack of dawn, heading for the supermarket in time for opening, loading up my car with trolleys full of food to last the whole day, and then off to the clubhouse where some of the other mums would take care of the cooking, the serving and the rest of it while I tried to get my focus back on the tennis.

Well, I say the tennis . . . I also had a water balloon masterplan. Just in case any kids came off court dejected by losing a match, I would keep a supply of filled water balloons behind the clubhouse all day, ready to distract and cheer up those who needed a boost. And that of course meant finding a couple of discreet, diligent older kids who were prepared to fill them without causing chaos at the beginning of the day. Keeping a sense of fun about the whole event was an essential part of getting everyone from grannies to little sisters to keep on turning up. But this was the first time, and I had no idea if I could pull it off . . . until I had.

The whole event galvanised me. Not for the first time, I realised that where *I* saw an opportunity for something, other people saw hurdles and complications. I knew it probably wasn't going to happen unless *I* got up and did something about it. Scotland just wasn't ready for tennis as a national sport back then, and there were no real links between schools and clubs in terms of community building either. It was up to volunteers to drive activity.

I discovered that there was a Midland Bank primary school tennis championship – a UK-wide event – but the schools that took part in it were the ones with tennis courts on their premises: private schools. That wouldn't do. So I set up my own Dunblane primary school team, entered it in the Midland Bank competition, and used the club courts for the matches. It was quicker to sort something out myself than to search around for someone else to do it, so I got used to the idea that if I wanted opportunities for my kids and my town's kids, I was going to have to create them myself.

As part of this move to try and make more happen for the club and the junior players, I decided to take my second coaching qualification. It was a week-long residential course at the same sports centre in Inverclyde where I had gone for my national squad training weekends as a teenager. My mum came to the rescue and looked after the boys during the daytime while Will was at work and I was busy learning. There were a few people on the course who I knew from my own playing days, so it was great fun, but I ended the week a little disappointed by its actual content.

I passed the course with relative ease, but once again I felt that nagging feeling that I hadn't really been taught what I actually needed to know. I probably passed the course because I was clever enough and had played to a high level – it wasn't because I had learned how to be a better coach. Yes, there was certain useful information – mainly technical and tactical – that I had picked up, but what I desperately needed help and advice on was how to practically apply the knowledge in a teaching environment. What I really wanted to see was a great coach in action, working with various age groups and levels of kids. I knew how much I had to learn and I wanted someone to emulate.

This kind of pragmatism was rarely addressed. We barely saw a child the entire week, so there was precious little practical experience or training. We practiced on each other, but we were all adults, all coaches and all decent players already. It felt as if I was being taught to be a dentist by being shown a lot of images of teeth, and being allowed to touch lots of the little metal implements . . . but going nowhere near a mouth. We discussed 'the tooth', but not the nerve system attached to it.

Nevertheless, the course gave me the confidence to carry on building the tennis community at Dunblane. It was still a rather low-key operation. I barely charged anything for my lessons as I felt that I wasn't as qualified as some of the other 'proper' coaches who worked at the big clubs in Glasgow or Edinburgh. It was a sort of vicious circle; I didn't charge much as I wasn't sure I was worth it, therefore I didn't earn much, which in turn reinforced my anxieties around other, slicker coaches. And of course the main result was that as a family, we were skint. Everything we did was on a shoe-string, or in some cases, a bit of an embarrassment.

One bleak winter's night around this time I had parked outside the clubhouse and gone to take a group lesson when I saw some guy reverse straight into the driver's side of my car. I saw it all from the court and was shouting at him to stop but it was too dark, too foggy and he obviously couldn't hear or see me. The damage was done. I had excess on my car insurance but it was something like £200 at the time and there was no way I could afford to pay that in those days, so I had to wait for his insurance to come through before I could get it fixed. The driver's door was jammed, so for weeks I had to climb over to the driver's seat via the passenger door, clambering over the gearbox. During this wait I drove down to watch some of the kids at the new indoor courts that had recently opened at Stirling University in 1994. As I was hauling myself out of my car, a tennis coach I knew from Glasgow pulled up in a great big shiny Audi estate next to me.

'What *are* you doing, Judy?' he asked.

'Oh, somebody bashed into my car!' I said, trying to laugh it off.

'Why don't you just get it fixed?' he said, grinning as if this was a great big joke.

I tried to laugh along, secretly mortified at the truth behind why I hadn't got it sorted yet. He popped his flash boot and got out a brand new hopper filled with brand new balls. I quietly sighed, and wondered if I should start charging proper money for what I was doing.

It took another car door situation before I had the courage to take things up a level. I was at the ATM at the Bank of Scotland in Dunblane and bumped into a boy who had been the reserve for our school team the year that Dunblane High School had won the schools' tennis championships. He was a footballer now – one of those kids who was good at everything: tennis club champion, golf club champion, squash club champion, and a great footballer to boot. He actually went on to play for Scotland, but at that time he had just signed for his first club.

'Congratulations!' I said. 'I heard you have just signed for Leicester City!'

He seemed pleased to see me, this eighteen-year-old who had been such a big part of my first coaching triumph. But he let on that he was a little dejected as he had been injured lately and not able to play. Then came the stinger.

'It's okay though,' he confessed, 'I'm still on six grand a week.'

I walked away, inhaling sharply. Six grand! I was lucky if I managed to make that in six months! From time to time I would wonder if I should be doing something else, to make a better salary. But the thought always passed. Perhaps it was to my long-term advantage that tennis coaching as a decent career was really only in its infancy; I was able to be a part of it from the very start. Scotland has long been a golfing nation, and all the golf clubs had pros employed to work in them, giving lessons, running competitions and selling equipment in their pro shops. But Scotland was still getting to grips with the idea of a professional set-up in tennis. Maybe the relative innocence of the sport back then helped me make the right choices. The culture of volunteers has faded away a bit now, and many parents have sadly lost confidence in playing with their kids themselves and opt to pay others to do it instead. A culture of obsession with excellence has diminished the value of the sort of fun that can be had in families and in the community with small-scale local events.

I must have been influenced by the relaxed, inclusive attitude towards sport that my own parents had demonstrated. They firmly believed in its ability to build communities and they passed that legacy on to me. I just refused to be put off by the idea that tennis was for privileged kids, or places with fancy facilities. I think there may well be a few people out there who still think that I brought my boys up to be tennis players out of some sort of frustrated ambition, simply because I was a player myself who might have been able to go further. But I didn't: I approached their playing as the daughter of two keen tennis players, not as the wannabe mother of two tennis stars. And the thought that I restricted them to just tennis back then is hilarious – they did absolutely everything when they were little!

They adored swimming, especially if it involved me bundling them and a group of their friends into the car to go to the water slides. Andy was fanatical about football and for Jamie it was golf. These were sports they did mainly with their dad but this was on top of the tennis, and an endless amount of general running around and trashing the garden, too. This constant sense of play meant that they became pretty good at their various activities, not because they were being 'trained' but because they enjoyed it, wanted to win and so worked out the best ways to do so. Whatever new games they were playing or making up, they invented a scoring system and followed it rigorously. I really don't buy into the idea that it needs to be all about top-notch coaches, expensive programmes, individual lessons and strength and conditioning sessions from childhood if you want to succeed.

When I think about what Andy did when he was younger, he didn't have any sort of individual fitness training programmes the way that twelve-year-olds do now if they are 'identified' by the system as a future star. He played football and football provided his 'strength and conditioning training'. He ran around for an hour or so, changing direction, learning how to be quick off the mark, honing his anticipation skills, using and strengthening muscles tennis might not employ and resting others. All of the things that come with playing another sport weren't holding him back; they were an advantage.

The opening of the first indoor tennis centre in Scotland at

Stirling University – only a couple of miles away – also made a difference in edging tennis to the top of the boys' interests. There is so much research to show that if anyone – especially a child – has to travel for longer than forty minutes to get to play their sport the chances are there will be a limit in how long they will keep it up. If your parents are doggedly taking you on two-hour drives each way to train, your chosen sport will lose its charms pretty sharpish, particularly if you don't have a social group training and playing with you. Any devotion has to be driven by your own passion for the sport, not an adult's ambition for you. The Stirling courts were ten minutes away. The fact that these facilities turned up almost on our doorstep when they did, enabling me to run my district programme from that base from such an early stage, played a crucial part in all of our careers unfolding the way that they have. You don't just need natural ability to reach the top in a discipline, you need opportunity as well, and it was a stroke of good luck for all of us that the tennis centre opened when it did.

As a family we were so fortunate to have those facilities at Stirling, but the boys were even more fortunate to have people around them eager to support their interests. They had grandparents who were always happy to have a kickabout or take them out to the golf course, or the play park or engage with their latest invented game. When we had the cash, it was off to the pool for the water slides and wave machines, or an occasional Hibs football match, and Will was brilliant at playing football with them for hours on end. And of course, they had me for tennis.

Well, they had me and all the other kids at the tennis courts. Older kids that I was working with were always willing to play with them, especially as the boys got better. And if there wasn't a spare court then there was table tennis, swingball or carpet bowls. This mix of ages and abilities didn't just improve their skills and knowledge of the game, it also gave them an emotional resilience that comes from having to experience winning and losing among your peer group, again and again – and face to face.

These days kids spend less time being physical and more time sitting at a computer. They learn to win or lose to the sound of a screen trilling at them. Developmentally, it isn't the same because the hurt never feels quite as bad; it's entirely private. You don't develop that ability to pick yourself up, dust yourself off, restore your pride and have another bash at it. A computer doesn't force you to work out a way to emotionally navigate a path through its response, sportsmanlike or otherwise. A computer might beep 'ta-da' at you, but then . . . well, you can just turn it off.

These were tough lessons for me to learn as well, because I was so often present when they were winning or losing these games, in a way that parents rarely are these days. I took four kids down to an Under 10s tournament in Wrexham. It was an Adidas Challenge, one of many which took place all over the UK. Andy was only about seven. He was still holding the racket with two hands, bless him! He was due to play a boy much older than him – probably about ten years old – and much bigger than him. I was watching from the café and trying to keep score from a distance, just to keep an eye out for any funny business as I suspected that a child so much bigger might be disconcerted by being beaten by a sprat Andy's size.

I was pretty sure that they had made it to match point and Andy played a perfect drop shot. The boy ran to hit it but only made it at the *third* bounce, so Andy went to shake hands. The boy wasn't having any of it though, and insisted that he had got to the ball in time. From a distance, I could see that the tournament referee was then called and it was each child's word against the other. Of course, presumably based on size alone, the referee assumed that the older boy was correct about the scoring, awarded him the point and a distraught Andy went on to lose the match.

Nothing like that had ever happened to him before and Andy was inconsolable. More angry than tearful. Obviously, I was furious, and wanted to storm over there and throttle this other tyke as I watched Andy trying to deal with the unfairness of the situation. But it doesn't do any good to create a fuss or behave inappropriately in front of your child. I slowly ground my back teeth and kept my mouth shut.

I've seen parents leap onto court after matches to call the opponent a cheat. The parent may have the best of intentions, but the child learns nothing of value. They see their parent shouting in anger, and absorb little beyond the fact that to lose a match is to prompt frightening behaviour in their loved ones. I have held my tongue many times, despite how painful it can be seeing your child slighted. I have seen kids not wanting to go home in the car with their parents when they've lost a match because the response it provokes in their parents makes the child feel they've failed. Tennis is a tough sport for a little kid – out there on their own on this huge court, with a complicated scoring system, without an umpire and no team support – but I came to understand that no child ever enjoyed it more because their parents kept forcing the issue. Again and again it was clear as a bell: the passion must come from the player not the parent.

Still, no matter how much I tried to step back, Andy developed the same competitive streak that had shone in my father and which I recognised in myself. Jamie was much more like my mum, happy to play and to play as much as the opportunities would let him. But Andy wanted to win everything, and if he didn't he would stomp off in a fury even from about three or four when he was playing cards or dominoes. I think the reason for this competitiveness was because he had grown up with an older sibling who was always slightly bigger and slightly better than him, for as long as he could possibly remember. They were close in age, so not everyone could immediately tell who was the older child, but Jamie still had that edge for at least a decade.

This constant availability of a willing and very able adversary contributed significantly to make Andy the mega-competitor he is today. He could never be the oldest, so he was forced – day in, day out – to find ways to be just as good. And he leapt at the challenge. Jamie would ride it out calmly if Andy flipped up a board game in his face, puce with fury. I think his brother's equilibrium actually enraged him even more. We used to say Andy had a witching hour between about 6.30 and 7.30 p.m. where he would just . . . blow. But as soon as it was over, he was fine again and it was time for bed.

Witching hour aside, it was of course a source of huge pride to watch them grow into such wonderful little sportsmen, and to enjoy spending so much time in each other's company. But there were times, and there were games, that nearly tipped me over the edge.

One such obsession was WWF: the World Wrestling Federation, which was big on TV at the time. Andy was absolutely mad about The Rock and Jamie loved Stone Cold Steve Austin. But it wasn't enough for the boys just to watch; so great was their passion that they had to take part. So they set about creating their own arena and their own bouts.

The first stage was – obviously – the crafting of their wrestling belts. This was the quietest part of the entire process, and it didn't take me long to realise that I should cherish this relative peace before the action began. They would sit at the kitchen table with some old breakfast cereal boxes, cutting the cardboard into the shape of large cummerbunds. Out came the felt pens, the glitter, the glue and the stickers, and the belts would be decorated ornately in a manner befitting a W W F wrestler from Dunblane. It was the full *Blue Peter*, as they measured each other up, got out the Sellotape for repeated fittings and eventually decided that they were ready.

At this point they would take off their tops for 'authenticity' and set about laying out the 'arena' – the two single duvets from their bunk beds laid together to form a square. Then, in their tracksuit bottoms and home-made glitter belts, on a floor made up of two identical Manchester United duvet covers, combat would commence. They would use loud American voices, announcing the contestants, and they would stand and bow before attacking each other with a viciousness I could barely believe siblings could ever have for each other.

As I sat downstairs at the kitchen table, my spreadsheets and semi-formed tournament plans laid out in front of me, I could hear the ceiling shudder above me. There was one occasion when the living-room ceiling actually appeared to bounce, and small showers of dust began to rain down in front of the TV I was trying to watch. I went upstairs to see what on earth they were up to. I opened the bedroom door – with difficulty – because the Manchester United arena was down on the floor again, wedged against the door. There was a stepladder from the cupboard downstairs in the corner of the room. And the lampshade was swinging wildly.

'What on earth are you doing?' I asked.

'We're having a ladder match,' came the answer.

'What on earth is a ladder match?' They looked at me as if it was shameful that I didn't already know.

'Well, you have to pin someone down for the count of three, and then climb to the top of the ladder and ding the bell.'

'The bell?'

They pointed up to the lampshade, now swaying as if complicit in trying to make the game sound reasonable. It was apparently playing the part of a large, boxing-ring style bell for the duration of this game.

'Could you try and keep it down please?' I asked, before closing the door again. I wanted to be furious, but I was actually chuckling to myself, secretly proud of their apparently limitless imaginations.

Children learn by example. They are inspired by what they see. The boys had watched the wrestling, and seen the bell and created their own game, just as they had improvised tennis or badminton using balloons or bean bags over the washing line, or two chairs and a piece of rope with a balloon when no courts or balls were available. As well as an example, kids need someone to spar with. You can do all the training drills you want, but it will never replace the emotional landscape that is created by play, and play was the fabric of their life.

Later, when I started working exclusively with girls, I often thought back to the WWF belts and the ladder game. The boys had seen men playing like this on telly, and they had no hesitation in believing that they could play those games too. They never doubted themselves. If you can see it, you can be it. And they could see male sportsmen all around them, so they believed it was within their grasp to be sportsmen. Were there many women playing sport on TV at that time? Very, very few.

But however much the boys were enjoying play, my mind was turning to what else I could achieve at work.

4

Determination, or the trouble with being a woman

In which I realise, for the very first time, that I may not be welcome on account of my gender and make a choice: don't get sad, get mad. Use it as rocket fuel for your determination, making sure your work is what improves, not anyone else's ego.

Once again, when I tried to reach towards that next professional goal, it was a woman who stuck her neck out for me and helped in ways I will never be able to thank her for. Having made the decision to commit to some further training, I enquired about what the next step was for me. The body in charge of such things is the Lawn Tennis Association, or the LTA, tennis's governing body for the whole of Great Britain.

At the time, their top qualification was called the Professional Tennis Coach's Award, a two-week residential course with a series of on- and off-court examinations at the end of it. But when I made the enquiry that day, the woman who headed up coach education at the LTA at the time took me aside and told me very specifically that they were putting together a new course called the Performance Coach Award, which would be a much more comprehensive qualification. It would be a bigger commitment though, with workshops and projects spread over the course of an entire year. She strongly advised me to wait and apply for that course. Her foresight resulted in a much better qualification for me.

I could never have undertaken the course without the encouragement of my husband and the help of my mum and dad. The boys were both at school by now, but there were still endless rounds of school pick-ups, activities to get to, dinners to be made and bedtimes. There was a huge amount to consider before I even had the guts to apply. First was the expense – the course was not cheap, especially for us at a time when we were still very strapped for cash. I saved for months, putting money aside wherever I could, and taking on any extra coaching I was offered. And then there was the travel. The ten workshops each lasted between two and four days and were dotted all around England, but never in Scotland. For a good year of my life I was traipsing up and down the country even more than I had been used to for tennis tournaments, and this time I was on my own. It was a feat entirely dependent on having a good support network.

I was more nervous than I had been for years when I attended that first workshop. There were twenty of us in the initial intake: eighteen men and two women. I had never done anything on this scale before. Would I be able to understand the content? Or manage the time commitment? Or cope with the coursework? These anxieties were compounded when, on the very first day, I was told by one of the tutors on the course that one of the male coaches who had applied for a place and not got one, had issued a formal complaint about me getting on the course instead of him. What could *I*, a woman with young children, possibly offer to performance coaching? he had written. The implication was very clear: this was not the place for me. A woman, indeed a mum, did not deserve a chance like this, particularly if she were taking the chance away from a *man*. It was the first time in my working life that a comment about my gender was made to me so openly. And I was shocked.

I didn't even know if the lack of women in tennis was specific to Scotland or if it was a national – or international – trend. I had been busy being a mum, and as a coach this was the first time I had ventured out of Scotland to learn. When I had gone into coaching a couple of years earlier there was no one else doing it, so there hadn't been anyone to run up against. I was making things happen where there had been a vacuum. When I took a team to a competition, as I had been doing over the last few months, it was usually the parents and grandparents who were there supporting the kids. I hadn't had the chance to learn anything about the infrastructure of the various district or county set-ups across the UK, what organisation or individual was driving them, or their gender. When I was back at home in Scotland, the utter lack of coaches had overridden any sense of gender bias I might have noticed. Being in tennis was an anomaly, so being a woman in tennis might have been an anomaly within an anomaly. But now I'd had the temerity to put myself forward and effectively say, 'Yes, I think I could be good at this. I think I have something of value to offer and I think I have every right to be here.'

Maybe this guy wanted to belittle me on behalf of his friend in the hope that I would quit. He didn't. Instead, he made me angry. Angry and determined. Instead of being the first step towards crushing me, it served as rocket fuel for my resolution to be treated equally. Instead of backing away, I started to notice how few women there were in professional tennis. On that course alone, the ratio was eighteen men to two women, and the other women there was only about twenty-two years old. She was lovely, glamorous and unthreatening – very different from me and where I was in my life. But a busy mother of two who didn't care what she looked like and who already had plenty of her own unconventional ideas about how to teach kids – well, that was a different matter entirely.

Now I not only had to complete the course, but I felt I had to do it against the odds: *despite* my colleagues instead of alongside them. Quite a few of the guys on the course were pretty heavyweight sorts, either in terms of their loud personalities, the fact that they were big name ex-players or because they were industry people I had known by reputation for some time. They were intimidating, and I suspect they knew that, even though I had played at a good level myself for years.

I worried about having to demonstrate strokes or do presentations in front of the group, refusing to let myself give up, but shaken by the knowledge that there was no one else like me on the course. Your normal instinct in these sorts of environments is to gravitate towards the people who are more like-minded, but I was never sure who that might be in this crowd. So I kept my head down and elected to focus on learning as much as I possibly could. The course tutors from the LTA were nevertheless a supportive team. Indeed, the head of the Coach Education Department was a woman, and she had stuck her neck out for me with her advice to wait for this course. But I remained dogged by a dread of being singled out, and every demonstration took place with an accompaniment of my inner voice whispering 'don't pick me don't pick me don't pick me', as my arms, hands and fingers pointed down as far as I could get them – the very opposite of the keen child in class who shoots their hand up at every opportunity.

So much of what we were learning was entirely new to me: the sports science, the psychology, the physical training, the biomechanics. I had no idea what biomechanics even were the first time the tutor started talking about it – it's just the mechanics of how living things move! Why has no one ever even mentioned this stuff to me before? I thought, as the lesson progressed. And why are they making it sound so complicated now? And as I sat there, trying to get my head round talk of 'upper body rotation' or similar, I realised that what they were actually talking about was simply what I called 'turning your shoulders'. If you're working with a child and you start throwing out biomechanical terms, they're going to have no idea what you're on about, of that I was quite sure. I'll carry on saying 'turn your shoulders', I quietly decided.

The more big words or complicated theory they threw at me, the more I was trying to process in my head what I could actually tell a seven-year-old. Of course, I needed to know a lot of this detail if I were going to operate on a professional level, but there was little or no allowance made for how to communicate it to our students, especially if they were under ten. That was the key factor missing from the course: everything we discussed was among us adults, and in adult terminology. We did not see any young players or talk about how to communicate with them, yet at the end of the course we were expected to produce a junior pupil and deliver a session with them on a specific topic.

When I got back from each training workshop I was absolutely exhausted. There was so much information for me to take in, along with the added task of sifting through it and working out what I could practically apply to my own coaching. I would sit on the train with my head spinning. It felt like attending endless university lectures – taking reams of notes to reassure yourself that you were taking it all on board, and then ending up with an enormously fat file of data that was all theory and no real insight.

Further down the line I would often think back and wish that someone had talked me through some of the more pragmatic elements of working with international juniors and professional players: what is the best way to deal with jet lag? What do you need to know about playing at altitude, or even about altitude sickness? What are the basics of racket stringing, and how to adjust the tension according to the weather conditions or court surfaces at different events? This is just some of the essential information that any coach training and travelling with a player at international level needs to know.

I wanted to learn from people who had actually been out there and done it, who could tell me what it was like to work with a player at a junior Grand Slam tournament or what the developmental stages of a stand-out little twelve-year-old were, but that type of experience and expertise just wasn't there. Just as Jamie and Andy had such easy confidence in their ability to play WWF because they saw it in front of them every weekend on TV, I wanted to see myself in my teachers, to imagine myself forging a path that they themselves had forged before me. I wanted someone to copy. Once again, I found myself muttering about how if you can see it, you can be it. But in this instance, there was no one and nothing to see. I was just going to have to convince *myself* that I could be it.

Right at the start of the course we were set a project that proved my biggest challenge yet. We had to film a lesson with a 'performance' player and submit it for presentation and review. During the lesson we needed to demonstrate our ability to look at the student's strokes and movement, and discuss what we planned to improve in the coming months and show them how. Sounds relatively simple, doesn't it? But this was over twenty years ago, a long time before mobile phone cameras and instantly uploadable videos. It involved actually buying a video camera, setting it up on a tripod or attaching it to the court fencing, making sure that the shot was framed properly and *then* filming the lesson.

A couple of weeks later, there I was, trying to set up the camera on the fencing of the soggy artificial grass courts at Dunblane, desperate to capture the perfect one-hour session with my guinea pig: seven-year-old Andy. It took ages to get the camera at the right height, and with a wide enough shot that the viewer could see where the balls landed. Eventually, we filmed our lesson and I went home to check out the finished version. I sat on the sofa, watching it with a growing sense of horror, imagining myself presenting it to the rest of the class and thought, Oh God, it just looks so amateur. It's going to seem utterly terrible compared to what that lot come up with.

So the next evening, I persuaded Andy to trek back out to the courts and do it all over again with me. He was less than impressed with the news that I wanted a reshoot, but was more patient with me that I'd imagined he might be. When you're that age you just want to play; you don't want to be hanging around with your mum while she faffs about to see if her work video is filming properly. And of course when you know someone's filming you it makes you a little bit self-conscious. Andy was no different. Tennis or no tennis, all this standing around doing a favour for his mum was boring.

As for me, watching myself back on the small video screen made my toes curl. I could immediately tell that I wasn't being myself; I wasn't being as natural as I would be when teaching unmonitored, with kids I knew and taught regularly, not a son I was trying to appease! I was so conscious that I was trying to put on a show, wondering if the video was catching us and how long I had left of Andy's patience, that I was far from my best. Still, as I watched it again the next evening, I thought that even though it didn't look great, we just had to go with it.

'This is the reality,' I said in the little pep talk I gave myself in an attempt to drum up a bit of confidence. 'This is the reality for me. I don't have sunshine, or indoor courts or anyone to learn from. I work by myself up here, and I have just as much right to learn as the others do.'

I had to force myself to stop focusing on what I didn't have. 'Think about what you *have* got,' I kept telling myself. What I didn't tell myself was that I had the future World number 1 as my guinea pig. Because I didn't know it then. As if anyone would have believed me twenty-odd years ago anyway – he was just standing around on the other side of the court saying, 'Hurry up, Mum, I'm getting cold.'

When the next training workshop rolled round and it was time to present our videos, I had my heart in my mouth as I presented mine, but was secretly quite chuffed with what Andy and I had achieved. I was expected to present the video to the tutor group of four or five of us, and then talk through what I was currently work-ing on, and where I planned to be with my player in three months' time. Those parts I could do. But once we had all finished present-ing, our tutor for this module came up to me and said, 'I'm afraid I'm going to have to ask you to do this with another pupil, because your player is only seven years old. You can't say at seven that a child is a performance player.'

I was aghast. Not because of any apparent slight on Andy's abil-ity, but because he clearly was exceptional for his age.

'Have you seen any other seven-year-olds who can play like that?' I asked the tutor.

'That's not the point,' she replied. 'He's far too young to be con-sidered a "performance player".'

These days there is no convincing me that a 'performance coach' only needs to be able to work with older teenagers. It's actually someone who can take the seven- or eight-year-olds up to fourteen- or fifteen-year old national or international competitors. The skill development, the commitment, the nurturing, the passion, the under- standing of what tennis demands of a player, the care. It is also worth noting that since about 2010, it has been the LTA's specific strategy to try and identify talented seven-year-olds. We are now a nation obsessed by spotting talent at that age. But it wasn't the case then. Back to the drawing board for me.

In the end, I am fairly sure that I passed the course because I was clever and could write good, logical projects on time. No matter how much I wanted it to be, it wasn't a course that focused on practicali- ties, so the final exams and project work were very 'schooly'. There were probably a few people on that course who were fantastic players but not especially academic in that particular grades-focused way.

I already have a degree, I would think to myself as more paper- work piled up for the projects. What I need are practical ideas on how to nurture people and how to get the best out of my players. I need to know how to organise and communicate better, to be able to look at someone and know: What is the absolute best way to help you right now?

I was pretty sure that my portfolio was good enough, but I was also aware that there was a final hurdle I had to pass which others might not break a sweat in passing. I had to complete a 45-minute lesson with a seventeen-year-old male player, and then take a group session with four pupils, all boys. There were no girls on the assess- ments. There were no girls even *mentioned*.

I was given a theme, I composed my lesson, and then I was moni- tored as I worked with the pupil. I am sure my lesson was deeply average, at best, because I was so nervous. Nowadays, I wouldn't find it so nerve-wracking. But that day I realised the most important thing wasn't what we'd been taught on the course, but what we did with it: how we could experiment and learn how to practically apply all of this knowledge. Anyone can understand the what and the why, but *how* to do it and how to *be* as a coach were the skills we could only learn once the course had finished. Mercifully, I passed. I was delighted that I had, but was still painfully aware of how much I still needed to know to be a decent coach.

Being a coach is not about swagger or bravado. It's not just about how well you can play or the knowledge and information you have accrued; it's about how you communicate it to your player and tailor it to their needs. And it's about your passion, commitment and emotional resilience. It only took me a few more years to realise that there was where my skills lay, and that we had more than enough of that emotional resilience in Dunblane.

Now I had the qualification to prove that I could stand alongside all these men and move to the next level with my own coaching. As the first woman to pass the LTA Performance Coach Award I headed back to Dunblane with renewed confidence. I carried on coaching in my district, working largely from the new tennis centre on the Stirling University campus. I would bring bigger and bigger pools of kids together, creating little matches further and further afield – almost at a national level!

Around this time another of my tennis fairy godmothers appeared in the picture. Her name was Gloria Grosset, and she was the secretary of the Scottish Lawn Tennis Association, the equivalent of a Chief Executive now. She called me up one day, and drew my attention to the fact that there was an advertisement in the paper for the role of Scottish National Coach. It had been vacant for about eighteen months, but they were recruiting again and she encouraged me to apply.

The role had a huge remit: from talent spotting the best under tens to putting together the senior (adult) teams in home international matches between the four UK countries, and everything in between. There was the added complication that you can't actually play tennis 'for Scotland' at international level; it is always team GB that is sent to events like the Olympics or the Davis and Fed Cups. The International Tennis Federation (ITF) rules that to be considered 'a nation' you have to have your own government. And as Scotland has its own parliament but not its own government, for ITF events Scots play as part of a GB team. We had friendly Home Internationals, but that was it. Team building aside, the other parts of the national coach's remit were to create a talent identification programme, and player pathway, set up and run the coaches' conference, and of course the district and national squad programmes. The role was financed by Sport Scotland and it presented more or less a blank canvas: perfect for me.

Six months earlier, I would never have even considered myself qualified for the role. But a combination of this woman encouraging me, calling me specifically to say, 'Why don't you go for this?' and the fact that I had now finished my course and had that extra bit of authority made me wonder if it just might be the time to try. Gloria really pushed me to believe that I could do it, so I took a deep breath and sorted out an application.

Part of the recruitment process also involved going for a full, formal interview, completing an on-court presentation (i.e. giving a lesson), and making a presentation about what you would change at Tennis Scotland, the country's governing body. Well, I had the Scottish bit and the tennis bit in the bag, but these were the days before PowerPoint and flash laptops and so the thought of giving a presentation left me about as excited as it had done while I was taking the

coaching qualification. It was going to be tricky. I just hated presenting or performing at any level. Now that I had the benefit of hindsight,
I could see that part of what had kept me from pursuing life as a
professional player had been the game's essential need to be viewed.
I loved the sport, I loved the strategy, the tactics and I loved the
competing, but I was far less keen on putting on a performance for
a crowd, which some players do instinctively. By now, I was as sure as
I had been when I had sought that duff teacher's advice as a teenager:
my role in tennis was as a coach, a confidence-giver, a talent-spotter,
a skill-developer and a creator of opportunities.

To fulfil this renewed dream, I knew I needed something
professional – a tool that would give me absolutely the best chance,
so I went into town and got myself a little mini flipchart. I didn't have
the money for anything more upmarket so I had to make do with
this tabletop flipchart and some really, *really* neat handwriting.
When I moved house recently, I found this flipchart again in an old
packing box and had a good flick through it. I was quite proud of
myself actually and found myself thinking: Do you know what,
there's a lot of stuff here that I would still do today. It was twenty-two
years ago, but most of it has either been put into practice nationally
or is something I would still develop in strategy planning today.

There were three of us up for the job in the end. Me, a guy from
Poland and one from Australia. On the morning of the interviews,
I realised that I had met the guy from Poland before at a coaching
conference, which instantly made me worry about how much more
experience he had than me, given that he'd worked all over the
world. As we got chatting, I found out that the Australian guy had a
similarly high level of experience. They were two really strong candidates in terms of international experience and worldliness.
But – as I kept telling myself – they didn't know Scotland.

I had a couple of other aces up my sleeve. The other two candidates knew no players locally, so they had to do their demonstration lesson with kids who were provided by the interviewers. However, I took two players who I was working with at the time. They both lived in Edinburgh, where the interview was being held, and their parents got them out of school and brought them up to the venue for me. I told them that it was just a demonstration, not that I was applying for the role of National Coach, to ease the pressure on them.

In addition, the other two candidates simply didn't know that much about the tennis scene in Scotland. These were pre-internet days, and Tennis Scotland wasn't in the press much at that time, so it must have been hard for them to build a picture of what was going on. But for me, well, it was my life. It was what I had devoted the last couple of years to, after a lifetime of playing myself. The more I looked into the role and what I could do with it, the more I realised how much the job would mean to me.

I'd only ever had two job interviews since I'd left university, and as I researched I stoked both my nerves and my excitement with thoughts of how much potential there was for me to really get something done in the role. Saying what I would do 'if only I could get my teeth into the Scottish National Coach's job' was the kind of conversation I'd have over a glass of wine with my old playing friends, so having to formalise that and put forward a clear case for what I'd do with the role was both exhilarating and terrifying and showed me how much I wanted the job . . . and how devastated I would be if I didn't get it.

The very same evening I was telephoned by the President of Tennis Scotland and formally offered the job. I was thrilled and so excited at having my first formal job in tennis. The new role, and a permanent salary, were a mixture of exciting and intimidating, especially as it happened at a time when the boys, aged eight and nine respectively, were just getting good enough to be looking further afield for their own playing.

It was a big change though. I had to make a swift shift from being an independent soul, doing pretty much what I wanted when I wanted, to working for a formal, government-funded organisation. And with that came responsibilities. When you work for yourself you can say what you want, but I quickly learned that you have to bite your tongue when you are representing a big organisation. There is so much more accountability: a specified aim, a budget, a strategy. Trying to make kids have fun running around all day no longer qualified as a valid goal.

My office was located at the Scottish Tennis HQ at Craiglockhart on the outskirts of Edinburgh. I would drive up there during the day to deal with the admin side of things, although any teaching I did was still at the tennis centre in Stirling, and as with anyone involved in sport with children, a lot of the crucial work I did was at weekends and in the evenings after school. Once I had got the boys to school I would often go to Edinburgh for a few hours before driving back in time for them to finish school and then heading out to Stirling for coaching. The days were longer and more hectic, and there was so much more travel than when I'd just popped to Torags or the Dunblane Tennis Club, but for as long as I felt that I was making a difference, I didn't mind. And it wasn't as if I were a music teacher with two sporty kids – it worked well that the boys were often training where I was teaching, or being taken care of playing other sports when I had obligations with other kids. We were busy, but we slotted around each other pretty comfortably.

There were other challenges, though. Scotland is a country with a land mass about the same as England's, but we had only one indoor tennis centre, and only 1 per cent of the population played tennis. As far as funding was concerned, this meant it was a real challenge being taken seriously in comparison to other, more established Scottish sports, but it also meant that simply covering the entire country fairly was a stretch. Once again, I told myself not to panic. Just because no 'mum' had taken on this role before, and just because there had been no one in the role for some time, didn't mean it couldn't be done. I had a £25,000 salary, an annual budget of £90,000 and no staff as yet. But I had energy, drive and an amazing taste of freedom. It was very exciting. The key was to start small and break the project into separate, manageable chunks and see what was feasible. Where could I actually make changes? Where could I have a genuine impact? And where would it count most? For the first time I realised that I was in a position to really make a difference. I would find the most promising kids, and the most motivated young coaches and create a team. It sounds so noble now, but I just wanted to surround myself with as much talent and enthusiasm as I could, in the hope that the positivity would spread, and we could build a fantastic workforce to grow the game.

One of the crucial elements of building a proper team was keeping the kids playing throughout the winter – if I really wanted to have an impact I couldn't lose half the group to other sports the minute the evenings got dark, damp and chilly. This meant keeping them training and competing throughout the winter months, but that in turn meant travelling year round, which of course stretched my meagre budget. I was the only person who seemed to have made the connection between consistent competitions and keeping the kids' attention, so of course it was down to me to make the finances elastic enough to accommodate this. At first, I just had to use parents wherever I could, but after a while I would beg friends to lend a hand. We'd hire a minibus and I would persuade a buddy to share the driving with me – this not only meant another adult pair of hands that I could trust, but if it was a mate I could share a room with it saved on costs and we'd have a laugh. Having someone I knew to help – and of course keep me company – also enabled me to keep in touch with friends when I was working all hours.

Another motivation for me was that I spotted the chance to give the women around me more opportunities and more of a voice. By now it was becoming crystal clear to me that women in tennis were rare, to say the very least, but the women who *were* there were diamonds. I knew that the two biggest career opportunities I had benefitted from were both made possible by other women, and within a relatively short amount of time came a third. There had been Anne Pankhurst, the woman who had persuaded me to take the bigger coaching course; Gloria who had persuaded me to apply for the national coach job; and now, within weeks, my friend Ellinore Lightbody, who had been running the national tennis scene in Wales and was now captain of the British Under 14 girls team, gave me my first opportunity to take a GB team to an overseas tournament. I had taken some of the Scottish kids to an occasional event abroad in the past year, but this would be a GB trip, a proper international LTA-funded trip, and a real step up for me.

Ellinore had offered this opportunity to me because I was a woman, and she, rightly, thought it was a good idea for the girls to have a female coach to accompany them. Again, the gender mismatch in the sport was made clear to me, and in grabbing this fantastic opportunity, I promised myself that I would create just as many for women in the future, whenever I could.

5

Heading for America, or how they do it in the Sunshine State

In which we head to Miami for a tournament and we discover that there are places where ambition is nothing to be ashamed of, but a positive mindset, a well of inspiration, and an asset. If only we could import it back home.

Accompanying the GB girls' team abroad was a fabulous opportunity for me professionally, but it was also a role I took seriously as a parent. It had only been the year before that I had waved my own boys off to their first tournament abroad, and I knew what a knot in the pit of your stomach that moment left you with for the first time. It was an Under 11s tournament, which meant that the boys were very young to be travelling without a parent.

But more importantly than that, I was very keen for the boys to get out of Dunblane that year and have some fun doing what they loved best. The tournament took place only a few months after the shootings at Dunblane Primary School, and every one of us in the town had been swamped by grief, or its nearby presence, ever since.

I remember moments of that day so clearly, and others are hazy with strange elastic patches of time. I had just dropped the boys off at school and had headed to Torags, where I had a call saying there had been a shooting at the primary school. I dropped everything, grabbed my car keys and ran. As I was driving the short distance to the school I kept thinking I might never see my children again. It was chaos, and there were too many cars on the road, everyone desperately trying to get to the school. Traffic was at a standstill, with the cars going nowhere, so I just got out, left my car and ran the last quarter mile.

It's terrifying to think how close Andy was to what happened. His class was the next to go into the gym. They were on their way there when they heard an unfamiliar noise and were told to wait in the corridor. A teacher went to investigate and suddenly Andy's class was being ushered into the headmaster's study. They didn't know what was going on – they were only eight – but they were told to sit down below the windows, or under the tables, and the teachers and dinner ladies got them singing songs to disguise the sound of the gunfire. I don't know how the hell those adults managed not to fall apart. Jamie's class was in a Portakabin classroom in the playground next to the gym when the shooting started. He remembers hearing a strange 'pop pop pop' sound but thought it was someone knocking on the roof of the cabin with a hammer, not gunfire. You would never think of gunfire, would you?

When I arrived at the school gates, everything was eerily quiet. The gates were closed and hoards of parents were standing there, in shock, terrified. It was before the age of mobile phones. We had no information, what could we do? We were moved to a small hotel close to the school and told to wait. And wait. We heard ambulance sirens and police cars arriving but we had no idea which class had been affected. We were so tightly packed in that room that I ended up sharing a chair with another mother, a woman I had been to primary school with, who had lived across the road from me when we were little.

It was ages until we knew which class had been in the gym. When they made the announcement I breathed a huge sigh of relief, just as the woman I was sitting with leapt up and gasped, 'That's my daughter's class'. Her daughter was one of the sixteen who were killed that day. I was horrified and completely overwhelmed, torn between my monumental relief that the boys were safe, and beset by guilt at how fortunate we had been, when other parents had lost their children.

There is never a day when I don't remind myself how lucky I am that my children survived. Even when they left the school premises they still had no idea what had happened in the gym, and although I told them that afternoon, it took some time for them to fully understand it, and longer still for them to be able to talk about it. This is why – no matter how hard it felt to say goodbye to them those first few times they went to tournaments abroad – I wanted them to relish every moment of fun, to seize joy wherever they could, and it is why to this day all of us feel a strong responsibility to show the world that the town of Dunblane is so much more than the memory of a horrific tragedy. It is survival, it is resilience, it is success.

That first event they went to on their own was in France, and was called Enfants de la Terre, part of a charity run by the former French player Yannick Noah. Great Britain was sending over a team of two boys and two girls, and the LTA picked both of my boys for the team. It was great news that they got to travel with each other, but a double whammy as far as the costs were concerned.

It was a great opportunity to go abroad as part of a team at that age, but still, my heart was in my mouth as I understood the wider implications of sending them. Transport was not mentioned at all in the letter that informed us that they had been selected; it was just a very calm, formal mention that: 'The trip leaves from Bisham Abbey on x date, you will need to be there at x o'clock.' Classic bureaucracy. Bisham Abbey, near Maidenhead in Berkshire, housed the GB National Tennis Centre. It was the home to many sports, and was the base from which the LTA ran all of its national age-group camps, from Under 12s to Under 18-year-olds. The trip was funded by the LTA because it was a GB team event, but we still had to pay for getting down to Bisham Abbey itself, which, with two pre-teen boys who would need adult supervision each way, was going to mean a minimum of eight flights to and from Scotland. After all, I couldn't just take a mini-break in the Home Counties while they were away; I would have to head down to drop them off, and back down to collect them. It was going to cost a small fortune.

This was the first moment where I stopped thinking about my national programme budget and realised that our own family budget was going to have to develop hitherto unknown levels of elasticity. I remember standing there at the kitchen counter that day, staring at the kettle as it boiled, the letter still in my hand, thinking, Oh, okay, this is what the next few years are going to feel like.

It's a moment that most parents of talented children will have at some point. You hit a stage where the children start competing all over the country and beyond if they are going to reach their full potential, but as they are still minors they need constant supervision. And all of this without the backup of prize money. In short, you have to start paying for experience, and in tennis, experience costs a lot. Unlike potential professional football players, who are whisked into an academy, provided with training, transported to matches and garlanded with kit – all the while sharing one ball between twenty-two of them for a single match – the tennis players of the future are funding their own coaching and competition, kit, and endless rackets, balls and re-strings.

The re-strings in particular were the bane of my life at this point: yet what was a money pit for me was a badge of honour for the boys. Every time they snapped a string on court, I would hear the whoop from the other side of the tennis centre, or they would come running towards the car that evening grinning from ear to ear. 'Mum, check it out, I broke another string!' they'd say, bubbling with excitement, fizzing with pride at their on-court prowess. I would do my best to smile back but it was really a grimace as I silently thought to myself, There goes another tenner. I'd grip the steering wheel hard, willing myself not to beg them to not break any more. Mercifully, in time they learned to string their own rackets and we even invested in a stringing machine for the garage where they would set themselves up and learn the intricacies of string types and tensions. If only there had been such a practical solution to all of the travelling costs.

I couldn't say no to them though, and of course we found a way to get them to Bisham Abbey for that first tournament abroad. It sounded like such an adventure and I knew that if I'd been their age I would have been desperate to go, but I still worried about them being safe. They were so little, and they had only ever been abroad with us for family holidays in the past. But every mum has to deal with that first sleepover and this was really just a slightly bigger version of that.

After copious warnings to brush their teeth, look after each other, and to keep their travel bags zipped up tightly at all times, I waved them off at Bisham Abbey as they headed to the LTA minibus, their little bodies weighed down by heavy racket bags and luggage. I had a lump in my throat, torn between pride and missing them already, but they didn't even look back.

They had a great time in France. It was a perfect little starter tournament, where they played in lots of matches, mainly at one central club but also at several satellite venues like school halls as well. Andy made the semi-final and lost to Gaël Monfils, a French player who is now one of the top players in the world and a great athlete. It was Jamie who won the tournament though, beating Monfils in the final, 6–0, 6–1. All I heard for about three months after their return was Andy telling him, 'You only won because I tired him out for you.' Sibling rivalry was perhaps the only thing that tormented me more than re-strings did back then . . .

The main thing I learned from their experience in France was that, because they'd had such a great time, winning matches and being accompanied by an encouraging, fun, LTA chaperone who understood both tennis and kids, they never feared going abroad in the future. There was no anxiety about the unknown; only a 'we can conquer the world' mentality, which was a huge step for them psychologically. I'm not sure I fully appreciated it at the time, as I was more focused on them having a fun experience and the practicalities from my end, but it was an enormous thing to do at such a young age – especially to also be successful and return feeling that they had survived a big adventure together. It was brilliantly handled by the LTA and they were never anxious, homesick or fretting about the language barrier or the food. For me, it was a moment of realisation: you have to let your kids go off and have their own adventures. It gave them confidence and a desire to do it again, but it also inspired me to try and create the same sorts of opportunities for the kids under my wing as the Scottish National Coach.

One of the things I found frustrating at the time was trying to explain to the team of administrators and people in charge of schedules at the LTA how difficult the travel was for parents on a limited budget – particularly for parents with two kids on the programme. It was amazing to see Andy and Jamie progress but the logistics were a nightmare. What if one child is going to Nottingham one weekend and the other has to be in Birmingham, or London? It can't be done! You can't be in both places! Especially difficult as Will and I had separated around that time. Yet what I came to realise was that many of the people back then making the decisions about the junior circuit and training camps had never gone through the experience as either a coach or as a parent. They just didn't know what it was like. Trying to explain these things to the layers of administrators was as much of a workout as any I did on the court!

There was a massive advantage to being up in Scotland. As we were so reliant on each other for endless lifts, minibus rides and hours of company and laughs, criss-crossing the country's motorways, we became like a big family, closer than so many other regional teams, which was the glue that held it all together when finances were tight or tempers were frayed. It was great fun and everybody looked out for each other, and I strongly suspect that those happy times have a lot to do with why so many of the kids who started at around the same time are still involved in tennis in some way today. Whether they're playing like my boys, whether they're coaching like Alan MacDonald, who was one of the older juniors back then and now travels as part of Jamie's coaching team, or whether they're captaining the GB Davis Cup team as Leon Smith does these days, the vast majority of that original gang are still playing tennis or working in the game now. And I believe there is one simple reason behind that: they learned to love what they were doing.

It was informal, recreational fun, and that emotional connection stuck. The sense of belonging was huge. I guess that is why it is second nature to me to try and make everyone feel as if they are all a part of one big team, whatever capacity I am working in now. People still come and talk to me about those days at Stirling in the nineties. 'I remember the day when you came down to the Doncaster tournament in the minibus, and you climbing over the fence to get into the courts so we could practise early in the morning.' It wasn't a high fence . . . we weren't doing any harm. We would just turn up before everyone else and if the courts were locked we would find a way in somehow.

I do think all of those hijinks have a lot to do with how the boys feel about the game now. They built an emotional and psychological resilience over those years. Being in Scotland and not having very much makes you appreciate what you do have. The distances we'd have to travel and the limited amount of time we could actually get on court made it feel like a treat not a chore. And having a slim budget and restrictive court time for me as a coach made me think carefully about what I wanted to get out of each session. I'd plan it and manage it meticulously. For example, I would think: If I only have these four kids for an hour, I need to max out on this hour. It also forced me to become good at dealing with big numbers on just one court. If it cost £12 an hour to book a court and I could get eight kids on it, it would only cost them £1.50 each. If it was one child, that was £12 gone – whoosh! – on that one person. So I learned to devise good quality sessions for multiple kids. Perhaps those hardships were the making of us after all.

The new job, the travel, the sense of community within our whole tennis group . . . by the end of the 1990s I was learning so much and we were all improving so fast that it slightly escaped my attention just how good my own boys were getting. They were aged ten and eleven by now, but by this point we weren't thinking: These could be once in a generation players for Scotland and the UK, we were still thinking that it was a hobby with huge benefits that was starting to get really expensive, but that we didn't want to stop them if they were doing well and having fun.

My philosophy had been to take things one tournament at a time – for all of us on the Scottish squad, not just Jamie and Andy. Over the previous couple of years I had started to think, Okay, what do the best Under 12s look like nationally? What do I need to know to be able to help my lot?

So that by the time they reached the Under 12 category, I knew what the circuit looked like and what the expectations were likely to be both nationally and internationally. The older kids in the group were forging a path for the rest of them, showing me what we were going to need for the younger children further down the line, as well as what I needed to put aside in terms of our budget as a squad, and as a family. Meanwhile, it was part of my remit as National Coach to keep trying to identify future talent, as well as nurturing what we already had. It was for this reason that in around 1996 I set up a further venture which I loftily named the Scottish National Development Schools programme, when more indoor centres started to open beyond Stirling. Another centre opened at Scotstoun in Glasgow, which gave us a further venue from which we could deliver training, so I set up another squad programme for Under 10s there. SNDS sounds quite grand, but they only really operated on a Saturday morning.

As National Coach, my philosophy was to invest in people and develop a team of excellent coaches, because more good coaches equals more good players. Right? And a couple of years into my stint as National Coach an opportunity arose to do just that and draw experts to Scotland after the summer. The idea was to create a Performance Development Programme in conjunction with

SportScotland. We had a number of very keen – and very part-time – regional coaches then, all operating at county level. Nothing national and certainly nothing international. I knew I wouldn't be able to do all the coaching and travelling myself, so I set about applying for the £10,000 funding. The remit of a national coach is broad and elastic: you are the strategist, the managing director, the keeper of the books, as well as the coach courtside, doing the hands-on work. I knew I didn't have all these skills and I found myself regularly in situations where I needed advice from experts.

Building anything – a talented child, team, business, yourself – demands investment and expertise. Learning how to go about building that expertise was one of the most valuable lessons I ever learned as a coach, and here I was being given the opportunity to invest in our team. I grasped it wholeheartedly. The funding for the programme enabled me to bring in experts from abroad and from down south on a regular basis to help the coaches: we had Ivo Van Haken, the technical director of a Belgian team, to work on technique; Istran Balyi from Canada to discuss periodisation – segmenting an athlete's year wisely – and long-term athlete development; Doug Gould, a tennis-specific sports psychologist came from the States; and Steve Green, fitness trainer to Tim Henman, flew up from London. This programme not only helped me build my skills but also to mentor and develop several coaches who have since had a significant impact on British tennis. Not least Leon Smith, Davis Cup captain, and Karen Ross, lead of GB disability and the coach to Scotland's World number 1 wheelchair player, Gordon Reid. Once again, the team, and investment in the team, was what brought success. In turn, this reflected well on the junior players themselves.

My plan must have worked: by 1998 we had some players who

were ready to be part of Great Britain's team heading to a huge Miami-based tournament called the Orange Bowl. Included were my Jamie and Jamie Baker, a lad from Glasgow who was part of the Scottish squad, having come out of the Scottish National Development Schools programme. The GB team was made up of two boys and two girls, and the entire trip was to be funded by the Lawn Tennis Association. I was asked again to captain the girls and seized the opportunity. The boys' captain was a guy called Andrew Lewandowski, who I got on very well with. He had done these trips before so he knew exactly what to expect and what all of the logistics entailed, which was reassuring to say the least.

It couldn't have been more perfect for me – a chance to take an intercontinental trip with a trusted colleague, and the added pride of the two GB lads, one of which was my son, being from my programmes in Scotland. To attend an event on that scale, to see the world standard of Under 12 players, and to meet other coaches and tennis professionals from one of tennis's key states, was a fabulous opportunity. I wanted to learn and the best way to learn is to keep speaking to people who have done it all before, so in this respect there really wasn't anywhere I'd have rather been at this stage. And while the professional experience alone was gold dust, the chance to see my Jamie play on this world stage was also a big incentive – as well as a huge gear change for us.

Jamie was of course beyond excited to be going. He was by now one of the best Under 12 players in the country – and he knew it – so getting selected in itself was not such a huge surprise, but the chance to go to America to play tennis was a huge deal and he was excited about every aspect, from the matches themselves to simply seeing the country that was already so familiar to him from TV and movies.

First, there was the seven-hour flight with four pre-teens to get through, and it was about as much work for us adults as it sounds. These were the days where there was no quick WhatsApp to parents to let them know we were fine, no FaceTime before bed and no instant bank transfers in case of emergency: it was a full three-week trip with all the attendant anxieties. These kids really were entirely in our charge and I felt a huge responsibility. Luckily, the previous few years of almost ceaseless travel in a minibus full of kids had left me with a keen understanding of what keeps them distracted. By this time I rarely left the house without a bag full of puzzle books, quizzes, pens, card games, whatever. There might be one slim magazine for me at the bottom, but mostly I wanted to keep them entertained, to keep nerves and homesickness at bay, to keep everyone calm and happy. Mercifully by the time we took this flight, Game Boys had been invented, and there was also the distraction of in-flight movies.

When we arrived in Miami, I was left speechless at the size and scale of almost everything we came across. I had never been to the US before and nor had any of the kids; it felt as if were in a different universe, not merely a different country. Just the drive from the airport seemed like an adventure, on those enormous roads filled with huge, stately cars. We were just staying in a simple Holiday Inn near to the competition venue, but it was still massive, and when we reached the tournament venue the next day, our eyes were on stalks.

The Orange Bowl was held at a five-star hotel called The Biltmore, which had a huge tennis complex and enormous, gorgeous grounds. The sort of place they invented the word 'sprawling' for. It was without doubt the most beautiful hotel I had ever seen in my life, let alone had business being in. It was proper, old-world luxury – the sort of environment where it was totally normal for a milkshake to cost $15. Surrounding the hotel, the luxury didn't stop. There were monster houses sitting on vast plots of land surrounded by ornate white fences and gleaming Doric columns. The opulence was compounded by the fantastical Christmas decorations everywhere. It was December, and despite being confusingly sun-drenched, Florida was very much in the swing of the festivities. These houses were not just festooned with lights and decorations, but liberally covered in fake snow as well – particularly disorientating for this group of visitors who were only just getting used to being away from real Scottish snow at home. There was one house in particular which fascinated us; we simply couldn't work out what the decorations were meant to be. They were white – fair enough, that's pretty Christmassy – but the main decoration on the roof was an incomprehensibly weird shape. It was a few days before we found out what it was.

Meanwhile, the draw for the tournament was enormous. The qualifying event had 128 competitors, made up largely of American kids, and was played the week before. The main draw – in which our boys and girls were competing – was made up of players who had earned a place on account of their national rankings or results in overseas tournaments throughout the year. There were 256 kids in qualifying and a further 256 in the main draw all over the world. That first morning as we walked around the tennis complex taking everything in, I could barely believe my eyes, and there was one thing in particular that seemed utterly foreign. The whole place was outdoors, in December! They could rely on the fact that the rows upon rows of tennis courts would be useable all year round because of the beaming Florida sunshine. What a bonus!

Around the corner there were yet more courts, and then between the hotel and Miami University, another of the tournament's hubs, was a further area called Flamingo Park which was teeming with, you guessed it, more tennis courts. There were probably more courts in those three areas than there were in the whole central belt of Scotland. It took a while for it to sink in. The weather is so good, people can play outside year round; it's a big country, and loads of people *want* to play tennis. It was a revelation after years in Scotland fighting to find a decent court to play on, fighting to be taken seriously as a coach, and fighting for scraps of enthusiasm or funding from governing bodies.

Even the practice week before the Orange Bowl began highlighted the different attitude here. There was a small warm-up tournament for a few days before the main event began, for the kids to get used to the heat, to get over any jet lag and to find their feet a bit. On the morning of day three we went to practise at a park near our Holiday Inn. It had perhaps six courts *and* a designated park keeper in charge of them. When he heard our accents and asked if we were over for the Orange Bowl, he could not have been more welcoming. He was almost cartoonishly jolly, this great big back-slapping chap with a booming voice. Everything he said exuded positivity, warmth and enthusiasm for what these kids were doing.

So of course we ended up going back a few times and getting to know him quite well – he came to be our go-to guy for weird and wonderful questions about Miami. It was he who explained to us what the bizarre Christmas decorations were on that mansion near to the hotel. 'Oh that guy!' he boomed. 'He's a big-shot dentist! That's a tooth!'

After a week or so the endless white-toothed smiles, the beaming sunshine and the radiating positivity began to rub off on us, too. The main tournament began and to my utter delight all four of the children did really well. I had such a wonderful time watching each of them progress, round after round, and seeing two of them reach the final. This was a huge deal and very unexpected. Out of over 250 competitors, one of my girls and my Jamie had reached their respective final.

The boys' final and the girls' final were at different venues so I didn't get to see Jamie's big game, nor did I see him during the tournament as much I would have if I had gone as a parent rather than as a coach. But there was the added advantage of him being able to just get on with things. And of course we were all staying in the same hotel so in the evenings we could all eat together, catch up and play endless games of cards.

We all learned a lot in Miami, but more than anything we learned that there were places in the world where loving the game and wanting to win were not strange or shameful concepts. Instead, perhaps, they could be encouraged and that encouragement could breed success. In Scotland we were used to frosty referees with lots of extra rules and the mantra that you should all 'know your place'. In America all we heard was: 'You guys are gonna smash this tournament! You go out there and have a great time! Be proud!' The idea that it was okay to have a sense of ambition ignited the children's imagination.

It is okay to want to be better and to do better. This was the first time they'd heard this attitude. And it was the first time that I saw something I had been trying so hard to impress upon them emphasised on such an epic scale. Of course, getting up almost every morning in December to blue skies and fantastic facilities helped to sweeten the message, but the point remained: wanting to win wasn't impudence; it could merely be positivity.

6

The hardest decision as a parent, or how I learned when to say no

In which I try to ignore my intuition and regret it almost immediately. No opportunity can come at the cost of a child's happiness, and having the courage to say no is a lesson once learned, never forgotten.

The year ended on a high, and it looked as if 1999 was going to follow in its footsteps when Jamie was talent-spotted that January at a tournament in Telford for Under 14s called Teen Tennis. It was a warm-up tournament for a big February event in Tarbes, and saw kids from all over Europe and beyond gather for a bit of match practice before heading to France.

Jamie was spotted by Ian Barclay, a UK-based Australian coach, who had coached Pat Cash when he won Wimbledon in 1997. He was quite an elderly guy – not one of the cool young coaches, but a wise, grandfatherly figure. He was working for the LTA at the time as lead coach at the National Tennis Centre at Bisham Abbey, a residential base for young players who were on the LTA full-time programme. They went to school nearby and received coaching and physical training under the watchful eye of Ian and his team. They were, however, all much older than Jamie who was still not even thirteen at this point.

I had met Ian a few times before when the boys had been down to Bisham Abbey for various national camps. Although those camps weren't run by Ian, he had been around, and was aware of the boys. He made a huge contribution to the boys' training in offering to analyse videos of their strokes and returning them with training advice. And he was a nice man, who understood that kids just need to be kids sometimes. A kind of grandfatherly figure who could see that these children had needs beyond tennis and that care was of as much value as training drills. I had gone down to observe some of those camps as part of my own job as National Coach, and he had been very helpful in terms of giving me tips about what kids should be working on at certain ages and stages, so I trusted him as a person, not just a coach. When he watched Jamie playing at Teen Tennis that January, he asked me what my plans were for him in the future. I didn't really have any; I was still making it up as I went along.

He broached the subject of Jamie coming down from Scotland to be based at Bisham Abbey, to train with him. Of course, it was a huge honour that Jamie was even being considered.

But there was a big niggle: Jamie was still very much a child at just twelve. It really was a huge concern for me that if he accepted this LTA-funded place (and not everyone did as it was still a considerable commitment), he wasn't left on his own, a little boy far away from home.

We made a tentative visit down south to go and look at nearby schools. I still had my doubts, but Ian had promised that he would

Yeah, it's true, I was being force-fed tennis balls before I could walk.

Learning to ski in Aviemore, aged six.

Developing motor skills and
confidence in the most natural way:
climbing trees on family walks.

Playing together in the great
outdoors. Sledging with my
mum and my brothers.

Trophy kid! Loving the wooden racket but my hair is awful. Aged fourteen.

Scottish Grass Court Championships final 1981.
Just before I graduated from Edinburgh University.

Our first picture together. Jamie aged fifteen
months and Andy a few days old.

Jamie, eighteen months old, watering the plants,
along with my broken old tennis racket, which he
insisted on dragging everywhere with him.

The way we were.

The way they were.
Typical boys. In the
garden with a football.
Love the muddy knees
and the Hibs tracksuit.

Top Gear?

My last day as Scottish National Coach. Finished as I started, surrounded by kids.

Taking a break from working on the Virginia Wade tennis clinic at Gleneagles to play with the boys, 1989.

The LTA gave me their Coach of the Year Award in 2001. It was my first black tie event! The thing I remember most about it was meeting John McEnroe.

Dunblane Primary School team 1994. Team sport creates sense of belonging and develops so many life skills for kids.

Andy and Abbie, the puppy my parents got for him when Jamie left for Cambridge in 1997.

Jamie playing in the Orange Bowl Championships in Miami, 1998.

Jamie winning the British Under 18 Doubles Championship with Tom Burn in 2003. Was it a sign?

A junior grand slam champion in 2004. From Scotland.
Who'd have believed it? Well me, maybe.

look after Jamie and would invite him over to his house to check up on him on an emotional level from time to time. He had a wonderful way with kids, and I had absolute faith in him. We took our time to decide. It was a massive, life-changing decision. After some soul-searching, we found a really nice boarding school. It was lovely, near to Bisham Abbey, and somewhere I could just about imagine leaving Jamie to head off on such a big adventure. Jamie was desperate to go because in his little mind he wanted to be a tennis player, and he thought that to be a tennis player you have to leave home and train with special people.

By May that year, we had visited the school again and the decision was made. Jamie would be living amongst a lot of other kids his own age there, so it solved the problem of him being so much younger than the boys training alongside him on the LTA programme at Bisham Abbey. He wasn't always going to be the youngest, he would have appropriate time and space to develop emotionally as well as to improve his tennis. So we were reasonably confident that this would be a good solution, or at least one worth trying, particularly as the LTA would be funding it as part of his inclusion in their training programme.

Looking back, if I had known then what I know now, I would never have even considered it. What happened over the next few months was one of the most heartbreaking experiences of my life, and certainly one of the most difficult as a mother. Hindsight is everyone's best friend, but oh how I wish I could have paid a little less attention to the flattery of professionals, and a little more to my raw maternal instincts. Now, whenever parents speak to me about moving house in order to be closer to a tennis opportunity, or remortgaging their home to send their kids away as young as that I say, 'Absolutely not, they are just too young.' And I *know* I am right.

But it is different when it's happening to you and your child. It is hard not to feel flattered when someone who has recently produced a Wimbledon champion is telling you that your son has enormous ability, has what it takes to make it to the top and simply needs some tailored training. If you're already feeling a little out of your depth, if you want the very best for your kids, it is all too easy to believe somebody who does, demonstrably, know what it takes. It is as if they have the keys to the magic kingdom and they're inviting you in, as simple as that. But . . . it's never that simple, is it?

Jamie had his bags packed months in advance, and was counting down the days. He was like a puppy – so enthusiastic about more tennis, more play, more of what he enjoyed. I don't think it's unusual at that age to be excited if someone offers you a big opportunity to do what you love, but he really was delirious with joy and I was delighted for him. As far as he was concerned it was basically a chance to do his hobby nearly all of the time.

Everything was set up for him to start in September. As the date drew closer we contacted Jamie's current school and said he wouldn't be coming back, explaining what he was off to do. At the end of term in June they had a little ceremony for him at the school and explained to the rest of the pupils what he was doing, where he was going and what an incredible opportunity it was. They made a big fuss of him at the school assembly, wished him luck, gave him a card and that was that.

That July, I went down to Bisham Abbey alone as I was due to take a group of Under 14 girls away for two weeks to Germany and it was still the launch post for those trips. While I was there, I made a point of finding the guy who was in charge of setting it all up for Jamie. Communication from the LTA had gone eerily silent. When I spotted him I asked him what was happening with the school for Jamie, as we hadn't had any paperwork or anything back yet. He said, as casually as could be, 'Ah, I need to speak to you about that.'

'Uh huh?' I replied, as the blood started to chill in my veins.

'Well,' he continued, 'there's been a change of plan. The LTA have decided that they're going to close Bisham Abbey as a centre over the next twelve months, so there isn't any point in Jamie starting in September.'

I looked at him, absolutely dumbfounded. 'This is the middle of July. We've taken our son out of school and set him up to go to this new school because you had promised him a training place down here. Now you're casually telling me – because I happen to have tracked you down – that there has been a change of plan?'

'Yeah,' he said, 'I'm really sorry, I've only just found out about it.'

'I don't believe that,' I replied. And I didn't. He was only telling me because I had cornered him. 'I just don't believe you've only just found out about it. When were you going to tell me? What are we going to do now? Jamie has had his bag packed since February. The school held a leaving ceremony for him and he's ready to start.'

Uppermost in my mind I was thinking, How on earth am I going to tell Jamie that this isn't happening now? But I was doing my best to keep my cool and salvage the situation where possible.

The new strategy was to close Bisham Abbey and to set up seven regional training centres around the country. 'One of those centres will be in Cambridge,' he explained, 'and there will be a place for Jamie there. There is a very good school nearby . . .'

'Uh huh?' I said. 'And what about Ian Barclay?' It was Ian's participation, after all, which had sealed the deal as far as we were concerned.

'Well, he'll come up and train with Jamie three times a week.'

This entire arrangement was a far cry from what we had agreed to. I was furious. I was shaking, flabbergasted that they could leave it that late to tell me what was happening. They must have known for a long time by this point: they already had these regional centres set up and ready to go. I was supposed to be leaving in the morning to take the girls on this trip and I didn't want to let them down, but heard myself saying to him: 'I feel like walking away and just leaving you to it. I'll just go home and sort my family out, shall I?'

In the end I agreed to go and do the trip to Germany just for the first week. 'I need to go home and put things right for my family,' I said, my heart hammering at the thought of what this would do to my happy little son.

When I came home and we finally told Jamie, he just put his arms on the table, buried his head in his hands and cried his eyes out. It was the worst thing I have ever had to do to one of my children. It absolutely broke his heart. We explained to him about the Cambridge option, and asked him whether he would like to go and look at that. There were one or two boys he knew who were starting there in September, but again, they were a little bit older than him.

So, filled with trepidation, we headed down south again, but this time I felt like there was so much more on the line. We looked at the tennis centre, at the lovely facilities. The school nearby was really fantastic, but the classes were divided differently there – Jamie would have been in the prep school at this place, whereas the other boys he knew would have been in the senior school, living and being taught separately from him. So, as well as being in a different school from the few boys he did know, he was also having to go in at the top of the prep school, which is the hardest time to try and integrate as a new boy. All the friendships there would have been made years ago and I knew it, even if he was prepared to try and brush that aside.

If you're going to make a decision like this – literally splitting your family in half for months on end – you have to be doing it because the child really, *really* loves their sport. And Jamie did love the sport. But the key for us agreeing to send him away originally had been the combination of factors: Ian Barclay was a hugely respected coach, but he was also a decent human being and a good substitute for a family member. And three visits a week, if that, was not the same as what we had been promised. Jamie couldn't see that then, though, and I didn't have the heart to hold him back. And that was probably my biggest mistake.

Even if Jamie had felt terrible and been horribly nervous about going away to a different, unexpected school, I think he still would have said yes to it because he wanted to be in the system, to play tennis, to be selected. He wanted to be special, to be at the top. I think that running through his mind the whole time was: I want to be a tennis player, I'm not going to be able to do it in Scotland. It's just my mum and some mates up there, no real opportunities. Particularly now that his eyes had been opened by all of the overseas trips.

So off he went. He was a classic mixture of nerves and excitement, and gave it a good go at first. Andy missed him enormously and even convinced my parents to buy him a dog, Abbie, to keep him company while Jamie was away. But with crushing inevitability it did not take long before the cracks started to show and we could tell that Jamie was miserable at boarding school. It takes time to make friends and integrate into an established group and he didn't have the time. On top of this, while the school was fantastic and the boarding house was exceptional, the tennis was not. The coach at Cambridge who was put in charge of Jamie's tuition had just come off the Tour as a professional player, and wasn't really a coach. His experience was as an adult male player, mixing with others like him, not as a figure communicating and nurturing a twelve-year-old boy. He was very nice but not the right person for that role. You don't become a good coach overnight; it takes years and years, and it takes a certain type of temperament, not to mention experience, to coach children of that age.

He made some changes to Jamie's forehand in the first couple of weeks which were totally destabilising. Anybody who knows the first thing about kids can tell you that if you take them away from their comfortable, known environment, from their family and their friends, the last thing you do is mess with their skills in the early stages of that emotional transition. This chap took away a strength from Jamie before Jamie knew him or trusted him. Jamie was selected for the programme because he was told he was talented, then spent the first couple of weeks being made to feel he wasn't that great after all. At that point tennis was all Jamie had, so far away from his friends and family, and it was as if that was being whipped away from him, too.

Jamie was a nice child, a good boy; he liked being liked and he was too young to question authority. He was never going to say, 'No way, this is my best shot, screw you,' and an experienced coach might have recognised he was uncomfortable with so much change so soon, and given him time to settle into the new environment. As a coach you need to build up a relationship with the youngsters in your care: the better you know them as people the more you can influence them as players.

This lack of experience in the coach, combined with the situation at the boarding school was a toxic mixture. Jamie needed time to settle. All the time that he might have spent getting to know the other children, forging friendships or developing a support network was spent playing or training with his coach or a small sparring group.

On top of this, he rarely had time for a proper meal – lunchtime was a packed lunch on the hoof, unable to eat with the others at school and in the evenings he often missed the main meal, too. He missed all the school trips and any sort of bonding experiences. Both the headmaster and the boarding house matron expressed huge concern at the hectic and demanding daily tennis schedule. Despite that three-week trip to Miami and a happy Christmas break at home, after about three or four months he was really struggling.

'Do you want to come home?' I would ask when we called.

'No, no, no. I definitely don't want to,' his soft little voice would say.

We would take it in turns – me, his dad, his grandparents, even Andy – to tell him it was okay if he wanted to come home. But he wouldn't. I could tell how unhappy he was, crying on the phone most nights. We all could, it was devastating. So we took it in turns to go down there and give him a bit of moral support. We'd all go down on the train at different times, just for a day and night to spend a bit of time with him and try to help him through.

January 1999 came round and so did the trip to the Tarbes tournament in France again. I saw Jamie at the Teen Tennis event the week before, and got a chance to watch him play a little in between my responsibilities with the girls' team. I could tell that little had changed in his well-being, despite a happy Christmas break at home.

When I arrived in Tarbes with the girls, Jamie had already been out there for a couple of days with the boys' group, but I knew we were designated to share a room once I arrived. My heart just felt lighter when I saw him again. On that first morning I woke up early and lay in silence, staring at the ceiling and wondering how best to help my son. It seemed impossible: I would see him heartbroken either way.

When he woke up, he just rolled over and looked at me with those big sad eyes and said a single word. 'Mummy.' Then he reached his hand out to touch mine. I could tell from that huge, lonely smile how happy he was just to be with someone he knew, and all I could think was: Sending him back down there is wrong.

Jamie wouldn't let go of me all of that week. I could sense how filled with dread he was about going away again. He stayed close to me at all times, which was entirely out of character – normally the boys couldn't wait to shake me off and do their own thing. When it was time for him to go back to Cambridge and me to go back to Scotland he really got quite upset. We left Tarbes and headed to the airport together and I snapped. Enough.

I just said to the coach, 'No, he's coming home with me.' And I looked at Jamie and said, 'Enough, you're coming back with me.'

Again, he just said one word: 'Okay.' And that was it.

I bought him a new flight and we headed home to Scotland together. I just had to make the decision for him and once I had, he accepted it without question.

I can't believe I made such a big mistake that year. And I will never know where the line between confidence and skill lies, and therefore what lasting damage was done to Jamie's game by that experience. What I do know is that he left for Cambridge a confident, competitive singles player – ranked in the top 3 in Europe for Under 12s along with Rafael Nadal and Richard Gasquet – and he returned with shattered confidence, now only at his best as a doubles player, with someone alongside him on court. Are those things connected? How can I ever have a definitive answer to that? But the change was marked.

When Jamie returned, he went straight back to the same school and all of his old friends, and only one thing changed: he didn't play tennis for months and months. He just played golf, decompressed in front of the telly, kicked a football around instead. He loved tennis, but what he didn't like was the life around the sport – it was too much for him, too young. I know that now, I can see it very clearly and I caution others wherever I can to avoid that path. There has to be a balance between sport, education and social life.

When you aren't experienced, you don't know that it might turn out like this, or how much is at stake. You are seduced by somebody saying your child is talented and special and you think: 'Okay, what do I have to do?' I wanted to give him every opportunity, but I didn't consider the costs to his well-being carefully enough.

But you live and learn, and I didn't make the same mistakes with Andy. He was at home throughout this period and saw it all unfold. He missed Jamie a lot, of course he did, but they saw each other a great deal because of playing in the same tournaments. I don't know whether they discussed it – I think when you're a little boy you might not open up in that way, or even really understand it at all. What I do know is how upset Andy was to see Jamie so unhappy. He was very aware of how miserable Jamie had been and it had a huge effect on him, seeing first-hand what that sacrifice for the sake of tennis could do. For several years he would repeat the same mantra: 'I'm never going away from home, look what it did to Jamie.'

Did it last though? Did it hell.

7

Leaving home, or how to have faith when others are losing theirs

In which I realise that there will always be times when family are the only ones who will believe in your potential, and that the only way to cure a case of 'It'll never happen in Scotland' is to forge ahead and create your own opportunities.

While Jamie was recovering from the Cambridge experience, I was becoming increasingly aware of the need to set up a base in Scotland from which we could deliver a more meaningful and effective programme. I had been Scottish National Coach for four years now, but I was still finding it very difficult reporting to a largely anonymous board who didn't understand what I was trying to achieve. Again and again my suggestions and requests were met with a lack of ambition and belief, a sense that no one was really interested – no matter how good our results.

I don't think anyone at an administrative level really grasped quite how good some of these kids were, that it wasn't just me blowing my own trumpet about my players or my own kids. We had a proper squad, and a reputation in Europe now, but still my reports were met with a sense of: 'Well, you would say that, Judy.' I wanted to grow the national programme but I needed a decent base to really put in the long hours so we could be in charge of our own courts, instead of being beholden to the university and my limited budget. All of us – coaches, players and parents – were prepared to do that, but the powers that be just weren't committed like we were: at Stirling University all of our training was dictated by availability of courts. Yes, it was called the National Tennis Centre, but we had to book the courts and pay for them like everyone else, and play second fiddle to the University's own court requirements.

If we wanted to practise on say, Boxing Day, we would be told it was out of the question as the university was closed over Christmas. Fair enough, but this arrangement simply didn't work for kids who were by now at a national and international level, who had a competition on the 27 December and wanted to prepare properly for it . . . if only the infrastructure around them would step up and match their level of commitment. I was also starting to suspect that the kids needed a bigger and more varied pool of players around them and to mix with older kids and adults, as learning those social skills is crucial to the life of a serious player.

Just as I was reaching peak frustration, I was offered a fantastic position at a new private sports club called Next Generation in Edinburgh – it was the first of its kind in Scotland and was run and managed by Scott Lloyd, the son of David Lloyd of the eponymous sports club chain. They were a dynamic team and offered me autonomy over the courts and the club tennis programme, as well as a lot more money than I was earning, just when I needed it. I leapt at the opportunity and handed in my notice as National Coach.

My brief was to create a performance academy, a structured programme for the better juniors so that they could be developed to a top-notch level out of this new club, so I set about hiring a team I knew well and could trust. The first key team member was Leon Smith, who had been working with me for about three years on the national squad programme. He was enthusiastic, switched on and had that sense of get-up-and-go that I longed to see a scrap of in most of the senior management I had been dealing with at the time. He had quickly become a valued member of my team on the national squad programme. Andy and Jamie idolised him, the younger kids loved playing with him as they all thought he was super-cool, and I had come to love him like an extra member of the family. I poached two other coaches I knew and trusted, and we set about building a club, a membership, a whole tennis community, based at the Next Generation Club.

It was a dream job at the perfect time and proved to be a huge eye-opener into the commercial tennis world and what could be achieved with a healthy budget and control of the courts. It wasn't to last though. After about eighteen months, I came back from the British Junior Championships in Bournemouth to discover that the club suddenly had a new after-school programme manager who had already taken it upon himself to change things around. As I soon discovered when I went to book some courts and found that they were now being used for other activities such as, well, trampolining, gymnastics and birthday parties. I don't think it was a gender thing, or even a hierarchy thing – rather, it was a case of the money being the deciding factor in how the courts were used. But no one had told me.

Big group activities are obviously more lucrative than teaching small groups of kids or adults like I was doing. And that was just the start of the incoming changes. It very quickly became a very different place for me to work: one focused on revenue rather than results. And that wasn't what I had been pitched. I had always been lucky enough to play and coach tennis for the sake of the sport rather than worrying about the bottom line of a larger business, and even when I did have to manage a budget, I'd found a hundred and one ways to stretch it, whether that meant roping in mates or selling hot dogs to fund the purchase of ping-pong bats. But I had certainly never felt the responsibility to make someone else money. It didn't sit well with me, when I could see that it was at the expense of the kids' training and the overall club tennis programme.

So I was very lucky when Tennis Scotland approached me to say that the person who had taken over my role as National Coach had only lasted six months, and to ask me to consider returning to the position. Given that I finally had a choice, I was able to negotiate a pay rise for myself and, crucially, a new budget which meant that I would be able to create opportunities for the players and coaches. More travel, more training centres, more backing. It felt good to return with a more substantial set of promises from the powers that be. It made me hopeful for the future.

A few months after Jamie's return, Andy followed in his footsteps and headed to Miami for the 1999 Orange Bowl Championships. He had shown limited interest when we'd been there the previous year, being a bit brief on the phone and happy playing with his mates. But when we came home that Christmas, with Jamie clutching the runners-up trophy, talking about how wonderful the tournament was and everything he had done and seen, Andy's interest soon rocketed.

When Andy went out to Miami, things had been already set up nicely for him by Jamie's success. He wasn't heading into the unknown, but was off to the sunshine having heard about it all before, safe in the knowledge that Jamie had done so well, and that there was nothing to fear. Anything was possible.

Indeed it was. This time I didn't go as captain, but took my mum for the last week as a holiday to say thank you for all of her help over the years. When we arrived, I wasn't overwhelmed this time; I was excited. I knew the lay of the land and was more relaxed as a result – and I'm sure this rubbed off on Andy, who had already been there a fortnight, having a blast. He immediately picked up on the American positivity that had made such an impression on Jamie, and had the time of his life.

As the week drew to a close, it became clear that Andy was in with a very good chance of winning. I was as nervous as I ever had been as I watched him play that final, but – as has now become a regular habit – I sat alone to watch, as far from my mother as I could. There's something about the way that she vibrates with every emotion, constantly twittering on about every tiny thing she feels. I find it too stressful, when I am already feeling every frustration and endeavour that the boys are going through on the court. It's been nearly twenty years now, but I still have to sit alone when they play big matches, trying to keep my expression as neutral as possible as I know how much every gasp or wince impacts on them.

In Andy's final he was playing the Czech player Tomas Piscacek, and we were watching from a sort of mezzanine patio on the roof of the clubhouse, looking down onto the court. My mother was at one end of the patio and I was sat at the other. The final shot was played – and Andy won! – and as I rose to my feet to applaud him with the rest of the crowd, the sound I was most aware of was an incredible shrieking coming from the other side of the balcony.

'He's won! He's won!' I could hear my mother yelling as she hurtled towards me.

Oh God, why the big exhibition? I found myself thinking, despite my pride at Andy's achievement. I guess we never *quite* grow out of being a little bit embarrassed by our parents . . .

The presentation took place immediately after the match and it was a moment of enormous pride for me to see Andy win a tournament abroad for the first time. He was beaming with happiness and we were all delighted to see that the winner's trophy itself was an actual silver bowl full of oranges.

In the hubbub after the prize-giving, while I was waiting to congratulate Andy myself, his opponent's coach came over to congratulate me, saying that Andy was a very special, very clever player. I thanked him, beaming, and he asked who else I coached.

'Oh, you won't know anyone else,' I said, 'I just coach in Scotland. What about you?'

'I've been working with Tomas for eighteen months,' he explained, 'but before that I spent thirteen years with Jana Navotna.'

Oh.

Only the year before Jana Novotná had won the Ladies' Singles title at Wimbledon. This guy had nurtured a young player to a Grand Slam title. It was way out of my league. I think that was the first time I paused, accepted how good the boys could actually be, and how I was now reaching a point where my lack of experience and contacts may well start holding them back. I realised with that comment that compared to the other coaches and support teams working with the best kids this age, I knew next to nothing, and knew next to no one.

'Oh my God, he knows exactly what to do. And I know nothing!' I mouthed to myself as that coach strolled away with a nonchalant swagger. It was time to up my own game if I was going to give the boys the chances they deserved. But I had no idea what to do. This panic, combined with the big decisions that I then knew were around the corner as far as Jamie's training went, threw me into paroxysms of worry for a good few months. This also coincided with the point in my friends' lives where we were all so busy that we rarely had time to see each other. Of course, there was the odd big old catch-up every few months, complete with wine and gossip, but by and large I felt rather alone during this time.

I was reluctant to burden my parents with what might seem like my professional anxieties – they'd had their own careers and they didn't deserve to be lumbered with my worries. It all felt overwhelming, I had no idea what was coming next, professionally or personally, but that winter I resolved not to overthink things. I had to trust my gut, to use my common sense, and to make sure I didn't panic just because I was heading towards the unknown. I was a grown-up; it was time to get my head down and get on with it.

I knew what the top Under 12s in the world now looked like, as some of my squad were among them, but in order to give them the best shot of climbing to the next rung of the ladder, I had to learn what the best Under 14s in the world looked like, so we could all be ready. I needed to know what I was aiming for and then put the right stepping stones in place. I realised I was going to have to try and invest in myself as a way of investing in the team. I had to learn more by seeing more, and that seeing more meant travelling more. Fair enough, I thought. It was a commitment I was prepared to make.

I worked out that if I could travel more with the GB Under 14 girls, I could see more of the Under 14 players across the board. I could expand my knowledge, and thereby the chances of the squad. For each age group I needed to study the players a few years older and anticipate the next challenges coming their way. It's the case with so many ambitions: a glance ahead at what's to come and you're equipping yourself for the coming battle. So that is what I made it my mission to do: investigate the world of junior Grand Slams, as that is the ultimate junior tennis goal. It was my goal to travel wherever, however I could in my capacity as National Coach. Naively, I hoped that, by now, with not just a couple but a significant handful of good up-and-coming Scottish players at international level, support and funding from sporting bodies might begin to perk up a bit. Far from it.

By the spring of 2000, the need to go and watch a junior Grand Slam tournament was becoming really urgent if I was going to avoid the squad being totally leapfrogged by other nations at the next stage. At this age, boys in particular are growing fast and I had no idea what they'd be facing in the following year or two if any of them made it to one of the major events. The obvious choice was the French Open at Roland Garros as it was the closest distance to travel, and a different playing surface from the more familiar grass courts of Wimbledon. I would be able to observe the best players in the world, familiarise myself with the event, speak to coaches, and take back this valuable knowledge in time to prepare my lot for what was – hopefully – to come.

The LTA had a formal opportunity for coaches to visit the French Open as part of their Coach Education Programme. I was a performance coach, I had players competing internationally, I wanted to learn and I had the determination to do my best for them. So when I was invited to apply for a coach's pass and sent off my application form, explaining my situation, listing my players and specifying their ages, I felt I was in with a good chance. However, I received a reply saying that this year there had been unprecedented demand for the places, and so the passes had been allocated randomly by ballot. They were sorry to say that I had not been awarded a pass.

Fine, I thought, knowing that my decision to start attending these tournaments had been made already. I'll go anyway. I scraped together enough money to go for two days, got myself to France and queued up with everyone else for a ground pass. I needed to watch these junior matches. I made my way to an early match where I knew the top seed in the boys singles was playing, a Serbian lad called Janko Tipsarević. He was a fantastic player, and already looked like a man compared to the gangly lads I had back at home. He even had tattoos! The experience was already invaluable, but there was a lot of work to do, I thought to myself as I frantically scribbled notes on Tipsarević's technique, physicality and ear piercings. Years before I had taken a shorthand course before starting at Edinburgh University. It was especially good for just these moments. And the bonus was that no one could read what I was writing. The spy!

At the end of the set I got up to move to another match. As at Wimbledon, the smaller courts are arranged with banks of seating rising back to back. As I stood, I looked over to the adjacent court. And there, within the crowd directly facing me, I saw the very woman who was in charge of allocating those few precious seats to GB coaches. She was sitting alongside her husband and her children, lanyards and passes around each of their necks. Unbelievable.

I applied for that pass, and I had a really good reason to get it, I thought to myself. So I'm damned if I'm going to let her know I haven't noticed what she's done.

'Bonjour!' I cried across the court between sets, with a cheery wave.

As I left Roland Garros that day, I made a mental note: If I wanted stuff done, I was going to have to do it myself. At the time, I would wonder if I was seriously mad to keep having this much belief in my little squad and this much ambition for Scottish tennis, but if I had listened to the people over the years who had rolled their eyes and said, 'Pffft! Scottish tennis?! Grand Slams! It'll never happen. We don't do tennis in Scotland', I would have given up that spring while we were nursing the wounds left by Jamie's painful experience. But something in me refused to surrender. A quiet voice that could never quite shut up, kept saying: 'But why not? What is there to stop us? Apart from some rubbish weather and not much money?'

With a determination to keep pushing forwards, things seemed to get a little easier. Jamie settled back into life in Scotland, Andy continued to progress through the latter stages of junior tournaments and I was still working hard with the national squad. I felt as if we were always on the go, with me like Mary Poppins and her carpet bag full of toys and games!

The best, most meaningful work as a coach is done with kids away from the court. When they open up to you when you're just playing a card game, doing a jigsaw or chatting to them over dinner – *that* is when you can work out what is motivating them or holding them back and how to help them move forward. It's much easier to forge a bond away from the balls and the rackets, and that's why I always drew a line when tennis was done for the day. We would head out for pizza or ice cream all together and just let them enjoy being kids. Every now and again I would get out my book or magazine and lift it up and there would be a little ripple among the gang. A sense of 'Okay, Judy's switching off now.' After all, you're on duty all day, all night in these situations. You're more than the coach. You're the minibus driver, the organiser, the ATM, the surrogate parent, and sometimes the human launderette!

It was such a great couple of years. Jamie came back to tennis in his own time. We were having fun every weekend, and best of all, I really felt as if we were making a tangible difference. The structure was unrecognisable from when I had started in the job. The kids were improving and loving being a part of something. We really were like a big family: the smallest group we ever took was four of us and I think the biggest was about seventeen. That's a lot of puzzle books, but it's also a lot of fun.

It was also around this time that I realised that it's not that easy coaching your own kids. And not that cool being coached by your mum. It is much more important to be the parent than the coach, so I continued to oversee their training and competitive programmes but brought in Leon smith to deliver most of the on-court work. Happy days.

Perhaps inevitably, Andy eventually outgrew the set-up we had. In February 2002, he was playing against Spain for the GB team, as part of the European Under 16s Championships in Andorra. At that stage, Rafael Nadal was playing for Spain and the two had struck up quite a friendship some years before. Rafa is a year older than Andy, so Andy looked up to him with admiration and curiosity. I guess he saw a template for what was possible.

In the final, there were two singles matches and a doubles match. Andy and Rafa both won their singles so the tie was decided by the doubles, which Spain won. After the presentation of the trophy the boys sloped off to play racquetball – a sort of squash/tennis hybrid played on an indoor court.

I wasn't in Andorra for that event, but when Andy materialised on the end of the phone later that night, he was talking so loudly and with so much energy that I almost felt as if I were there. It was a long time before the boys had mobile phones so he had called up on a payphone, reversing the charges. He wasn't one for phoning home that often and my attitude had long been 'no news is good news', so when I heard it was him, I suspected nothing more (or less) than a lost wallet or missing passport.

So I took a breath and said, 'Oh hi, Andy. What's the matter?' I shouldn't have judged him by the standards I had set for myself in Barcelona all those years ago. Within seconds I was holding the receiver a foot from my ear.

'I've been playing racquetball with Rafa,' he ranted down the phone, 'and do you know he doesn't even go to normal school?!' was the opening gambit. 'He trains on clay all day in Majorca and he gets to hit with Carlos Moyá and people like that! And what have I got? I've got the university, and no one but you and my brother. I want to go to Spain, I *need* to go to Spain!' And so it continued. For some time.

He was more excitable than truly angry, but I could sense that there was now genuine frustration in his voice. Rafa had obviously unwittingly painted this amazing picture in his mind of hitting with Carlos Moyá (who was number 1 in the world at the time) in the sun and never having to go to real school.

As a fourteen-year-old who had been in the same place with the same opportunities for almost a decade, compared to Rafa who was playing hours of top-quality tennis per day, getting to hit with the best in the world, Andy now realised what he was missing out on, and Jamie's awful experience away from home was now sufficiently long enough ago not to feel relevant.

Andy's refusal to go away to train had long been more about heading down south than actually leaving home. He was now a good few years older than Jamie had been when he had left, but his mantra had never changed: 'I don't want to train with the LTA: look what an awful time Jamie had.' But now Andy had had his eyes opened: there were facilities beyond the UK where he could train.

Secretly, I was quite pleased to hear him shouting like this. I had long known that we would eventually run out of options for him in Scotland – we didn't have the expertise, the facilities, the sparring partners, and so much else that was needed if he was going to fulfil his potential. But there was no way that I could be the one pushing him to look elsewhere. So thank you, Rafa, you did us a huge favour.

Over the coming months, we agreed to let Andy look at a few schools abroad, and it was quickly clear that the best fit was the Academia Sánchez-Casal, just outside of Barcelona in Spain. Andy already knew a couple of lads who had gone to train there, and he had heard good things. Good things that were more than justified by our visit: it had clay courts, hard courts, a gym, accommodation and an American High School franchise on site, as well as a club-house, a football pitch and equestrian centre. Yeah, no wonder he liked it.

What I liked about it was that it wasn't just an academy for hothousing children – it was a functioning tennis club, too, with adults playing, people having fun playing tennis with each other, and all of the social benefits that go with those two things. I wouldn't be sending a son to be pushed too hard at the expense of everything clsc again.

On the second day of our visit, Emilio Sánchez, a former top ten player and co-owner of the academy, asked if he could play a couple of sets with Andy. 'Of course, whatever you want,' I said, before heading to the clubhouse with my book so that I didn't cramp any-one's style by being the beady-eyed mother on the look-out.

When they returned, Emilio said to Andy, in front of me, 'Andy, you go and take a shower while I have a talk with your mum,' and pulled up a chair next to me. 'Well, that has never happened to me before,' he said.

My stomach lurched. Andy was such a hothead at this stage, and when he played competitively his temper was at its worst, especially if he was losing. Oh no, I thought, he has behaved really badly. I was convinced something had gone horribly wrong.

When I returned my focus to what Sánchez was actually saying, I realised that he was explaining that they had quickly reached 3–3 in the first set, then it had all changed. 'It only took him six games to work out how to beat me,' he said, smiling. 'He is so clever; it is very rare to find someone so young who both understands the game, and has the variety to play it, to pick you apart, to make you struggle.'

Emilio was now in his late thirties, but had previously been a top ten singles and doubles player, and he had extensive experience of top-class tennis and an eye for strategy. Which Andy had apparently intuitively worked out within six games. I wasn't quite sure how to respond when Emilio told me that Andy was a special player, a future champion and that they would love to have him at the academy. My voice said thank you, but my brain was fizzing – how on earth were we going to be able to afford this?

The first thing we had to do was work out a costing: how much we would need for a year at the academy, expenses for a whole schedule of competitions and then flights to Barcelona and back several times a year. Luckily the campus was right behind Barcelona airport, almost sharing the same land, so there would be no trains or taxis on landing, but still – airfares were a consideration as he would need to travel, and I was determined that we would all visit regularly. After discussions with the academy and a lot of time at the kitchen table with a notebook and pen, we worked out that we would need about £35,000 per year. That was £35,000 we didn't have.

Our first obvious port of call was the LTA. It was evident that they didn't have a suitable training environment for the age and stage that Andy was at now, and they knew it, so perhaps they would fund him elsewhere. We made an appointment with their Head of Performance and Will and I flew down to Stansted on the cheapest flight we could find, and took the train and tube to their London headquarters in Baron's Court. I can't remember what time the appointment was, but I do remember the agony of being kept waiting for forty-five minutes, and the panic about possibly missing our train back up to Stansted, and the rebooking of a flight if we missed it. We sat and we sweated.

Eventually we were called in to make our case. I have never been terribly good at asking for anything, but luckily Will did most of the talking. And he did a great job.

We weren't asking them to fund everything: we just wanted to know if they would be prepared to make a contribution. We explained that we needed £35,000 and reinforced the fact that Andy was by now ranked number 2 or 3 in Europe in his age group. There was not another British player who was even close to that – surely they had to help him?

But they were very reluctant to commit to anything. We were flummoxed. Was it because we were Scottish? Was it because of the experience with Jamie? Was it because I was a national coach? Even bearing in mind all of those things, surely Andy deserved a chance on his own merit? At that point, fifteen years ago, they were an organisation with so little track record of actual success in tennis – Tim Henman was a top 10 player at the time, but he hadn't been trained through the LTA. Suddenly they had a player who was pitching well above his weight internationally, was prepared to make this huge commitment to the game and . . . they weren't sure? But we are a Grand Slam nation, we pleaded, as a country we are punching well *below* our weight considering we have Wimbledon. We have no one else making an impression like this right now.

After what seemed like endless toing and froing, we were offered £10,000 towards the total cost. I barely remember what I felt as I was so shocked at how little that was compared to the potential budget they had, but I do remember Will, quite rightly, saying, 'So what you are telling us is that you don't believe in him?'

'No, we do believe in him,' came the answer, 'but there are no guarantees are there?'

When is there ever a guarantee? How could they reduce this to little more than a numbers game? It was a child's life and an exceptional chance, and we were left sitting, begging, panicking.

'If Andy were a footballer at this age, at this level,' said Will, 'you lot would be breaking down our door to sign him up.'

He was absolutely right, and I think everyone in the room knew it. But the answer came back, immovable: 'Ten thousand pounds is the best we can do.'

8

Empty Nest Syndrome, or how I say *adiós* and *au revoir* to the boys

*In which I try to navigate the emotions, the practicalities
and the finances of training for two different boys, with two
different playing styles, and two different personalities, and
how ambition only works alongside adaptability.*

With our hopes of support from government bodies now at an end, it was down to the family, specifically me, to try and scrabble together the remaining funds for Andy's training in Spain. So I began a campaign of writing to absolutely anyone I could think of and asking for help. Night after night I would sit at the kitchen table, trying to think of who to write to next, how best to persuade them, and how to convince the family that we were getting somewhere. It was a period of endless letter-writing, endless rejection and endless hope that someone, somewhere might take a punt on Andy.

I was writing to sponsorship managers at any local or even regional business I could think of. I didn't really understand the process of fundraising at the time. I would write to someone in their marketing department in the hopes of getting money from them, with the promise of some sort of marketing or brand exposure in return. The trouble was, when the player you are 'pitching' to the companies is a junior, there is very little marketing exposure to be had. There are no column inches, there is no TV coverage, even something like them wearing a branded patch on their sleeve will be seen by very few people. I knew Andy's potential, but the way they saw it was: what were they going to gain from it? The all-pervasive message became clearer and clearer: it's just not going to happen.

My letters were met almost universally with replies saying thanks, but no thanks. I had no idea what I was doing, but I knew I couldn't give up. I tried to find people to advise us on what to write, how much to write in each letter and what tone to strike – but looking back on it, there were definitely times when I was writing pages of waffle to people to whom it meant absolutely nothing.

This was long before the age of google, where a world of expertise is only a click away. I didn't know anyone with a child in this position and I had no idea how to find anyone who had. The loneliness was spirit-crushing. I just had to keep at it, regardless of the steady drop of rejection letters on the doormat, morning after morning.

We had been working with a sports management company called Octagon for a couple of years and they had set up contracts which provided free clothing and rackets. That was a help for sure, as were the small pockets of sponsorship they negotiated from tennis brands like Robinsons, and the odd contribution from benefactors they knew.

We were trapped in a middle ground where what we needed to get Andy to the next level was hideously expensive, but he wasn't yet earning any money or getting any real attention. Every racket re-string made me wince at the price, every competition place was another entry in the 'outgoing' column of the expenses sheet, every train ticket or tank of petrol another cost that had yet to be accounted for. Tennis becomes so expensive, so fast, when you start to compete regularly, but the only way to get good enough to even come close to winning prize money is to keep competing regularly. It was as if it was sucking every resource, but still no prize money in sight. And why *should* he have to start earning prize money yet? He was still a kid! There are much healthier – on the whole – systems in other sports. Young footballers are scooped up and made part of a junior team, all expenses paid and the pressure taken off for a bit. They aren't expected to be earning a crust in childhood.

Eventually, after taking advice wherever I could, I realised that the best course of action was to try to build some sort of profile around Andy, instead of just sitting at home, thinking. I set my mind to approaching local newspapers or TV, accepting that the nationals weren't going to be interested at this point. There was no social media for me to build a little site for him, nothing but a will to keep going until we got somewhere. In the end we decided we had enough money for him to get started and to cover the first six months, so we thought we'd just suck it and see . . .

Several months later we had a lucky break, and were invited in to the Royal Bank of Scotland. One of those endless letters was about to come good. At the time RBS did absolutely nothing with tennis and certainly not with youngsters, but someone further up in the organisation knew of me from my playing days, and had heard how well the boys were doing. It took this, a chance from an almost total stranger, to sway someone's opinion. A chunk of funding from them gave us the boost we needed, and once we could show others that they had faith in Andy, we were able to scrabble together some more money. Small charitable trusts and local firms gave us £100 here and there, and eventually, with a little bit from Tennis Scotland and a little bit from the SportScotland lottery fund – and absolutely all of our savings – we eventually got enough to cover year one. A few months later another helping hand rescued us: my Great Uncle Arthur left me £25,000 in his will. It came through about six months after Andy started in Barcelona and proved an absolute godsend.

So at the end of August 2002 Andy was off to Spain. I went over with him to get him settled in – which basically entailed working out what we had forgotten to bring, getting that in a rush, then getting some supplies from the supermarket and double checking that he wasn't having any second thoughts. That bit didn't take long: he was so happy to be there that when the time came for me to head back to Scotland he barely gave me a backwards glance.

The facilities at the academy were fantastic and as far as emotional well-being was concerned, the set-up was significantly healthier than it had been for Jamie in Cambridge. Jamie had gone directly into quite an old-fashioned boarding school environment where he didn't know anyone, trained at a separate tennis centre where he only knew a handful of people and was incredibly isolated, far out of his comfort zone as a result. Despite being further away from home, Andy's situation was way more comfortable. Obviously he was a couple of years older than Jamie had been, which certainly helped, but he also knew a few players there and was very happy to pal around with them from day one. And unlike the UK, where tennis back then was still predominantly a sport for privileged kids, Barcelona was the hotbed of European tennis. There were clubs and academies all around, tournaments going on almost constantly, with a seemingly endless pool of potential competitors, and above all, a world of like-minded people. The days of convincing those around you that tennis was not a ridiculous waste of time – and money – were over.

Andy was going to school daily, as well as training for several hours every day, too. But he was also sharing a room in the on-site accommodation block, making friends with kids his age, and learning a bit of Spanish and French. What better way to prepare for the international tennis circuit than being in an international training environment.

The social side of things was great for him, too, given that he had only just turned fifteen. There was school and tennis training Monday to Friday, but on Saturday mornings tennis was optional and on Saturday afternoons there was always something organised – a trip to a funfair or the movies, to the shops or a game of football. There was a sports club within the academy where they could indulge in table tennis, exercise classes, beach volleyball and more. This was also open to non-residents, who would come in to unwind after work. The reminders were constant that sport was fun, that you could find pleasure in your chosen discipline and indulge in other skills, too. It was warm in Spain, but it was far from hothousing.

We desperately wanted that freedom for him; we wanted him to have as normal a childhood as possible, so it was important for us to know that he could play football as well as tennis and to do all these things among friends. As I can now appreciate, getting that balance is essential: sport demands so many sacrifices of you later on in life that you have to enjoy whatever you can, whenever you can, for as long as possible. Raising a sports superstar from early childhood with victory – rather than the happiness of the child as your mission, is always going to be a false economy. The child will either buckle under the pressure before reaching success, burn out too soon after reaching it . . . or be miserable.

If you want your child to improve, it has to be because they want it, not because they are trying to fit in, or to please a coach they don't know. You cannot ram professional sport down anyone's throat, each player has to work it out for themselves over time, particularly as it is a process that usually begins in childhood. But back then, as a parent, it was a complicated balance to strike – we wanted to find whatever opportunities we could to help the boys be the best that they could, whatever it took, while keeping unreasonable pressure at bay and their heads screwed on. To create an environment where they knew they could reach for the stars *and* keep their feet on the ground.

The latter part was more than taken care of by life at the academy: the international tennis environment there had very little time for Andy's temperament. By the time he left for Barcelona, he had become a very hotheaded young player. He was fine off court, rarely a peep, but on court he could be not just bad-tempered but often badly behaved – a result of his intense competitiveness. This, added to the fact that he had become a big fish in a very small pond – particularly in Scotland – meant that his temper often flared unchecked.

In Spain, however, no one was interested in tantrums: they got him absolutely nowhere. He had gone from training with kids his age to training with guys aged between nineteen and twenty-six – these were players ranked 300 to 700 in the world. They didn't care that he was a big fish back home, because he was an annoying little sprat to them. If he started sulking on court, they paid zero attention. So he soon learned that to sulk was to waste time.

Plus, the way that they were coached meant that he didn't have time to be annoyed – there was always another ball coming from somewhere. Sánchez was a big fan of using what were called 'basket drills', where the coach didn't engage in a rally with his pupil, he simply fed balls from the basket next to him – non-stop. This meant there was no time to dwell, to answer back, to get fiery or upset. And Sánchez clearly worked out that this was a great way to train both Andy and his temper.

He also rated Andy's ability highly enough that he was given opportunities which some of the others at the academy didn't get. When top players came to practice there, he was always given the chance to play with them – not for long: just a set, or a hit with them for half an hour or so. But it was the inspiration which created the sea change in Andy's attitude. He would see a genuine world-class player, be treated as a peer on court, and watch not just their game but how they carried themselves. Those guys were there to train. They wanted sparring partners. They were at work, with no time for ego battles or tantrums. And for Andy to see that – not just once, but time and again – that was gold dust.

That first year in Spain, Andy was happier than I could ever have dreamed he would be. The Spaniards talk about training the heart, the head and legs: the legs, because you have to get fit enough to keep going when you're exhausted, the heart because you have to have the spirit to never give up, and the head because you have to be able to stay calm and cope alone on court. These were the lessons he was learning.

He really was lost in tennis – even at the expense of some practical details. The academy was one of those places where your laundry was done on a Monday and Thursday. You had a laundry bag, which you had to fill and leave on your bed for collection. They were training on clay a lot, which meant that the kit was absolutely filthy – half of it was bright orange by now! Suddenly, Andy was away from home, having to remember to fill his laundry bag and get it ready on time. Did he manage? Did he hell. The second time I went to visit, the floor was so covered in dirty, dusty clothing that I could barely wedge the door open to get in the room. And the stink was something that still haunts me!

It was in these life-management lessons where Andy had to do the most learning. After a while, he was becoming genuinely exhausted. He was thriving, but shattered. He was still taking school classes as well as being out in the sun training for three or four hours a day. In the past, it had been a struggle for us to get him to do ninety minutes of training maybe four times a week, so on a physical level this was an enormous step up. And at home all of his other fitness training was done on the football pitch – it was very organic and unstructured as it had combined fitness with play and enjoyment, as well as focusing on a broad range of training from cardio strengthening to hand-eye and foot-eye coordination.

But now he was older, and in Barcelona his gym sessions usually came at the end of the day. They weren't personalised to him – everybody just did the same thing in the evening, after schooling and after all of those hours on court, and *then* he had a further school class from six until seven. He was fifteen, he was growing, he was having to manage his own life, and he was having to do it all while surrounded by people speaking multiple foreign languages. By the end of the day, he was knackered. Added to this, he had only the slimmest grasp of how important it was for him to take care of himself physically, that this amount of exercise needed an appropriate amount of rest and sleep, and the right type of nutrition. His hands were getting blisters and his diet was appalling: I think there is a strong chance that he would have lived off penne pasta with tomato sauce and chicken for lunch and dinner every single day if he hadn't been set a better example. It was a struggle to persuade him that even a small side salad was worth it in those days.

Quietly, I was immensely relieved that these were the kind of mistakes he was making. Nothing truly serious: he was experiencing what most kids do when they head for college or university, just a few years earlier. He was loving it, but he couldn't sustain it all. And when he started to travel more for tournaments, it made his full programme of commitments even harder to sustain. The only solution would have been to employ a tutor to travel with him, which was a further expense for what felt like a relatively inconsequential result.

When I went over to visit, one of the coaches explained to me that they were trying to get him to go back to his room to nap after lunch. But boys that age don't want to nap! It was an impossible ask. So after that first year in Barcelona it seemed as if the best solution was to let him drop the schoolwork. These days it's a question I get asked a lot: why did I let him finish formal schooling at only sixteen?

By now Andy was an exceptional tennis player. By letting him drop formal schooling we were in effect staking almost everything on the tennis working out, but I felt he was learning so much in every other area of his life, and if he had a change of heart it would be so much easier to go back into education than it would be to go back into tennis training, especially at that high level. He doesn't have any academic qualifications, but I reckon he's got a zillion other skills now. There's more than one way to get an education.

Back in Scotland the house felt very quiet – and very tidy – without him. 'Jamie will still be around,' I had told myself, but without Andy, he was actually around a lot less. He was sixteen now, working on his Higher exams, and having made his way back to tennis over the years he was now looking at applying for a tennis scholarship at an American university. The US collegiate system is based much more around team play than in the UK, and doubles, which suited Jamie's playing style very well already, was a big part of that. It made him attractive to several US universities and just like I had at the same age, he hoped to be offered a place on a scholarship. He was playing both singles and doubles by this point, and was successful at both, although still a long way from focusing exclusively on doubles as 'his' discipline. He may have had a natural aptitude for it, but, particularly in the UK, it was less of a specific sport in its own right back then, and he was good enough at both disciplines to be in the British junior team, and travelling to overseas tournaments.

But it wasn't all about tennis for him any more; he was playing a lot of golf, too, and had a handicap of three by now – a level that grown men who spend their every spare moment playing golf would give their eye teeth to reach. That he had reached this standard, without even trying that hard, was vindication of my theory that letting kids play the sports they are interested in can only have wider benefits – especially if you have developed great hand-eye coordination at a young age. With all of this going on for Jamie, and the memory of Cambridge, there was no jealousy on his part about Andy going abroad to train. He was enjoying living at home, working hard at school, as well as travelling to tennis events and the odd golf tournament – and getting great enjoyment from both sports. With him on the golf course or away at tennis tournaments for so much of the time, and no Andy to pick up or take to training, to matches, to see mates – the whole family dynamic felt very different.

A couple of years later Jamie changed his mind about studying and pursuing tennis in the US, electing instead to go and train in France once he had finished school. I had been sure that he would head to the States: he had got four Highers – as required for applying to US universities – and then he took the SATs when we were at the US Open Juniors in 2003. He had caught the eye of some great scouts and received a number of offers for full tennis scholarships from good US colleges. But then he surprised us all by saying that he didn't want to go.

I was never quite sure what changed his mind: if it was too far from home for him after his negative experience in Cambridge, if he simply didn't click with any of the places where he was offered a scholarship, or if he, as I had at the same age, simply felt that it was too much of a leap into the unknown. Andy was only a cheap budget flight away, but the US was a bigger step altogether. I knew that for as long as he wanted to play tennis, it was only fair that we created the same opportunities for him that we had for Andy. I would have to come up with funds for coaching in Paris, a city where there were no tennis scholarships at that stage.

The trouble was that Andy's training in Barcelona was using up most of the family finances, and Jamie training abroad without a scholarship would double our outgoings overnight. There was no question of Jamie going to Barcelona – not just because of the massive overall costs, but because even by then it was obvious that their games were very different. The style of play, the court surface and the coaching in Barcelona that specifically suited Andy's game was no good for Jamie. Jamie needed somewhere with faster courts and coaches who understood his game style.

It's fascinating to see how differently they play: two boys, barely a year apart, each playing the same game with an utterly unique approach. Andy is right-handed, Jamie left-handed, and that is just the start of it. Even then, Andy was a classic baseline counter-puncher who would run around all day long, and Jamie a more traditional flair player who wanted to rush to the net at every opportunity. There was no one-size-fits-all solution to this conundrum.

In the end, we found an academy in Paris that we liked. It was owned by a Frenchman named Patrick Mouratoglou, who many years later went on to become Serena Williams' coach, and the head coach was Australian Bob Brett, who had worked with Boris Becker, Goran Ivanišević and many more over the years. Jamie went to try out and discovered that there were several others he knew from the ITF junior circuit there. Before long he had his heart set on it, and it was up to us to make it happen. It was a situation when I really needed a fairy godmother moment, and as luck would have it . . . a fairy godfather appeared in the form of my uncle who very kindly gave me £10,000 to get him started.

We also managed to find a sort of French exchange solution to Jamie's room and board: he stayed with a local French family with four kids, whose parents wanted them to speak English. He had subsidised rent in exchange for chatting to the children in English, and soon settled in well to Parisian life, looking after himself with an ease and confidence that he certainly hadn't had back in the Cambridge days, and which made Andy's scruffy ways seem even more chaotic. While Andy was still living in Planet Mess, struggling with the concept of getting his own kit washed, Jamie was zipping across Paris on the Métro, picking up French, and discovering a new, much happier way of life.

Meanwhile in Barcelona, Andy was continuing with almost unimpeded progress through the ranks. When he had set off for Spain there had been no specific goal or strategy. None of us, parents or coaches, had issued ultimatums about having to reach a certain ranking by a certain date, nor had we expected him to win tournaments to justify all this expense and prove it was worth it. It was Andy's competitive spirit alone that powered him higher and higher.

It's so much easier to be the kid rising through the ranks than the one who is trying to stay up there. As you head up the world rankings – especially as a junior – you have nothing to fear; it's all to play for. But once you get to the top, you have a lot to lose. And something that Jamie had already experienced in spades and learned to deal with was something that Andy had never even encountered: adversity. Until now.

9

Never underestimate the power of adversity, or how we finally break through

In which injury forces us to find a way to put despair aside, to refuse to accept the first answer we're given and to unearth the huge psychological positives in having to overcome adversity. And within months a big win and a whole new world of challenges present themselves.

For Andy, adversity did not appear as an emotional challenge but a physical one, when he confronted serious injury for the first time in his career. Throughout the course of 2003, now aged sixteen, he had been having some problems with his knee, and every trip to the physio came back with the same answer: it was patella tendonitis, which is basically an inflammation of the tendons around the kneecap. Treatment was simple: ice the knee, a bit of rest and then back on court. Or so we thought.

By the autumn he was starting to play some men's tournaments – starting with the International Tennis Federation's Futures circuit, where the prize money was considerably more than the junior offerings of twenty quid or a voucher for some new training shoes. He was chomping at the bit, and couldn't wait to get stuck in, especially as I had now taken on the extra commitment of hiring his ex-coach Leon Smith, who had known Andy for years and been such a huge part of his development. It was the first time Andy had an individual coach, someone just for him, instead of being part of a larger training programme. The plan was that Leon would travel with him as coach and hitting partner, because now Andy needed somebody with him who could focus on him at each stage and to tailor a competitive training programme to his needs. He kept winning and he kept improving. So it seemed impossible, reckless even, not to provide this specific support. It meant putting someone on a salary for the first time though, which was an enormous leap of faith for us in terms of costs and required me to take a big financial risk. I just had to hope my confidence in the idea wouldn't be proved wrong . . .

His knee pain, however, kept on flaring up, despite Andy winning his first men's tournament in October 2003, on the ITF Futures circuit in Glasgow. It was only about £600 in prize money, which was a drop in the ocean given the money we were spending weekly, but it marked a huge turning point for him psychologically. He was *earning as a professional player.*

Just two months later he was playing in another ITF Futures tournament in Spain, when he took the previously unheard of step of retiring mid-match. Far from clearing up with a bit of rest, his knee pain was just too intense to continue. He made the difficult decision to stop, in case something more sinister than inflammation was going on. And he was right.

We immediately took him to see a specialist who X-rayed the knee. As the expert held the image to the light, he told us that he wasn't sure if it was a bipartite patella, or a broken kneecap. My stomach lurched: either way, it sounded horrendous. He advised us to have an MRI scan as soon as possible. Of course, scans are the most expensive – and effective – way of investigating an injury (and were so much less common back then), so it was back to the Scottish Institute of Sport, which had recently been set up to provide sports science and sports medicine support and resources to selected athletes. We asked if they could help us with the costs. It was £400 we simply didn't have and we didn't have the time to wait for an appointment on the NHS.

As if the stomach-churning anxiety of having to ask for more money, and this time for a serious injury, wasn't enough, the consultant's appointment that we had after the scan was a further torment. The consultant quickly confirmed that Andy had a bipartite patella, which meant that his kneecap was separated into two parts. Rather than one bony 'cap', it is two separate pieces joined at the sides by cartilage. In short, when Andy bends his knee, the bone looks like Kermit the Frog smiling. The condition is congenital, not an injury from playing. As he had grown and begun to put more pressure on it by playing at a higher level, the knee had begun to scream under the pressure.

As I was sitting in the consultant's room with Andy, numb, trying to work out how on earth he had been playing all of these years with a condition like this, the expert delivered his final blow. A casual, 'Well, I'd be very surprised if he'll ever be able to play tennis at a high level again.' In that moment, on that sofa, I absolutely could have swung for him. As Andy's face fell on hearing the news, it was as if I were seeing it in slow motion. The dreams, the ambition, the hope, just draining from him.

'We'll just *have* to find a way to deal with it,' I replied, with as much brisk optimism as I could muster on watching my teenage son crumble at the prospect of never playing again. I had, of course, absolutely no idea what to do. Andy was still growing so there was no way it could be operated on soon, if at all. And in the face of such hapless pessimism from this consultant, I had no idea who we could turn to for help. All I knew was that Andy was now at home, unable to play, miserable and depressed. We were going to have to find someone to help us, and fast.

This was thirteen years ago now. Internet search engines were not quite what they are today, and social media was . . . well, it wasn't. Nevertheless, I began my search for an athlete, any athlete, who may have had a similar condition and yet continued with their professional career. I began by asking my contacts if they knew any experts in knee injuries, in any context at all, and then tried to refine it from there. I called everyone I knew, anyone who would take my call. I would ask about their experience with professional athletes and patella conditions. The tennis world knows what the sport demands of your knees, and in a strange way it is very similar to football, with lots of twists and turns and sudden explosive movements.

I discovered a German footballer with a tripartite patella, who was playing at an international level, which in itself gave us the hope that this news didn't have to be career-ending. Then, after calling more contacts who suggested other contacts and so on, we came across a tennis player in Miami who had been diagnosed with a bipartite patella at the age of nineteen. We begged them for details of their consultant and sent over Andy's scans as soon as we had a name.

The response was mixed. The consultant did believe that Andy would be able to play again, but explained that there was no magic cure for such a condition. It was merely a case of creating the right rehabilitation programme, building all of the muscles around the knee and enough strength to compensate for the physiological weakness. It sounded like a long journey to recovery and our first experience of a rehab programme. We understood the importance of taking care of your body as you reach professional level, and fully understanding all of the strengths and weaknesses therein. If you're a professional sportsperson and your body doesn't work – you don't work. It is as simple as that. From now on, Andy was going to have to both train and play taking into account the situation with his knee.

Andy stayed at home for this rehabilitation, as there was no way that we could continue paying the academy as well as the consultant's bills, plus I wanted to keep an eye on him. One contract we couldn't get out of was Leon's though, as we had only just signed him. It seemed like madness that we had a private coach at home with Andy for most of the day, but in hindsight it probably kept us all sane. For starters, Andy had company, and then there was the fact that he had an adult around while I was at work, to make sure he actually did the rehabilitation exercises, some at home, some in the gym, some in the pool. The routine of exercises was very specific, set out by the doctor and physios at the Scottish Institute of Sport. Some involved movements so small and intricate I am sure they would have become movements towards the PlayStation if there had been no one around to keep him focused. Leon was on a pretty steep learning curve of his own at that time, albeit not the one he had imagined when he had originally set off for Spain. Aside from anything else, both of them became exceptionally good at sports which required minimal movement, especially snooker and darts.

There was also a lot of tennis on TV, which Andy began to watch with an analytical eye. He had always been very astute tactically, but now he seized the chance to refine that instinct. He had a little book in which he would make notes as he watched matches – the front of the book was for technical observations and patterns of play, while the back became a list of ridiculous remarks the commentators had made that day. I would come home from work and ask what he'd been up to, and he would have all of the details ready to go.

'Went to the gym, went to the pool, stuffed Leon at snooker and watched Agassi versus Safin. And when I play Safin this is what I'm going to do . . .' The notebook would be opened. 'I'll serve wide to the forehand, slice short and . . .' There would then follow some wisecracks about the commentators, littered with: 'You'll never *guess* what he said today . . .' and endless eye-rolling. There was one in particular who would regularly make basic mistakes or especially inane comments, but that's perhaps something neither he nor Andy would thank me for being specific about.

The way Andy saw it, this time spent watching matches was the equivalent of being in business and being able to see all of your rivals in negotiations while you sat at home with your feet up and plenty of time on your hands. Nowadays, I am constantly surprised at how rarely promising juniors watch their prospective rivals on TV. What better way to learn than watching the world's best players?

By the spring, he was able to start hitting balls again, albeit without much leg movement, and by May he was nearly there. The whole rehabilitation period had been an intense education for all of us. And just as Jamie's previous brush with adversity had informed Andy's decisions and approach to the game, watching Andy go through this was also of value to his brother. The very process of becoming a professional athlete is learning how to deal with adversity: to deal with defeat and disappointment, and to understand the importance of knowing your body's strengths and weaknesses. But opportunity can be found in everything: Andy learned so much in that time. It is almost as if after a period of intense acceleration with his game on court, he needed to stop, rest and emotionally catch up with his new responsibilities. These days, even the slightest twinge and he is off to get scanned immediately so that he knows exactly what he is dealing with. But these days he can afford it. Back then, every consultant appointment or physio visit was another knot in my stomach or another night's sleep lost.

To this day, I am not sure if either of the boys knows the horrendous financial stress I was under during those teenage years. In November 2003, I had borrowed a frightening amount of money to be able to pay for both Jamie's Parisian training and Leon's individual coaching. I could barely even let myself think about it; I just had to keep working and working. And I had no idea if I would be able to pay it back. We didn't know if Andy would ever play again, let alone win and be able to earn money from playing professionally.

I was living hand to mouth, pay cheque to pay cheque. Every hotel for every tournament was the absolute cheapest. I became expert at finding deals at restaurants – 'kids eat free' or '2 for 1 dinners'. Rarely had I had to be so creative with how the money stretched. I seldom had new clothes and never had any time off. I was constantly going to the bank, filling in more forms, being assessed again, having to explain myself from the beginning all over again, and hoping that I'd be able to borrow against the house one more time.

I had stopped telling my folks or anyone around me how deep into debt I had let myself get, so I was carrying the burden alone. I knew what it felt like to stare at the ceiling at 3 a.m. wondering how on earth this was all going to work itself out. So I got thinner, I got more tired, and all I could ever ask of the boys was that they tried their hardest. I just knew that I had to give them the chance and hoped that one day it would work itself out. There was no plan B. So it's a good job plan A worked out!

Within three months of being back on court, Andy won the US Open Junior Championship – his first Grand Slam title. And everything changed. For all of us.

The experience with his injury had taught us so much – as a team, as a family and as individuals. Not just about injury and how it is part and parcel of the athlete's life, but about the psychology of dealing with adversity, about not accepting the first answer that an expert gives you and, crucially, about patience and resilience. By early summer 2004, six months after he had been forced to stop completely, Andy was playing again, and by September he was on his way to New York for the US Open Juniors with the Scottish squad.

We were, as ever, a little gang travelling together. There were three Scottish players – Andy, Jamie, Jamie Baker, as well as an English lad called Tom Rushby who shared a coach with Jamie Baker in Loughborough. We travelled together, we stayed in the tournament hotel together, the Grand Hyatt, and we ate all our meals together, relaxing and keeping an eye on each other like a family. I had also brought another young coach called Alan MacDonald with us, as part of my ongoing mission to make sure that wherever we could squeeze the budget to fit, we'd take younger coaches on trips to build their experience for when they had to lead trips of their own. I think I realised the importance of succession plans even then and now, thirteen years later, Alan is my Jamie's full-time coach on the ATP circuit.

So that was our team. But this time we also had a secret weapon.

Her name was Pamela Stephenson and she was a video analyst. This was a long time before all tournaments had their data crunched live by companies such as SAP or Hawk-Eye, and even now the players don't have access to all that information as it's owned by the television companies or the event itself. Video analysis was in its infancy, but I was convinced that it would help us, and having seen a presentation on it at the University of Wales in Cardiff, I had persuaded the Scottish Institute of Sport to let us invest in someone to help us.

The presentation I had seen showed footage of a squash match, with the court divided into nine 'zones', and the data analysed to see what player B would do each time player A hit the ball into a certain zone. It was remarkably effective at amassing evidence and establishing predictability. Basically, it did what the naked eye usually can't, and allowed you to head into a match with a pretty good idea of how your opponent is going to respond to specific shots. Which of course means you can plan your strategy very effectively, giving you the best possible chance of dominating the game.

The system was new and still pretty rare. The footage was often just taken from an old-school clunky video camera strapped to the back of the fencing, as high up as you could get it. But the principle was what counted – it wasn't as if you could ever get a junior tennis player to watch the whole of a match anyway, their concentration spans weren't that long! I was a huge convert, especially after having made that tape as part of my coaching qualification. In fact, I was such a fan that I was often spotted by other coaches and players stalking the courts with my enormous camera, earning myself the nickname 'The Spy'. I was still working at quite a basic level, though, while the professional video analyst's job was to condense the key elements of the match into about ten minutes, to make as much of an impact in the player's mind, really reinforcing what their opponent might do and getting them as prepared as possible. Pamela was our woman and we were thrilled to have her. She would film the matches of the opponents. I would then watch the match, identify the tactics and she would pull out all the relevant clips to show our player.

I had also picked up an extra skill in recent years. During my time at the Next Generation Club I had taken a sports massage course. It was more out of necessity than anything else. We were doing so much travelling as a team and we'd find ourselves in an unfamiliar place, in need of a physio to give the sore, exhausted players a rub-down after a long match but without the first clue where to find one. If we couldn't find someone else to do it, I'd do it myself. It had become a terribly familiar mantra by now!

With this team, I really saw the trip to the US as a mission. We were like a little army, and we were going into battle. How strong could we be? What could we hit the enemy with? What could they hit us with, and what would our tactical response be?

Between us, we did a great job. Jamie Baker made the last sixteen of the singles, Andy and my Jamie made the semi-finals of the doubles. And, only 14 weeks after his rehabilitation had ended, Andy made it to the singles final. It was a sixty-four player draw, which meant having to play six matches instead of the seven in the men's event, but it still felt like a long, tense fortnight.

On the morning of the final, I had barely slept for nerves. After what had seemed like hours lying there in the dark, trying not to wake Andy, I grabbed my laptop, crept out of the room and headed downstairs to the hotel lobby. Desperate to find a way to not just occupy my frenzied brain, but to somehow do something useful, I decided to watch some of the footage of Sergiy Stakhovsky, Andy's Ukrainian opponent, playing his previous match, in the peace of the early morning.

What I hadn't anticipated was the steady flow of Brits heading downstairs to check out in time for flights back to the UK. That year, Tim Henman had made it to the semi-finals of the men's singles, which had led to an influx of various dignitaries, publicists and general hangers-on who had hopped on the Friday flight after Thursday's quarter-final, ready to watch him play the semi on the Saturday. He was the nation's big tennis star at the time and there was no shortage of interest in him and his career. Sadly, he had lost that semi-final, which meant that those who had flown out to watch were flying straight back home the next day.

At first, I just thought it was a busy time of day for the Hyatt, but as I sat, crouched over my laptop in the strange artificial light of the lobby, I looked up to see the Chief Executive of the LTA stepping out of the lift with his suitcase. He caught my eye and walked over to say hello. When he saw my laptop he asked what I was up to at this time of the morning and I explained that I was watching footage of Andy's opponent that had been provided by our video analyst.

'Goodness,' he said, with a wry, almost indulgent smile, 'you're taking this all a bit seriously, aren't you?'

I smiled back at him. Not because any single inch of me felt like smiling, but because I simply couldn't think of an appropriate response. *Of course* I was taking it seriously. I was the Scottish National Coach, and we had a player in the final. How was that amusing to him? I was both bemused and disappointed in his attitude. I bit down on my back teeth, hoping he wouldn't notice my jaw muscles flexing, and wished him a safe flight.

Slowly, dawn broke properly and eventually it was time to head to Flushing Meadows for the match. My nerves were now so frayed that I decided the only reasonable thing I could do was to focus on getting the support around Andy that he needed from others, rather than trying to provide it myself. For many years I'd been aware of how your kids pick up on your body language, positive or negative, so I thought it best to keep my input minimal. Andy had stopped working with Leon a month before the US Open. The one-on-one relationship between coach and pupil is not easy: it's intense. On the circuit you spend every waking hour together, and that can take its toll on both of you. We had not yet replaced him. Instead I had brought Alan MacDonald, one of the boys who had been part of our squad a few years earlier. He was the one I charged with practising and warming up with Andy – I sensed that if I had sent his brother Jamie in to do that role, it would just have stoked the anxiety for both of them and ended in a fight. They needed not to be winding each other up on court. Off court was a different matter.

As the match drew closer I sensed the tension mounting and took Jamie to one side.

'I can't go into the men's locker room,' I said. 'So you need to, and you need to stick to Andy like glue.'

He nodded. Of course he was going to do it. The boys were so close, and this was different from sparring on the tennis court. Being there for each other at times like this – well, it was like having a super power.

'He's going to be nervous, so just play cards with him, whatever. Just keep him relaxed and distracted. If he doesn't want to talk, don't try and make him talk. If he wants to play PlayStation, go with that. Just try to help him pass the time.'

And off Jamie went. I didn't see him again until just before the match began and Andy was walking on to the court. As for the match itself, I can barely remember it. It seemed to float by, as the points turned into games, games turned into sets, and all the while I tried to stay as calm as possible so as not to affect Andy's concentration in any way at all. But almost without me realising it, the crowd erupted and

Andy had won. The cheering was deafening and the elation was over-whelming, but within minutes of Andy leaving the court he was surrounded by security guards and media. We now had a new prob-lem on our hands: being the champion meant that he was now scheduled for a full day of international press interviews on the Mon-day, but we all had flights booked home that Sunday night and we had checked out of the hotel. When I tried to find the LTA's PR person who had flown out to New York just in case Tim Henman made the final, I discovered that he, too, had flown back to London. Apparently no one had expected that much from Andy, so we were on our own.

There was no way that he could miss out on Monday's media sched-ule, it was part of the contract for taking part in the tournament. So that Sunday night I found myself, not exactly celebrating (okay, maybe I had one glass of fizz), but changing flights for our entire squad of six and rebooking the hotel, while racking up a phone bill informing par-ents and navigating unfamiliar media. After negotiating a raft of written, radio and TV interviews across the city, the boys went sight-seeing and I went back to the hotel to pack. A mum's work . . . We did, however, manage a squad party in a typical New York diner on Broad-way, where the waiters and waitresses were young aspiring actors who sang and danced at the tables. It's important to celebrate success. Too often there isn't time, you just pack up and fly to the next event. But that night was a lot of fun. And perhaps worth all that stress!

When we finally got on the plane twenty-four hours later, it was a blessed relief to close my eyes and relax for a few hours. But they were the only few hours' rest I was going to get for a while, as things were not much calmer when we landed back in Scotland.

As we navigated security checks and finally made our way through customs, sleepy and discombobulated, we got to the doors to take us to the Arrivals area. There was the sound of a scuffle, and flashes of light coming from beyond the frosted glass.

'Mum, something's happening out there,' said Andy, anxiously. We assumed there was some sort of security alert and held back a minute, looking around, waiting for a sign that it was safe.

But we were too slow. The doors opened just as we paused behind them, exposing us all to what lay on the other side: a huge barrage of media. Reporters calling Andy's name, photographers and their flashes popping and humming in our faces, followed of course by the attention of everyone else in the terminal who might otherwise have been none the wiser. The place was all but at a standstill.

Strangest of all was that it took each of us a minute to work out what on earth was going on. We were stunned for a moment, used to our little bubble, staring at them, speechless. Then, slowly, it sank in.

'Andy,' I said quietly, 'this is all for you.' He smiled back at me, nervously.

When we finally got into the waiting car, my mum and dad, who had come to meet us, told us we might not want to go straight home. Apparently the few remaining members of the Scottish press who weren't at the airport were now in our front garden, jostling for the best shot of Andy arriving home, and the first interview with the new star of British tennis.

But how do they know where we live? I thought, actually a little scared, and certainly rather overwhelmed. It was only then that I realised what a huge story this was for Scotland. Dunblane is a tiny town that had for so long only been known for one thing – one very sad thing – and now there was a kid here who was a champion. Of course everyone wanted some good news! Being a champion is a bigger deal than even I had realised. And to think I had believed we were prepared for anything when we had set off a fortnight ago.

On our return, there was suddenly huge interest in Andy, and all sorts of requests for him to do various things. There was no prize money for winning the US Open Juniors – although the tiny solid gold tennis ball that was the trophy was gorgeous – so it was a strange combination of attention and perceived success without any of the solid progress that an adult win would have brought his career. We were still skint, still trying to persuade governing bodies that a kid from Scotland could be a proper tennis champion, and I was still battling the perception that I was not much more than a really pushy mum.

We had returned from New York on the Monday night, exhausted from the previous forty-eight hours, and I immediately had to prepare a presentation on the National Tennis Strategy for a meeting at SportScotland on the Thursday. I was apprehensive about the meeting, as nearly ten years of dealing with them had taught me time and again that tennis was not a priority for them. But we had never been in a better position than after Andy's win, and I was determined to put together a blinding presentation.

Years of experience had made it clear to me that, when presenting to SportScotland, one has to assume that they know nothing about your sport. I was looking for a lot more funding for the squad as we now had a handful of top junior players who required training bases overseas and an international tournament schedule, not to mention support for restringing, physiotherapy, video analysis and even basic things like constantly having to get names engraved on trophies (which of course always had to be returned the following year for the new champion). The costs were getting bigger and bigger.

The Scottish Institute of Sport was a relatively new body within SportScotland. In order to be eligible for their support, you had to be in the top 50 in the world in your sport. And we now had three boys in the top twenty juniors. This was more than France, Russia and the United States at the time, and they were hugely successful tennis nations. Surely the powers that be would understand that, I told myself, as I reeled out the facts and figures.

But as I gave my presentation to the chap heading up the meeting that day, I sensed that whatever we were doing, it wasn't impressing him. He was the interim performance director with a background in cycling. Maybe he understood Olympic sports intricately, or was an expert in team sports, but he had no concept of what it required to become a pro tennis player, and made it more than clear that he just wasn't interested. He knew little of the demands we had on us as a sport or the costs involved in transitioning a top junior into the dog-eat-dog world of men's tennis. Nothing I could say seemed to capture his imagination or make him reconsider.

In my opinion, he had absolutely zero interest and therefore zero ambition for tennis in Scotland, and he seemed to think that my ambition was more than a little curious. Was it because I was the mum of two of the boys? Was it because these were young lads being trained by a woman? Or was it because he simply didn't care? I will never know, but whatever the reason, his dismissal was swift and comprehensive.

Without hesitation he told us that we didn't meet the criteria for national funding.

'These boys are only top twenty juniors,' he explained.

'Of course,' I answered. 'But that's when they need help. You don't need support if you're one of the top fifty players in the world at adult level – you're a multimillionaire by then!'

I tried, again and again, to impress upon him that our hard work was starting to pay off, that we just needed help for a few years before the boys graduated to the ATP Tour and were able to earn proper money and attract sponsorship.

'Look how close we are,' I begged, 'we've got a junior Grand Slam champion now!'

'We're not interested in junior Grand Slam champions,' he replied. 'We're interested in Grand Slam champions.'

The words horse and cart sprang to mind. And so did two other words . . . words I can't print. You're not listening, I thought to myself. You only want to support people who are already successful, or fund sports you are interested in yourself. I'll never know the motivation behind it, but I'll never forget the relish with which he dismissed me. We had been on cloud nine since getting back from the States and I had spent a long, jet-lagged day on that presentation, but within seconds all of that positivity was whipped away.

Perhaps it would have been easier to forget if I'd been in the meeting by myself. I could have told myself that maybe I'd imagined it, that I was being oversensitive as the boys' mum. But I wasn't alone. As had long been my policy, I had taken a junior colleague with me to learn the ropes for such meetings, and this time it happened to be a young female coach.

The minute we left the room she turned to me, aghast.

'I cannot believe what just happened,' she said. 'Is it always like that?'

I was so relieved to hear someone else question the tone of the responses we'd had. It wasn't an individual paranoia – someone else had seen the way we had been treated.

'It wasn't just me, was it?' I replied.

'No! But how do you put up with it? It was as if he was . . . just blanking you.'

And with that question it dawned on me that I didn't have to put up with it. At last I had reached a wall, and I could go no further. If our national sports bodies were not going to believe in us when we came home with international Grand Slam titles, how could I ever persuade them to engage with tennis as a sport for Scotland? Where can you go from there? For one final time, I had been made to feel uncomfortable that two of the players were my kids, when I had spent the best part of a decade making sure that I was scrupulously fair at every stage. I loved working with all of those kids, and I had put my heart into building a successful national squad.

Did I still want to do this job, I thought, when it's such an uphill slog with so little support? It was an enormous risk to confront a future with no job. Could I really quit, just because I was finding it tough, at exactly the point where our finances were at their most perilous? Yes. This was a threshold I just couldn't pass. I firmly believed that the boys could make it to the top and I had to believe that the US Open success would open doors for both Andy and Jamie in terms of sponsorship and opportunity. I handed in my resignation for the position of Scottish National Coach that week, and began my three months' notice period with trepidation, but also with relief and determination.

It was a strange time, those months after the US Open: I had told myself for so long that we would turn a corner soon, but it seemed that instead of bringing us success, or even a little bit of respite from the financial anxiety and fight for acceptance from governing bodies, the US Open win was simply bringing bigger challenges. I started to question if things would ever change for the better. I didn't sleep properly for months. And then, for the first time, the focus turned to me.

At the end of November that year, we were told that Andy was going to be awarded Junior Player of the Year at the Scottish Sports

Awards. It was a big awards ceremony held at a fancy hotel in Glasgow, and sponsored by the *Sunday Mail*. It wasn't televised, but it was the sort of thing widely covered by the press and attended by a raft of sports professionals. It was also the type of event where the women wore a lot of sparkle – long dresses, heels, bling, that sort of thing.

Andy was away playing at a tournament in Spain so he wasn't around to pick it up, and none of us wanted his achievement to go unnoticed on the night, so I went with my dad and picked up the award for him. I was hugely nervous about the event in general, but especially about having to get dressed up and sit with people that I didn't know. The whole thing was entirely out of my comfort zone: my job had been performed in sportswear for over a decade, and I simply didn't own the kind of clothes that were expected at a do this formal. More importantly, I certainly didn't have the budget to buy something appropriate.

I could hardly rock up in a shell suit though, so I did my best. And my best was a smart, pale green corduroy jacket from Marks & Spencer. It was £29.99 and that was absolutely every penny that I had to spare. As such, it left me with no leeway to buy anything else, so I wore it with a longish denim skirt and some pretty ancient black boots. But as we sat down to dinner, it was impossible not to notice how underdressed I seemed in comparison to the other women in the room. I was there to pick up an award, I told myself. And nobody knows who I am anyway, they're not going to care.

As the evening progressed, I paid close attention to the mood and the layout of the room so that I could avoid as much embarrassment as possible when it was my turn to head up to the stage. The evening's presenter was Tam Cowan, a well-known Scottish comedian and football pundit. He was a perfect after-dinner speaker for an event in front of a bunch of men. It was a pretty male-dominated room, but it was not an event *for* men. It felt like it though, with the underlying atmosphere of 'sport equals men'. But this kind of laddish banter was nothing I hadn't heard before, and I wanted to show the room that I could meet their tone and hold my own in the company there that night. I knew Andy's award wasn't coming up until the second half of the evening, so I had a little bit of time to prepare a comeback for whatever inevitable quip came my way.

It had only been a couple of months since the success in New York, but we had quickly learned that the one question that would now be a constant in our lives was: 'So, when's Andy going to win Wimbledon then?' and it looked like that night would be no different. I was pretty sure Tam would ask me that, so I paid close attention and established that his home football team was a mid-table team called Motherwell. I felt ready to answer back if he gave me any grief about Wimbledon, and focused on navigating the stage to avoid tripping up the steps or wandering off out of the wrong exit.

When I went up and collected the award, his remark followed the congratulations like clockwork.

'Never mind the US Open,' he said with a grin, 'when's Andy going to win Wimbledon then?'

The crowd laughed.

'Well,' I replied with a raised eyebrow, hoping I was playing along and showing the crowd that a mum could meet the banter with a sense of humour, 'I think he has more chance of winning Wimbledon than Motherwell do of winning the European Cup.'

The laugher continued. A smile broke across my face. But not across Tam's. He looked me up and down, pointedly.

'Could he not have bought you anything decent to wear tonight then?'

The laughter turned to the roar that a rush of blood to the head can create, as I felt my face turn crimson. I had no reply now. But even if I had, I wouldn't have had a chance to use it, as Tam gave me no opportunity to answer back this time. He grinned at the crowd, then returned to his script quickly, leaving me to be ushered, mortified, from the stage.

It would be impossible to underestimate the impact that one moment had on me. I'm almost embarrassed to admit how much it affected me. I just wanted to get off the stage and stay off stages for ever. It compounded every anxiety I had ever had about dressing up and going to a public event like that. It made me avoid them wherever possible for years. After years of being a confident, adventurous spirit, I began to dread and then to avoid, walking into rooms where I didn't know anyone. I turned down countless events, which should have been fun, for fear of not having the right clothes or not knowing what to say when put on the spot.

When Andy and Jamie started to win more awards, they were often away when the time for presentations like this came around, and I tried to do the right thing by collecting them when I absolutely had to, but for a long time I didn't even consider attending – simply because I didn't have the 'right' image.

These days Tam Cowan has his own radio show. I caught a little bit of it in the car a couple of months ago and just hearing his voice takes me back to that denim skirt and corduroy jacket. He probably has no recollection of that night at all, let alone any sense of its effect on me. He was simply used to a male audience, and unaccustomed to a woman answering back, even if in jest, in an attempt to engage with the tone of the evening. I learned long ago that people never forget how you make them feel. He made me feel terrible and it affected me for years. It's why I try to make my pupils feel special whatever their age, gender or ability.

As the year ended, I confronted a future with no salary, very little support and seemingly never-ending outgoings. Mercifully, I still had a tight-knit group of friends as supportive as they are hilarious – and it was they who largely got me through the tough times. Then, a chance phone call changed everything.

10

A lifeline, or a new life altogether

*In which an unexpected meeting turns our prospects
around fast, but leaves us exposed to a media we are
unfamiliar with and unprepared for. Where Andy has
the chance to let his tennis do the talking, I am not
afforded that chance, and struggle to find a voice
amidst the hoopla of the professional game.*

I never found out how Maggie Auld got hold of our address, but
her letter landed on the doormat out of the blue one day, shortly
before Christmas of 2004. It was a lovely, handwritten letter in
beautiful old-fashioned handwriting. She simply said that she was
Scottish, a huge tennis fan, and very much wanted to do something
to help Andy with his career – and would I be happy to discuss that
at some point? From time to time, I would get a similar letter from
a stranger, and I always replied politely although they usually came
to nothing at all.

So I replied to the letter and said that yes, I would be very happy to talk to Maggie about Andy. A few days later, I called her and we had a lovely chat. She seemed absolutely genuine, rather than merely the kind of 'benefactor' who wants to offer fifty quid and then expects free Grand Slam tickets for life – several of whom I had heard about on the circuit. She told me that she would love to contribute something towards Andy's coaching, and I tried to be as gracious as I possibly could, all the while telling myself not to expect anything. No numbers were mentioned on the telephone, so she could easily have been a dear lady who simply wanted a chat with someone whose son she admired.

I tried to forget all about the call, and to focus on the new year and the inevitable round of funding approaches I had ahead of me. As Andy's spring tournaments loomed, the travel looked like it would be further afield than ever before, and Jamie's time in Paris was showing no sign of coming to an end either. I felt sick day and night, wondering how I could stretch our meagre finances. Once again I realised that I couldn't rely on anyone else having faith in my kids, so if I wanted to make it happen, I was going to have to brave it and do it myself.

A few weeks later, with no notice, a cheque for ten thousand pounds arrived. As I opened the envelope I gasped. It made no sense – this was as much money as RBS were sponsoring Andy *per year*, and this woman simply wanted to give it away? There had been no other single moment in the entire span of my life, or the boys' careers, when we needed an unexpected benefactor more. And here, out of the blue, she had appeared. I slumped onto the sofa and fanned myself with the cheque, part of me still wondering what on earth we might have to do to repay such kindness. But when I made contact with her to confirm that this was her cheque and to thank her, she asked for nothing in return. It genuinely was a gift. I made a promise to her that whenever Andy played in London, we would meet, and that they would have the best tickets I could possibly arrange. As it turned out, we only had to wait another six months.

By autumn 2004, Andy was back in Spain training at the Sánchez academy and working with a very experienced coach called Pato Alvarez. Pato had worked with greats such as Ilie Năstase, as well as Sánchez himself, and was a pretty elderly, pretty eccentric South American. What he didn't know about tennis wasn't worth knowing. He just had the basics nailed: simple stuff like movement to and from the ball, which he'd make you look at with entirely fresh eyes. Even years later, Andy still talks about how much he learned with Pato.

But, of course, that didn't mean it was an easy ride! Andy was now at a delicate transitional stage between junior and adult tennis, one at which many young players drop out. He was seventeen, so nominally he still had a year left in him on the junior circuit. But he had now played all of the best juniors and won a Grand Slam, so there was little left to learn in that environment. However, the leap up to men's tennis is a challenging one.

A lot of kids simply don't adapt to the adult game or to the life and business of a pro player. You have to make this shift as your sport, your hobby and source of joy and confidence, transforms from fun to a livelihood. You're no longer playing other kids, largely age-matched to you, you're playing grown men maybe a decade older than you, with a decade's more experience. These guys are playing with an entirely different set of motivations – they want to win so they can get a decent car, so they can afford to start a family, so they can buy a house where they want to live. The mindset and the attitude at adult level is entirely different, and not everyone can make that switch.

Andy had already had some success on the ITF Futures Circuit, so Pato's strategy was to enter him into what were called Challenger events. While Futures tournaments are the first rung of the men's tennis ladder (mainly for those ranked 500 to 1500 in the world), Challengers are the second rung (mainly for those ranked 100 to 500) in the world, with the ATP (Association of Tennis Professionals) Tour as the final rung of the ladder. Andy was ranked about 540 in the world, so he was within touching distance of the Challenger Tour, but he would still require a wildcard into some qualifying events. But Pato was adamant.

As 2005 dawned, Pato took him to South America to play in three of these events, but he came back disheartened at his lack of progress and drained by the increased international travel. Andy was used to travelling in a squad, among friends, as he always had done with the Scottish squad or GB teams, and with my bag of puzzle books and card games. In those early days, he was given the chance to unwind over a pizza and some goofing around with his mates in the evenings. Now, he was taking transatlantic flights with a guy of seventy-odd and spending long evenings in budget hotel rooms alone. It wasn't exactly fun and it did nothing for his morale.

That South American trip lasted for three weeks, and Andy only won one match of the four that he played. He was very down-beat on his return, not just about his results, but about the prospect of further trips to the other side of the world, with no one to hang out with and opponents of totally different ages and ambitions. Pato's only other client was a twenty-seven-year-old Chilean player who was hardly the sort of guy Andy, still a teenager, felt comfortable spending downtime with, let alone confiding in. And there was a language barrier.

I went to Barcelona to visit him as soon as I could after he returned from that trip, as I could tell he was feeling really low. Pato was planning for the next trip to include some European Challenger events, and I was concerned that this wasn't the right thing for Andy at this stage. But Pato was convinced that the alternative option, the Futures Circuit, was 'a very bad level' and that he didn't want Andy to languish there. After talking to Andy again, I questioned Pato once more, but he was convinced.

'He has to learn Challenger level, Judy,' he would tell me. 'He will learn quickly, trust me. He's so close. He's going to be better than Henman, and soon.'

It still seemed like a jump too soon, but Pato was insistent. And his background and experience were undeniable. If I couldn't trust someone who had seen this many players transition at this level, who could I trust?

'Do what you think is best, Pato,' I told him. At least the financial burden had lifted. I hugged Andy as I left, reassuring him how much faith we all had in him. Just a little longer . . .

Meanwhile, as Jamie's men's ranking was not as high as his brother's, he was still touring the junior circuit from his base in Paris, with the goal of getting his International Tennis Federation (ITF) ranking to about forty, which would mean he'd have a safe spot at the French Open Juniors in May. He was competing in an entirely different schedule of tournaments because of how completely different his game was developing from Andy's: where Andy prefers grass and slower surfaces, Jamie was by now much happier on faster surfaces, so his tournament choices reflected that. Every flight, hotel and entry fee still had to be paid for, not to mention meals, phone calls and the rest and, as ever, I was busily balancing the books while trying to maintain a calm front at home. I was able to do a lot of that spring's travel with Jamie, though, and he was really enjoying it. Andy was not having such a good time, though. When he returned from a string of European clay court events at the end of April 2005 he had barely won a match all year. He was struggling with the lack of success and the lack of fun on the road. He told us he didn't want to continue working with Pato, so I headed off to Barcelona to deal with another difficult situation.

I was perfectly happy to let this go. I could see the age gap was a problem, and nobody handles constant losses well. As ever, I stuck to my overriding principle: Andy's success should never come at the expense of his happiness. He was now a kid in a man's world, no pals or family around, deflated. But there seems to be something in his make-up that means he has to hit a real low before he can summon the fight to play his best again. Just as he had experienced the frustration and anxiety of injury before his US Open win, he had to endure his losing streak with Pato before finding the spirit to play his best tennis for some time in Paris. Or maybe having friends and family around made him feel secure and confident again. Emotional support should never be underestimated. And, just as Pato had predicted, Andy rose to the challenge, reaching the semi-finals. So now Pato had gone, I stepped into the breach. He hadn't done anything wrong; it was simply that Andy needed more than the coaching input. He needed someone closer to his age and some familiar faces around him. Pato understood that and things ended amicably. I'm very proud that this is the case with all of the coaches that have worked with the boys over the years. It is rare for any of us to actively fall out with someone, but you do have to keep moving on – players need different influences at different stages, and so the job continued to be about finding the right people and the right places at the right time. A sort of cross between headhunting and matchmaking.

Reaching the semi-finals felt like a triumph for Andy after the last few months in the doldrums. I have to be honest here and say that I was devastated. He ought to have won the whole thing, but it's hard to see it objectively. I tried not to show it as we walked back to the lockers. For Andy, it had been a positive experience. It was as if something in him had clicked back into place that week, because as he walked off the court after being beaten by Marin Čilić, the eventual tournament winner, he simply said to me: 'Never mind, Mum. It means we get back to the UK earlier for some grass court practice. Queen's is much more important.'

Unusually for a junior, Andy was asked to do some press at Roland Garros after his match, and this was to mark his first negative brush with the media. In the interview room, one of the French reporters asked Andy about his now-rising status on the circuit and how it was going down back home. Or at least he meant to.

'How does it feel to be the great English hope?' he asked.

I could see Andy bristle. I wanted to put my hands over my ears. What was he going to do now?

'I'm not English, I'm Scottish,' corrected Andy, who at this point had been interviewed only a handful of times and had no idea how quickly things could be picked up and used to suit the newspapers' purposes.

'It's the same thing,' said the interviewer.

'So you're German then?' Andy replied.

Oh God. Here we go . . . He was, of course, antsy at a line of questioning that seemed irrelevant to the tennis. But it set a small benchmark for journalists who would now know where to go if they wanted to get a post-match rise out of him.

It didn't take long for the jubilant mood to return though, and after a short while we were bundled onto the Eurostar, heading to London. The next big hurdle was right around the corner: Andy had a wild card entry into Queen's, an ATP tournament in London considered very prestigious as it's one of the Wimbledon warm-up events. It was the very next week.

By 2005, there had been an almost complete change of leadership at the Lawn Tennis Association, and a former player called Mark Petchey was now head of Men's Tennis there. He had also agreed to take care of Andy's training costs in Barcelona for the last few months. He was someone – finally – who had real faith in Andy, and had told us to keep in touch with him if we needed anything. Given that we were heading straight back to London and another tournament, I took him at his word and gave him a call as soon as we made it to the UK side of the tunnel. With a change of surface it would be good to practice as soon as possible, so I asked him whether there were any grass courts available for Andy to hit on over the next few days. The answer was simple: 'Leave it with me, Judy. Bring him to Queen's for 10 a.m. tomorrow morning.' God, the relief!

Sure enough, when we arrived the next day, a court had been arranged, Mark had sorted hitting partners for the week, and we were told not to worry about anything for the duration of the grass season. The possibility of him having a mentor figure in the UK who genuinely believed in him – a young, approachable guy with a family of his own – felt like moving into the sunshine after long years in the shadows. Andy had always found great support in Barcelona, but now, on home turf, there was someone he could turn to for backup and leadership. It was exactly what we needed. We had rented a small basement flat in Wimbledon for the three of us for

154

the whole of June, and it felt as if this might be the summer that our luck finally changed.

A second factor convincing me that this was going to be our summer was that with Andy now playing in London, I could finally arrange to meet Maggie Auld, the woman who had sent us the gift of £10,000 to help with Andy's training. I managed to get her and her friend seats for Andy's first match at Queen's and arranged to take them to the players' lounge afterwards. I had no idea whether Andy would win or not as this was such a big step up for him, but I knew he wanted to meet her. I knew that she lived in London and I desperately wanted to thank her in person, and to give Andy the chance to say thank you, too. I was sitting elsewhere for the match, so I didn't get the chance to speak to her until afterwards. In fact, I had no idea what she even looked like until she and her friend came up to me in person. And when I did see Maggie, I was shocked. It was abundantly clear that she was extremely ill.

She had given no indication of it on the telephone, but she was very frail, with yellowed eyes, and she was relying quite heavily on her friend. As they did not mention it, I elected not to mention it either – I didn't want to make either of them feel uncomfortable. Instead, we tucked into what have now become my favourite post-match treats: a pot of tea and some mini chocolate eclairs. They were both wonderful company and seemed truly delighted to meet Andy, who was thrilled to have won his match.

The following morning, I received a text from Maggie's friend, who explained that Maggie was indeed dying of cancer, and it had been one of her greatest wishes to help Andy and to see him play. She died the following day.

She will never truly know what a lifeline she threw us as a family. There were very few avenues left to us when she first got in touch, and by the time she saw Andy play, he had turned a corner more comprehensively than even I appreciated at the time. A few weeks later, I received an email from her husband, explaining that he had been with her in the hospital at the end, and one of the last things she had said to him was to 'take care of that boy – he's going to be a star'.

To this day, I still meet up once a year or so with Maggie's friend. I last saw her at the ATP Masters Finals in 2016, when both Andy and Jamie became World number 1 in their respective disciplines. Once again I expressed my regret that Maggie never saw what they could achieve. 'She just knew,' she always tells me. 'Maggie just knew.' Perhaps she did. I will never forget how she stepped up to help at a time when we so desperately needed it.

Within weeks, Andy was well on his way up the men's rankings, taking part in his first Wimbledon, where he got to the third round, and lost in five sets to a top 5 player. The transition from junior player to fully fledged adult player was starting.

He was making the transition; myself less so. That first Wimbledon was an enormous learning curve, only for reasons I had never anticipated. I suppose we had all spent so long dreaming about getting to Wimbledon that we hadn't given much thought to what it would be like once we got there.

The pressure on Andy was intense. The UK media were excited to have a new hope to follow, and follow him they certainly did. We had thought that our little rented basement flat, walking distance from the All England Club, would see us through the grass court season without incident. But within a few days of the tournament beginning, there were white vans parked outside, on the other side of the road. It was only after images of me or Jamie heading out first thing in the morning to buy bagels appeared in the national press that we realised the dark windows of the vans were in fact blacked out, to hide photographers. We were being papped! After that, those were probably the best of the snaps they took that summer – the on-court ones, on the other hand, were terrible.

Tennis is a unique spectator sport in that there are regular breaks for the players, during the match – twenty seconds between points, and ninety seconds at each changeover. And the BBC is a unique broadcaster in that it doesn't cut to advertisements during those breaks. This makes Wimbledon coverage particularly focused on the crowd – especially the famous, the glamorous, or in my case, the unusual. The summer of 2005 was the first time I had sat in the player's box during the Championships, so it was the first time I had encountered the attention of the cameras.

Yes, I was a fresh face in the box, but I certainly wasn't a particularly interesting one. Or so I thought. But there was coverage of me during Andy's matches from the very first game. I think it is because the mother–son dynamic is an unusual one in sport. We are used to seeing the energy of a father–son dynamic, or the encouragement of a father with a daughter, but people seemed not to know what to make of a competitive mother who is unashamedly ambitious on her son's behalf.

Most sports journalists are male, most sports editors are male, as are most of the photographers taking the images on court. This means that an image deemed 'curious' or 'original' is only deemed so having been seen by a chain of male professionals. I'm sure if more women, or mothers, had been involved in the publication of these images, they would have said, 'What's the big deal? That's what I look like on Sports Day.'

Instead, that summer, almost every single image used of me supporting Andy had me snarling, baring my teeth or looking pained.

There was very little that was relaxed or celebratory despite me being among people I knew and feeling hugely excited and proud most of the time. Each published picture served the public another gurn, another fist pump, or another grimace.

But those first few matches were so exciting! Andy was finally there, with a team who believed in him and a world of possibility at his feet. I cheered, whooped and fist-pumped as much as I had been doing for the previous twelve years. Lost in the game, I was having a blast. Then we came home to see the highlights on TV. And what a jolt that was.

It is an impossible battle to try and work out where each and every camera is during the match – you can't try to control your face any more than you can control when the photographers are pressing their shutters. But that fortnight I wished I could have done. It seemed to confound people that a woman could be there supporting a man, and be in a position of power or influence that wasn't romantic. That I could have professional value, or even maternal value, and that I was not ashamed of my ambition or excitement, seemed to relentlessly flummox both media and public.

At first, I was confused by it and then, when I saw the images as they rolled in day after day, very upset. In time, I have come to understand that it is – or at least it certainly was – socially unacceptable to a lot of men, and even some women, for me to be a competitive, driven woman. But it always felt fine for me. From those very first matches with my dad – who saw playing to win as the most fun we could have – to watching Andy's rise to the All England Club, I have seen no shame in wanting the same for my sons as countless fathers do for theirs, on court or off.

If I had been a man, I am pretty sure that no one would even have noticed me at Wimbledon that year. The only tennis father who has caught anyone's attention for years is the Williams sisters' dad, Richard, and that is because of his larger-than-life personality and media interviews, not because of his gender. Had my gender been different, so would my reception have been: the cameras would have found a celebrity, an ex-player, or a wacky Union Jack hat and followed that for twenty seconds every few games. But that year, it was me.

It would be a lie to say that it didn't have an impact. The pictures in the papers were bad enough, but the moment that really hurt was when I saw footage of myself on the BBC's *Today at Wimbledon* round-up. Having been at the All England Club for the match itself, we rushed home, excited to see the coverage of Andy's second win. Then, as the games unfolded into sets, the blood turned an uncomfortably icy cold in my veins as I realised how I looked on screen. I had wanted Andy to see me as I cheered that afternoon, to see how proud I was however he did. I'm so small, I had done everything I could to make myself large in the crowd – cheering with my hands cupping my mouth, waving my arms whenever I felt appropriate and lifting my hands way above my head to clap at every big point.

Then the BBC showed it in slow motion.

I had been wearing a vest top that day, which was revealing enough when every excited move I made was replayed in slow motion to the nation before bedtime. But the worst of it all was the apparently endless shot of me clapping with my arms raised up above my head. Each time my slo-mo hands met, a ripple of flesh juddered down my arm. It wasn't a great look. In fact it was grotesque.

This was less than a year after the Tam Cowan debacle, and I still wasn't especially confident about public appearances, aware of the gap between how I looked and how people expected me to look for certain occasions. In a tracksuit on court, no problem. But where there were rules or perceived ideas about what was appropriate, I was still struggling. And this coverage only compounded that. Part of me felt angry – I knew I had, on some level, been stitched up, because I knew that tennis dads weren't getting this treatment. But part of me just felt sad. I just wanted to support my son, enjoy the occasion. And now I was on national TV looking like a demented fan. I wanted to ignore it, to rise above it, but I knew it was what people were talking about – the grimace, the ambition, the 'she seems like a right piece of work'.

I never wore vest tops again, I took to clapping like a seal, and I tried to keep a lid on my emotions. It felt completely unnatural – and it didn't last long. But it was another introduction to what was to become my world. My actions and my appearance were going to be in the public eye and every detail scrutinised.

There were, however, strange consolations – and things I nearly missed out on so great was my aversion to dressing up. As I tried to acclimatise myself to life at Wimbledon that first week, I received a message from a former president of the LTA. He had four daughters, two of whom had played tennis at the same time as me twenty-odd years previously. I hadn't seen him for a long, long time, but had known him quite well back then.

Not only was he a past LTA president, he was also Deputy President of the Royal Shakespeare Company, so I was quite surprised to get the invitation from someone so establishment saying that they would like to have tea with me. In the Members enclosure, no less, where the VIPs invited to watch the tennis from the Royal Box are entertained. When at first I said I wasn't sure about the invitation, trying to explain that I would be too nervous between matches, he really was quite persuasive. Except of course it nearly didn't happen. When I got to the door, the doorman took one look at my jeans and hoodie and said that I wasn't allowed up. I was mortified: I had no idea about the strict rules they had in that section of the club. No denim. But part of me was relieved. Relieved that I wasn't going to have to sit there among the smart set, exposed to even more curious stares and feeling uncomfortable.

But within moments my host had appeared, all old-school British charm, telling the doorman – who to be fair was only doing his job – that he was quite sure 'it will be perfectly fine to allow Mrs Murray in on this occasion'. I couldn't help but smile at his chivalry, but anxiety started to simmer again once we reached the table and I saw that it was set for four. One of the other guests, it turned out, was Sir Ian McKellen. I was bowled over. How on earth was I supposed to banter with Gandalf? In my jeans and hoodie? I should have known better than to doubt the company of two of the most charming men in the country, as it turned out to be a lovely afternoon, and I am so glad that fretting about appearances or social skills didn't deprive me of the pleasure.

That tea-which-almost-wasn't taught me where my fears lay as Andy moved onto a global stage: it wasn't on the court, it was in the media and surrounding circus. Increasingly, it was the terror of wearing the wrong thing, going through the wrong door, or putting my foot in it. And saying the wrong thing became increasingly likely that summer as I learned about the dark art of doorstepping.

My only previous experience of the press appearing apparently out of nowhere had come the year before when we arrived home from the US Open Juniors. Back then, they had been on our front lawn, so at least I could identify them. At Wimbledon, I discovered that they could be hidden as just another face in the crowd. I would go and watch a match, then be heading down the stairs to leave the court with the rest of the spectators, when occasionally someone would start talking to me.

'Great match, didn't he do well?'

'How far do you think he can go?'

'Are you proud of him, then?'

They were usually innocuous comments or questions, the kind of thing that members of the public would often ask me and still do. I never wanted to be rude, particularly as the very idea of having fans was a new one to Andy or any of us. So I would reply, sincerely, and then see in the next day's paper that I had apparently 'given an interview'.

It was Greg Rusedski's wife who explained to me what was happening. She warned me that certain members of the press would work out what matches I would be watching (it wasn't hard, after all!) so they would know what gate I would be exiting and when. They would be there, simply melt into the crowd and start chatting as if they were regular punters. Before you knew it, embellished comments would appear as if by magic in print. These little tricks shook my confidence in the people around me, making me wonder what else I could be getting wrong as my vulnerability increased. The briefest of moments that I would otherwise have brushed off stung, and left me feeling uncomfortable, but unable to put my finger on why.

I was becoming more and more wary of those around me, to the detriment of good relationships I did have. And Andy was struggling with the media, too. No one prepares you for that kind of sudden exposure and it took a while for me to work out what needed to be done, but by early 2006 there only seemed to be one reasonable option: if we were now going to be in the public eye, it was time to get some professional help.

11

Creative differences, or how to find the best for each of your children

In which I realise how fast things can change, and that careers will never stop demanding creative responses to individual problems, seeking new answers and different approaches for different people.

The final straw was Andy's experience at the Australian Open in January 2006. It was the first time that he had played at the tournament, and given that it was only six months on from his first Wimbledon, he was still a new kid on the block, unused to the media, the pressure, and unfamiliar with the vast majority of competitors.

After a spate of run-ins with the media, he was becoming far too guarded. He felt that if he didn't speak, people picked his appearance apart, and when he did speak they zoomed in on his language, his accent, saying he was grumpy or he had a problem with women.

He was still smarting from an uncomfortable experience with the press corps at the ATP event in Auckland, a fortnight before the Australian Open. The conditions were tough. It was incredibly windy, which affected the ball toss when serving and caused many more breaks of serve than you'd usually find in a men's match. When asked about all of those breaks in a post-match interview, he had quipped that it had been a bit like a women's match, where multiple breaks of serve are commonplace. Within hours reports were out saying he'd had a pop at the women's game. The tension was mounting and a narrative was starting to form in the press. He was getting known for being difficult, so the press waited for him to be difficult, at times even baiting him. And so the trend continued.

Andy's focus was always on his tennis. He didn't really understand why this small gang of twenty or thirty journalists should be so important when there was a huge world of players, coaches, industry specialists and of course tennis fans who mattered so much more. But life's more complicated than that, as he was increasingly finding out – to his cost.

At the Australian Open in 2006, he was scheduled to play on the Tuesday – the day after Tim Henman had lost. He was playing Juan Ignacio Chela, an Argentinian ranked 46 in the world to Andy's 64. It was not a match that Andy was expected to win. It was potentially winnable, but far from a dead cert. But if he did win, he was due to play Australian superstar Leyton Hewitt, which would have been a huge match and a huge story as Leyton was the home favourite and one of the world's best at the time.

Andy played and lost, and was subsequently led into the media suite for his required interviews. The tone of the interviews was a little harsh, as there had been a lot of excitement around the prospect of him winning, and it felt like he had 'let the side down'. The press wanted answers. The most obvious answer was that he had been playing a much more experienced and higher ranked player, but the journalists were pushing, and Andy felt that they were pushing too hard.

'Look,' he said – admittedly gruffly, 'this guy is 46 in the world. I'm 64. I'm only eighteen. This is my first Australian Open and you're putting too much pressure on me.'

I can remember it as if it were yesterday, as I still have a DVD of that press conference. It is a perfect example of how not to handle a difficult situation. Because at this point the press turned on him, accusing him of blaming them for his defeat.

It's easy for me to see that he wasn't trying to blame them for the actual result, but was just trying to call them out for being unrealistic. What he was trying to say was: 'Don't write it up as a defeat in an easy first round, because it was never that and I'm still just a kid.' But that's not what he actually said, and it's not the tone in which he said it. And they were a pack of twenty-odd British journalists who had gone out to see the Brits and had been disappointed. They were frustrated, they were looking for a story, and they chose to focus on Andy's temperament in the absence of anything juicer.

That evening he – thankfully! – took some advice from the media advisor at Tennis Australia, and accepted the opportunity to go back to the press the next day and apologise. He understood that the animosity between them couldn't be left to fester. And I understood how he'd unintentionally got himself into such a mess. The level of expectation that had sprung up from nowhere over these six months was now at fever pitch, and he was having to learn how to adapt all over again.

Prompted by this, we started to look at other press conferences, to record interviews with people like Andy Roddick who was really great with the press and made it look fun and effortless, or Roger Federer, of course, who is so relaxed that he does interviews in several languages while looking as if he's having a massage. We tried to analyse how these people spoke, what it was that they were communicating beyond their words, what they chose to say and what made them so at ease. It was simple and obvious: they all had something that Andy didn't. Experience. And he knew it.

So as he headed to San José for another ATP tournament, he was the most guarded he had ever been. This time, he travelled with a smaller group than normal. Mark Petchey, who had been his personal coach since the previous summer, was unavailable, as we had all agreed that he would not work during his kids' school holidays. It was just Andy, Kim – who was by now his girlfriend of a few months – and James Auckland, a former British pro who had played doubles with him in the tournament and decided to stay on and support him in the singles final after they lost at the quarter final stage.

In typical Andy style, after a huge low, a period of being knocked down and feeling overwhelmed, he had quietly headed off on his own, regenerated, and come back stronger. It was here that he won his first ever ATP title.

Obviously, it was a long-dreamed-for moment to hear that Andy had won his first ATP men's title. All those cold winter training sessions, the endless travel and the nights spent staring at the ceiling wondering if remortgaging the house again was really worth it suddenly seemed a thing of the past. Andy had done it! He could win at ATP level and he had done it after a couple of really tough experiences, which would have left others battle-scarred and distracted. That was impressive, and typical of Andy's stoicism. But the circumstances in which I received that news, and the impact that it had were never part of the dream. In fact, for Jamie especially, they were somewhat nightmarish.

Jamie and I were staying in our usual budget Travelodge during his tournament in Sheffield. I went to sleep the night of Andy's final match with my phone turned off. As ever, my attitude was, 'Well, there's nothing I can do from here anyway, might as well try and get a good night's sleep.' On top of that, I was sharing a twin room with Jamie so I didn't want to wake him before a big match with texts buzzing away or whispered phone calls at three in the morning.

When we woke up, I checked my phone and there was a text from Andy to say that he had beaten Leyton Hewitt in the final. Of course, we were thrilled! I told Jamie when he woke up and we were both absolutely delighted, buzzing for him . . . but also very aware that Jamie had a big match that day too. I didn't want to dwell on the news; I wanted him to have his own space to get his head clear and to be as prepared and confident as possible when he stepped out onto the court. Ha, as if! It was he and I alone who cared about that.

As we arrived at the tennis centre in Sheffield, we saw vans of TV crews arriving, which was highly unusual for a tournament of this size. And when we got inside, we quickly spotted that there were cameras being set up around the court. It did not take long for us to work out why: they wanted a story on Andy, and they were going to use Jamie's appearance to get it. For the entire match, the hum and buzz of the cameras followed Jamie as he tried to play his best. But knowing that the lenses were following him, to get a shot with which to accompany a piece about his younger brother, was – of course! – a horrible distraction. He knew they weren't interested in him or his match. How can you be the best version of yourself when everyone around you is only using you for comparison? It is an impossible task. And he played terribly.

In the interviews following the match, he was asked repeatedly about Andy, Andy's success, and Andy's prospects. He was genuinely thrilled for his brother – he had seen the effort he had made to get there, he had been closer to it than anyone, but he still had the right to be seen on his own terms. That match had been huge for Jamie, but it was now squandered and he was left having to discuss his little brother.

It was an extraordinary day. A uniquely difficult moment in family life. This unit of ours, which had been so close, for so long, was now feeling stretched and pulled apart. It was a taster of what life was going to be like for Jamie from now on. He was horribly torn: he never wanted Andy to do anything other than brilliantly, but understandably he wanted to focus on his own game, and be respected for his own achievements. Worst of all, we had no way of knowing how to deal with this. There were no comparable dynamics in tennis – or certainly none that we knew of. A lot of people compare the boys' careers to those of the Williams sisters, but they reached the top virtually hand in hand, their ascent almost completely level for years. They didn't suffer these early bumps, comparisons and difficulties. Once again I found myself wishing there was someone to talk to or a manual on how to deal with these tough situations. Parenting is hard enough, but everything for my boys felt magnified. Jamie must have felt very alone. I know I did. And I know that Andy felt the pressure, too.

It was time to take better control of things to prepare for the grass court season of 2006. It was time to set about making plans: I couldn't sit around complaining or contemplating – it's not my style – so I decided to get learning. One of the first things I did was to take a course on communicating with the media. There was nothing to be gained from simply feeling hard done by. Perhaps understanding the situation better would help me to regain some trust in the press, and help Andy relax around them.

By now, I was struggling as a parent to read the coverage Andy was getting. I knew he was a good kid who wanted to work hard and be treated fairly. I also realised he was having to grow up in the public eye and that's not easy. But as a professional adult whom he still relied on for guidance and comfort, I needed to work out a way around this horrible situation. There seemed to be a stand-off between him and the press. His relationship with the media had deteriorated very quickly. But you can't fix someone's behaviour simply by telling them to change. I had as much hope of getting Andy to be more chilled by asking him to simply smile more on court as I did of persuading the media to give him an easier ride just by asking them politely. Sure, I still felt like Andy was a kid, but he was nineteen now, in an adult's world, and we had to engage with the press on adult terms.

There were a number of female tennis journalists, such as Alix Ramsay and Eleanor Preston, who had kept an eye out for me over the last year or so. They would tip me off if someone was snooping around, looking for a story where there was none, or let me know if someone was planning a piece about the family and scoping around for gossipy interviewees. They were very good to me; they understood the pressure that I was under to behave the 'right' way, as well as continuing to look after the family. Perhaps it was because they were women and they could empathise better with this curious attention my support for the boys seemed to attract. And it was Eleanor who suggested that we take this public relations course together, as she was looking to expand her repertoire into player management and event management from a media and PR perspective.

As a newcomer to the media game, I was finding it hard to understand that what I was casually saying to a journalist, while trying to be polite, or answering their question specifically, could end up in print with a completely different tone, different context, being transmitted to the nation. And I knew for sure that Andy was also struggling with this idea that what you say to one individual is effectively what you are saying to the world. The course was bespoke to us. We told them in advance what we wanted to learn and the company tailored the three days to us and us alone. We learned the basics of how the various media outlets operate and how to work with them on things such as image building and damage limitation. Once it was explained to us how journalists are trained and what they are after, we understood better how to manage a productive and positive relationship with them, how to handle difficult questions appropriately, some dos and don'ts of what to say and what not to say under pressure, and what not to talk about . . . namely football and politics!

It was one of the best decisions I ever made. Learning what I needed to help myself was easily transferrable to Andy's situation, and I was able to explain various angles to him, helping him to better manage his own responses in future. And the whole experience gave me the confidence to look people in the eye again after a bruising couple of years. It was the beginning of my transformation from someone who was too scared to have tea wearing a pair of jeans, to someone who would happily turn up on *Britain's Got Extra Talent* just because I'm a bit nosey about some of the contestants and fancy a look behind the scenes. For Andy and Jamie's careers it was invaluable; for me, it was transformative.

This sense of empowerment beyond the tennis court was something I needed to build for the escalating business and financial demands that Andy's recent success brought us. Sure, he had started to win, but he was hardly earning big bucks. We were still incurring massive costs each week, and now, when money did come in from sponsorships and prize money, it created a huge volume of work in terms of tax and accountancy – and most of it was international.

I started to lead a sort of double life at this point; I was no longer just a tennis coach, but someone trying to learn how to manage the life and business of a pro player. Andy had a management company at this point, but players can choose different types of management according to their budget, their ranking, their ambition or personal preference. We were mindful not to hand absolutely everything over to one company. Earlier we had suffered considerably as a result of misplaced trust. It happened at a time when we were vulnerable, and I desperately needed support and guidance in taking the boys and their playing to that next level. I had never felt so out of my depth or so close to losing faith in human nature. My judgement of people was something I had always seen as a strength; how was it now my biggest weakness. Trust is so important in this business, and it took me a long time to recover from this situation. Even now, I find myself cautious about trusting newcomers, wary of their intentions. So different from the easy faith I had in people long ago.

We were working with the Ace Group – a sports management company – who were pretty much a two-man band. We'd chosen this deliberately as it meant Andy was the focus of their efforts, but the disadvantage was that they couldn't provide all of the services that a bigger group might. This left a lot down to me. I had to get to grips with setting up a website, working out how to do basic accounting and navigating the simplest way to complete tax returns in several different countries. I was doing less and less coaching, and spending more time finding and managing other coaches, physiotherapists, fitness trainers, financial advisors and agents. Suddenly, business, strategy and management were now as much a part of life as the game itself.

There was only one son I was having to do this for though, as Jamie was finding himself in a different situation altogether. While Andy had been having this monumental breakthrough in his career, Jamie had been going through something of a lull. He had returned from training in Paris, where he had been playing the ITF junior circuit and taking part in some men's Futures tournaments. By early 2005, he had decided to leave his training base in Paris. His coach and two of his training partners had left the academy. He was back in London, sharing a flat with some other players in Southfields near Wimbledon, and training as part of a squad of four with one coach.

But it hadn't taken long for me to realise that the training wasn't good enough in that particular arrangement. There was little attention to detail; Jamie was just drifting and starting to get a little dejected. What was keeping his confidence up were his regular wins in doubles. As the year wound to a close, it became clear to me that while his singles level was Futures, he could happily be playing doubles – where his serve-volley game and natural flair were better suited – on the Challenger Tour.

However, as is very often the case, he still saw himself as a singles player. He saw it as more important than doubles, as if to enjoy the victories in doubles matches was somehow an act of surrender. Doing both was making scheduling a nightmare for him though:

for each tournament he would have to be onsite in time to play in the qualifying event for the singles, often on the Thursday before the event opens, then stay long enough to compete in the doubles finals the following Saturday. This meant that he would be at tournaments for ten days rather than a week at most, and that he was often needed at the early stages of the next event's singles qualifying rounds while he was still playing doubles at the previous one.

Sure, there is not as much prize money in doubles, but it was increasingly obvious that his game was far better suited to it. Back in 2006, there was no one in the UK going for an out and out doubles career. He saw it as a result of being a poor second best. I saw it as a massive opportunity. Early that year, I started to look at the careers of successful doubles players, the biggest of whom at the time were the Bryan brothers, American twins who had played together for years. They were obviously very marketable because of this and had carved out a very successful career both on and off the court.

The more I studied the doubles circuit and the way that it was changing to be taken more seriously, the clearer it seemed that there was a real chance for Jamie here – not just to compete at a higher level or to win more matches, but to do it on his own terms, playing to his own strengths. Where Andy has more of the grit and tenacity under pressure – he actively enjoys it when his back is to the wall and fighting his way out of trouble – Jamie was not as confident, and he hadn't been for years. As I've already said, much of this I trace back to him going down south to train at such a young age. But a lot of it is down to the fact that he did not have the key advantage Andy did: an older brother treading the ground before him, making it all look that little bit less terrifying. It wasn't just his game that was better suited to doubles, but his temperament, too. Having someone alongside him brought the best out in him.

So I put together a sort of presentation to show him that he could make a successful career in doubles. As a Grand Slam nation, GB players can count on a certain number of wild card places at major tournaments prior to Wimbledon. They also have the chance to play in the Davis Cup and earn decent fees for that, as well as building up some exposure at those sorts of events, and working towards getting some decent sponsorship. One day in early 2006, at the Bridge of Allan Tennis Club, near our home, I put my argument to Jamie and Colin Fleming, a Scottish lad a couple of years older than Jamie and his doubles partner at the time. They seemed pretty keen, unflustered by the suggestion, and agreed that they were up for pursuing a career in doubles and looking for a doubles coach. At this point, taking the focus off playing singles seemed like no great hardship, and a chance to excel elsewhere seemed to appeal.

A few weeks later, I was at a Masters event in Monte Carlo with Andy, geekily spending a bit of time watching the practice courts. This had long been one of my favourite ways to indulge myself on tour – checking out how other coaches worked with their charges. I was fascinated to see the drills they used and to observe their body language and how they communicated with their players. I made lots of notes and picked up loads of ideas. I loved a quiet afternoon doing this, and spent a happy couple of hours watching a guy I had never met before working with an Israeli doubles team. I was so impressed with how he was running the session; he demonstrated a great combination of patience, authority and attention to detail. Everyone was completely absorbed in the session. It was run with military precision.

Afterwards, I approached him, introduced myself, and said that

I had a young son who I thought could be a great doubles player, and was looking for a coach. 'Yes, I know Andy,' he said, as quick as a flash. He seemed a little confused by the suggestion.

'It's not Andy,' I replied. 'It's my older son, Jamie. He has a completely different game.'

At this, he was intrigued. He was Louis Cayer, a Canadian coach who had relocated to London three years previously but had – amazingly – never been asked by anyone to work with a British player. He seemed interested in the idea of working with Jamie, but was committed to other players until at least the end of May. He suggested I send a video of one of Jamie's matches to him, and offered to analyse it, to feed back his thoughts, and give us the best chance to see if they would be a good fit. It seemed like the perfect solution.

What he came back with was very impressive. It was a comprehensive report, with an amazing number of observations. He had looked at the video, freeze-framing bits and drawing lines on the frames to illustrate court positioning – whether they were too far back or not in line with each other, their movements after serves and so on. He made it very visual, very easy to see and to understand what needed to be done. This helped us appreciate his insight as well as his ability to communicate. And the attention to detail was excellent; he had clearly taken a lot of time to make his thoughts as clear as he possibly could. He seemed to have noticed so many things about Jamie's game that I hadn't. I have met very few coaches in my life who would go to those lengths for a prospective client, and I liked the way he addressed the problems in hand. Basically, he told us that they were all very simple things to fix, and he had ideas of how to do it, but that while he would like to help out, he couldn't do anything until the end of May. Then he gave us a breakdown of his costs ... He was expensive, but he was a great coach, and I figured that as both he and Jamie were based in London by this point, there would be no expense on accommodation or travel, so we could just about stretch to it – for a while.

I figured out that we could afford about six weeks of his time. As it turned out, the scheduling was perfect as he would step in just in time for the grass season. I found one of the Scottish coaches to work with them, too, as a hitting partner, and also as an opportunity for him to learn as much as possible from a pro like Cayer. It was a change in direction for everyone, a bit of a leap of faith for all of us involved, but then, only six months after the anguish of that match in Sheffield, and only eight weeks after working together, Jamie made the final of an ATP tournament in Los Angeles. This was a fantastic result, and such a fast turnaround! For his confidence, for the validation of the new approach, and to level things out a bit as Andy continued up the singles rankings. Above all, it meant that he was now well out of the Futures level events, where he had been at risk of languishing as a singles player. My big worry had been that he would simply become very good at being average, and never improve enough to make a living from the game. An even bigger worry had been that he would accept that for himself. I *knew* that he had the skill to be a really great professional tennis player, but unlike Andy who'd not had quite such a bumpy ride, Jamie had been at risk of letting a toxic combination of low confidence and bad circumstance get in his way.

Being able to hit a ball extraordinarily well is not enough to become a top player: you need the mental stamina, the emotional resiliance, and of course the luck and guidance, too. My concern for Jamie had never been that he wasn't good enough, but whether he could handle the life and business of tennis. The ups and downs, the rough and smooth of professional sport. But now he had matched his skill set to a type of play that suited him. He had been the one to choose that path, and it was starting to work for him. Result! Relief!

My suggestion for him to commit to doubles was a good one, but the real key to Jamie's success was Louis Cayer, not just the technical and tactical expertise but the psychological impact he made on Jamie's game. Jamie and Louis have gone on to enjoy a consistent coaching relationship of a kind that Andy has never really had. Players need different influences at different stages of development. It's unusual to find one coach who can provide everything from teenager to top tenner.

The relationship between player and coach is a delicate one, and one that does need to change over time as the player matures both physically and emotionally and moves up through the various levels of competition. When Andy was still a teenager, Rafa Nadal's uncle Toni told me that he believed that all coaches need to inspire a mixture of fear and respect in their players, and I believe that he was right – particularly with regards to younger players. You need to be able to convince a young, fit, enthusiastic youth that your greater experience, your emotional insights and your wisdom are worth listening to – that there is a strategy at play, even for the most impatient player, or indeed that psychological hard work is just as valuable as fitness training for the more emotionally volatile player. You need to sell yourself through your actions and achievements, but you also need to inspire that tiny drop of fear. Your player has to want to impress you – to work his butt off for you – every day in training. If they have worked out how to get round you as they would an opponent, or if they think your commitment doesn't match theirs – your time might be numbered.

Then there are the lifestyle choices that being a coach demands. Sometimes a player can find the perfect coach for them, but they might have a young family and be unprepared for the disruptive lifestyle that following a pro around the world entails. Or they may prefer working with younger players, nurturing them from childhood, or training a small squad of players rather than feeling the pressure of being responsible for one player alone. Perhaps above all, you have to find someone that you can face having dinner with most nights, someone with whom you can shoot the breeze, whose company, advice and even jokes you can enjoy. The pitfalls are almost endless, so any fruitful coaching relationship is to be treasured. Louis is someone who not only made a radical difference to the course of Jamie's career, but has also gone on to be one of my closest friends. I was even 'best man' at his wedding!

It was at this point that the coaching methods for the two boys diverged more than ever before. They have stayed very different ever since.

12

When winning isn't everything, or learning how to keep going

*In which a big win and a big loss don't have the effects
we anticipate, and I learn the value of taking a step back,
having a look at the long view, and stopping to
appreciate how far we have all come.*

Whatever it was that Jamie rediscovered when he started training with Louis – it worked. Because in July 2007, he surprised us all by becoming the first of the two boys to win a title at Wimbledon, something which no one was expecting, least of all him. That he entered the mixed doubles event at all was a spur of the moment decision. That he won was even more of a bolt from the blue.

In the case of most doubles tournaments, you have to enter well in advance, but mixed doubles is the one event that you can simply sign up for on site, and the championships at Wimbledon are no different. Jamie happened to be getting out of his car in the competitor's area at the same time that Serbian player Jelena Janković was getting out of hers. They had known each other a while from the circuit, and started chatting. He asked her if she fancied playing together, and she said she would. They entered the event that very day, the first Wednesday of the fortnight, and – having never played a single match together before – ten days later, they were Wimbledon champions. There was no master plan, nothing to prove, and no one to prove it to, and in my opinion that was the secret behind the sudden success: they were simply having fun.

In contrast, that year was the first one that Andy would have got a seeded position at Wimbledon, but he could not play. In the days leading up to the Championships, he was forced to accept that a wrist injury, which had been dogging him for a while, was simply not going to be healed in time for him to be able to take part. But he was very much there, enjoying his brother's matches where possible, and watching and learning as much about future opponents as he could from the sidelines.

We had thought that Andy's injury would make for a frustrating or depressing fortnight, but Jamie's success soon put paid to that, and before I knew it, I was sitting in the crowd during a Wimbledon final in which my son was competing. Then the realisation struck me: he might actually win this. The moment seemed to have over-taken me, and instead of being my usual self, I was just staring, barely even watching, numb with excitement and wonder.

They were 5–1 up in the third set, and Jamie and Jelena still just looked as if they were having an absolute blast. But I could barely feel my hands. This is Wimbledon, I thought to myself. It's actually the final at the All England Club, and Jamie is about to win, he really is. It's going to happen.

It was only about eighteen months since I had suggested to him that he focused on doubles. It felt like yesterday. So much had

First Wimbledon champion in the family. Jamie wins the
mixed doubles with Jelena Jancović in 2007.

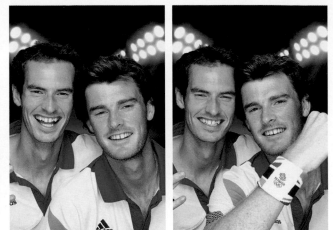

Defeat in the 2012 Wimbledon final to Roger Federer was almost unbearable. So near, yet so far.

Photo booth. Olympic style. Oh brother.

London Olympics 2012. Revenge and a gold medal. Andy beats Federer for the Olympic title at Wimbledon.

The US Open that same year. A first Grand Slam. On American soil and on hard courts, where he has always been most comfortable.

Watching big matches
is like a heart attack and
severe nausea all at the
same time. It's no fun.
In fact, I'm surprised
I'm still alive

Victory. Pride. Joy. Relief.

GB Fed Cup and Davis Cup captains. Me and Leon Smith running a kids' training session in Scotland in 2015. Back to where we started almost twenty years before.

GB Fed Cup team 2013 just before our World Group playoff against Argentina. Anne Keothavong, Laura Robson, Johanna Konta and Elena Baltacha.

Fed Cup taught me lots about working with girls. Like...sport and glamour can mix.
And the importance of the team selfie.

My favourite tennis picture of the boys. Says it all.
Davis Cup champions, 2015. Together.

Me and my van. Taking my sport into places you wouldn't normally find it and building workforces in local communities with Tennis on the Road.

Strike a pose little ladies. Having a blast with the Miss-Hits programme I created to make tennis more fun for girls.

Jamie's first Grand Slam title. The men's doubles at the 2016 Australian Open with Bruno Soares.

Mother's pride. Filming the awards ceremony at the ATP Masters finals where Jamie and Andy were both crowned End of Year World Number 1 for 2016.

Outstanding Contribution to Sport at the Sports Industry Awards, 2016. The Murray Family. Almost made me cry. I said almost.

changed for him; he was like a different man – yet he was still only twenty-one. And just as I stopped to pause to take in what he had already achieved, the crowd erupted: they had won.

This victory was like a burst of sunlight after endless clouds. Jamie deserved every moment of joy and praise he got. Yet again, he had done what he so often has in his relationship with his brother: he quietly went ahead and showed Andy that it could be done, that they had it in them, that anything was possible. Just as the nation's expectation was tightening its vice-like pressure on Andy, Jamie stepped up and forged the path ahead for him. As with those first trips abroad, the excitement of the Orange Bowl in Miami, or the experience of training away from home, Jamie headed out of the traps first, leaving Andy to follow in his own persistent way, in his own sweet time.

That day, Andy was watching Jamie's win from the BBC Radio 5 Live commentary box, as he had by now accepted that if he was visible to the cameras, they would film him and his reaction. He was so edgy and nervous for Jamie that he didn't want to be seen, and he certainly didn't want to distract Jamie's play or Jamie's moment in any way. He came out of the commentary box at 5–1, 30–0, in order to see the final points, and was so overjoyed that he was crying. He knew exactly what that win would mean for Jamie, and indeed what it meant for him. The days of Sheffield and San José were now long behind them.

These days, the boys rarely watch each other in person, but often on TV or by live stream on their computers. But they will sometimes turn up under exceptional circumstances. For example, when Jamie and Bruno Soares won the Australian Open Doubles in 2016, Andy had been watching back at his hotel, as he had to play his own singles final the following day. But when it got to the third set and

Andy started to sense that they might win, he ran from the hotel to the tournament site late that night all alone. He called me – I was away with the Fed Cup team at the time – gabbling: 'Mum, I've got to go, I'm heading over,' and I didn't have time to work out what he was talking about until he had completed the fifteen minute sprint and was there, watching the last few games, seeing Jamie receiving his trophy, and then heading back to the hotel without ever telling anyone except me that he was going to be there.

I love knowing when their schedules coincide and they're travelling to the same tournament. No matter how much else has changed, the thought of the two of them out on the road together, supporting each other, and competing in the world's biggest events and flying the flag for Scotland, is a real source of pride and comfort. Back in 2007 it felt as if the challenges were only going to get smaller from now on. But the biggest – for all of us – were yet to come.

Andy was there for Jamie that Wimbledon, and thrilled by every second of it, but he was having a far from easy time himself. The previous year his coaching relationship with the wonderful Mark Petchey had reached its natural end. Mark had guided him amazingly through that incredibly difficult transition from top junior into the world's top 60. Now Andy had set his heart on working with an American called Brad Gilbert. Brad was a seriously top level coach – he had worked with Andre Agassi, Andy's big childhood hero, and had been a top twenty tennis player himself. That was going to cost big bucks, but we were all sure it would be worth it. The whole tennis journey had been about investing in the right people at the right time, and this was no different. He could be a game-changer.

Brad had written a book called *Winning Ugly*, about playing smart and finding a way to win, even if you weren't at your best or you weren't the 'better player'. This had really struck a chord with

Andy, and he was determined to get his guy. I'm sure you've got the picture by now: Andy likes to make his own decisions, but once he has his heart set on something, he will do anything possible to make it work, whatever that takes. What Andy wanted now was to train with someone who had the experience of taking a player to the very top. So we found a way to contact him via Andy's management group at the time.

At first, they met for a chat, they had a bit of a play, had the chance to see how a relationship might feel. Things were looking good. But there was the cost to consider. Even though Andy was now beginning to earn decent money, it wasn't anything like enough to pay a coach like Brad. Financially, things had really turned round for Andy after the summer of 2005: he had picked up some prize money from Queen's and then from Wimbledon itself. This, combined with two other great sources of income – a sponsorship deal from Fred Perry and the offer of more and more wild card places at Challenger events in the US, which he was now winning quite regularly – meant that the heart-stopping anxiety of the previous years was now largely over. Coaches are by a clear margin the biggest expense for a player, because it's not just the coach's salary that the player is expected to pay, but all the attendant expenses as well: accommodation, international travel, food, phone bills and all the rest. This is where individual sports like tennis differ so dramatically from team sports such as football. You are responsible for all your costs and your income is determined by your success.

An example of this was in 2008 when Andy reached the quarterfinals of Wimbledon. His prize money was around £90,000, and by almost everyone's standards, that is a huge amount of money – far more than a year's salary for many of us. I can remember Andy asking me to pick up the prize money for him. In those days, if it was your home nation you were given an old-fashioned, handwritten cheque. I went into the All England Club the day after the match and was driving home with the cheque on the passenger seat. It was more money than I had ever seen on a cheque. I couldn't stop looking at it as I wove my way through the traffic with it sitting next to me like a wealthy passenger. I reached forward to turn on the radio, keen to hear the sports news. Within moments, perspective was slipping into place: the reporters were discussing Frank Lampard's new deal with Chelsea. It was to be for £125,000 a week. A week! Andy's winnings would be split into salaries for a fleet of people – coaches, physios, racket stringers, fitness trainers, website managers and PR advisors.

But the mission for Brad Gilbert in 2006 continued nonetheless, and we were very lucky that the LTA was headed up at the time by Roger Draper, a chief executive with a dream to develop world-class players. He had already invested in some top drawer staff. Andy was in the world's top 100 now, so he was firmly on Roger's radar, and he offered us the financial help to get Brad on board. He knew there were no guarantees, but he wasn't afraid to take the risk. A sponsorship deal was worked out, with Andy giving some time and image rights to the LTA, who in turn would contract Brad for thirty or so weeks of the year. Once again, feeling the support of the LTA when we needed it was a huge relief, and it was also a sign of recognition for Andy, some acknowledgement of what he had achieved and what they now saw as his potential.

However, as was so often the case with Andy, their coaching relationship ran its course relatively quickly and was coming to a head shortly before Wimbledon 2007 – the one he couldn't play in because of his wrist injury. Andy had torn a tendon in his wrist. It was his twentieth birthday, he was in Hamburg for an ATP tournament,

when something snapped in his wrist about five games into his opening match. He retired from the match and was taken off for a scan.
Although the slit in the tendon was tiny, wrists are crucial to tennis
players – it's where the body takes most of the impact after all – and
we all realised that his recovery was going to take some time. Yet
again, it looked as if injury was going to stymie his progress.

That evening he was devastated. It was a big birthday, my mum
and I had come over to celebrate with him and the team, but he had
his wrist in a cast and a more than heavy heart. I was aching for
him; he had been doing so well, he was really growing and progress-
ing and now this. Another setback. Or as I like to see it, another
obstacle to overcome.

We were determined to make the best of the evening though,
and in my memory it will always be special for two reasons. Firstly,
it was the night that the family was introduced to sushi for the first
time, and secondly we had an unexpected guest at our table. It was
Brad's idea to take us out for Japanese, as he was convinced Andy
would love it, and it's also a good, healthy meal for athletes. It's now
Andy's absolute favourite food, and these days, he'll head out for
sushi whenever there is a special occasion to be celebrated. Back
then, we were all baffled by the menu, especially my mum who kept
grabbing my sleeve and muttering about why there wasn't any 'normal food'.

Just as we were getting to grips with the menu, Brad, who was
sitting opposite me, gasped at something over my shoulder. I turned
round to see what had startled him, and saw a guy bigger than anyone I've ever seen in my life. He looked like a Bond villain. He had
enormous shoulders, was hugely tall and was rippling with muscle
like some sort of cartoon character. The woman with him was of
almost similar dimensions. I was as baffled by them as my mum

had been by the menu. But Brad left his seat, headed to the bar and started talking to them.

He came back to the table and said to me, 'That's Wladimir Klitschko, the boxer. I have asked him to come over and have a word with Andy.'

Andy is a massive boxing fan, and has been since childhood. When he gets the chance to meet a boxer, it's as if he's that little boy in the cereal-box WWF belt all over again. So when Klitschko appeared at his side and started chatting away, he was spellbound. The guy had such presence. They talked for ages, discussing Andy's injury and sharing his experience in managing injuries and setbacks. There were lots of boxing anecdotes and Andy was very inspired. He seemed much more upbeat and philosophical when the night ended back in the hotel lounge with us all eating the chocolate cake his gran had made and brought over all the way from Dunblane.

The next few weeks were tough psychologically, as Andy had to learn yet again how to rehab another injury. He started trying to practise after a month or so, just using soft foamy balls which would be easier on the wrist. But he could barely hit a forehand. Time crept on, progress was slow and as I was watching him practise two days before Wimbledon, I told it to him straight: 'You've just got to stop. You're not ready.' He could only hit his forehand with slice, which basically means you hit down and under the ball, and would normally only be used in a defensive situation. The injury wouldn't allow him to hit up and over the ball with top spin so he couldn't be aggressive at all.

Brad saw it differently, though. He was courtside, coaching Andy, and he was determined that Andy should play. I am not sure if he felt pressure to produce a result while under contract, but he wasn't letting up. Andy's first round match was due to be against Nicolás

Lapentti, the Ecuadorian player, and Brad was insistent. 'You can beat him without a forehand,' he told Andy.

But it wasn't about that. Someone had to think outside of that immediate Wimbledon pressure and step in. I could see Andy talking to Brad between play, and then looking back at me on the balcony. He was anxious – really anxious.

It had taken a lot of effort to get Brad on board, and I am sure that he was doing what he thought was best for Andy and his morale. But he was a strong-willed man, and everyone ultimately has their own agenda unless they're family. As family, I had no vested interest in Andy beyond love, and my only real job was to make sure that he was happy and healthy. And the minute I asked him, 'What do you think about playing?' I could see that he wasn't happy. Torn between knowing he wasn't yet fully fit and following his coach's advice. That night we created a list of pros and cons to help him make the right decision. The cons won and the next day, he pulled out of the tournament. It's always tough to miss Wimbledon – it's the highlight of the tennis calendar. But that year, with Jamie's incredible win, is remembered for good news not bad. But it was the beginning of the end of Andy's relationship with Brad and it had run its course by the end of the year.

As a sportsman you become acutely attuned to your body and its needs. Injury can be so demoralising, but for long-term good you often have to sacrifice short-term gain. In 2009 Andy faced another wrist injury and it threatened his appearance at the Davis Cup tie against Poland in Liverpool that September. It was a crucial match: lose and the GB team would be relegated. Andy had been suffering since August and he was pretty certain he wouldn't be able to play, but he agreed to travel with the team for the practice week as his physio was attached to the team along with a team doctor who could help him treat the injury and track his progress.

As they neared the date of the tie, both the team doctor and team physio declared him unfit to play, yet Andy felt the captain and coach both weigh in and try to persuade him to play: GB couldn't win the tie without him. Andy was young, vulnerable, and felt under extreme pressure to play. He eventually agreed to have his wrist strapped and be dosed up on pain killers. He played three matches in that tie but the team ultimately lost. The night before the last match (with Poland leading 2–1) I decided to drive back to Scotland, convinced that Andy was not going to play on the final day. His wrist was inflamed, he was in a lot of pain and it just made no sense to inflict further damage. As I pulled into the drive a text pinged through. It was Andy: 'Can't sleep. They're going to blame me if we lose. Everyone will say it's my fault for not playing.' The pressure on him was intense. I felt utterly powerless, miles away at three o'clock in the morning. Playing those matches seriously aggravated his injury and he was out of action for three months, which affected his end of year ranking and most of all his confidence. It also radically affected me as a coach and a captain, and taught me to always listen to my players first and foremost.

It can be hard to stand firm when others are depending on you, and as parents, coaches, friends, we have to learn how important it is to always, always listen to the player and trust that they know their body better than any of us. The power of peer pressure can be overwhelming in any industry, and looking beyond the immediate moment and seeing the long-term, bigger picture is vital, no matter what the circumstances.

Just over a year later, Andy had a shot at his first Grand Slam final, in the 2008 US Open. I would love to be able to regale you with every detail of the match, but once again a big career moment turned out to be just as memorable for the family dynamics at play. This time, I had flown out with my dad on the Wednesday as Jamie had reached the mixed doubles final, and we wanted to be able to support him.

While we were in the air, Andy had beaten Argentinian Juan Martín del Potro in the quarter-final and went on to play Rafa Nadal in the semi-final a couple of days later. He was by now working with Miles Maclagan, and doing pretty well, but that Rafa match was horribly tough going. Rafa was so dominant back then that it would have been a fierce battle under any conditions, but the weather was terrible, causing the match to be suspended until the following day – just as Andy was leading. It was the first time that Andy had to deal with an anxious overnight delay in the middle of a huge match, and it was difficult for all of us. I hated being a parent, and being nearby, yet unable to do anything useful. Adversity performed its usual spell on Andy though, and just when I started to fear he might buckle under the pressure, he rose to it instead – and won. Despite the best efforts of my dad to inadvertently wreck it all!

There was a good group of us there supporting him. My brother, who was by then a golf pro in Dallas, had flown down, and of course Jamie was there as well. I was sitting with Andy's team; my brother and dad were two rows behind us. Because of all of the bad weather and the fact that the tournament was trying to catch up with delayed matches, the semi-final against Rafa was transferred to one of the smaller courts, which made things feel a little off-kilter, particularly as the players' box was very close to the court itself. Almost on the baseline. Usually, it is a bit removed, which I prefer as you can be seen but not heard. That day . . . far from it, and it couldn't have been a worse set-up as my dad hit his spectating stride.

All of my match-watching life, I have always tried to betray nothing other than positive emotions – particularly if it's a big match. I know some of them might seem a little excessive but you'll never see me show any negativity: never a shaken head, never a furious wince or a despondent hand gesture, never a tut or a sag of the shoulders. My dad is not held back by such fluffy sentiment though. Added to that, of course, he shares Andy's ferocious sense of competitiveness. So, while he was watching the match, he was letting fly with the heavy sighs, the head dramatically tipped into hands, the stage whispers about how 'that shot should have been easy!' and a few eye rolls for good measure.

He probably didn't even know he was doing it. And maybe he thought showing such passion was actively supportive. He was wrong. It was hitting Andy right where it hurt – his focus and his confidence. After a couple of sets, Andy stood at the very back of the court, where he was clearly audible to us – and us alone – and whispered hoarsely to me: 'TELL GRANDPA TO STOP PUTTING HIS HEAD IN HIS HANDS.'

I could picture exactly what Andy was seeing from his vantage point at the other end of the court, and the minute Andy looked away from me, I spun round to see my dad in a flurry of negative gesticulations. It must have been utterly infuriating for him, poor kid. I caught my brother's eye and whispered as fast as I could, 'Get Dad to put his bloody hands down.'

My dad behaved a little better for the rest of the match, and Andy survived to make his first Grand Slam final. For me, it was the day that I realised you can sort the money, you can sort the kit, you can sort the coach . . . but from childhood onwards, the one thing you can't sort is your parents' behaviour.

Andy faced Federer in that 2008 US Open Final and the match came and went pretty quickly. A classic example of experience versus inexperience. For Federer it was his fifth US Open title. He looked totally at ease with the occasion, while Andy never really settled into it. He faced him in a second Grand Slam final at the 2010 Australian Open, and lost again. By now, these close calls were becoming really tough emotionally. The set-up at these big tournaments is such that if you are the runner-up, or on the team of the runner-up, you are largely forgotten. If you lose in any of the earlier stages, it somehow doesn't feel quite as depressing – the locker rooms, the players' lounges, the media suites – they are all still buzzing as you collect your prize money and get going, on to the next tournament. But when you come second in a Grand Slam, the player areas are all eerily silent. And every single thing is geared around the winner. You have to do your media straight after the final and you head to the locker room alone. At this Australian Open even the players lounge had been transformed for the party for staff and was full of people celebrating. There was literally nowhere to sit and wait for Andy.

When Andy lost that match in 2010, I just wanted to get out of the arena and give him a hug. I knew how tough it was for him to be so close and yet so far. Again. And the burden of expectation was weighing on his shoulders heavier than ever. After giving him a while to do his press commitments, I decided to go and find him – it wasn't as if there would be anyone around to stop me after all.

I saw his team at the corner of the bar as I headed out of the player's lounge, and asked where Andy was. 'He's in the locker room,' one of them replied, and I couldn't believe it. I knew he would be alone and devastated in there, and wanted to be furious with them for leaving him by himself. I stopped myself, remembering that I always saw these moments from a mother's perspective, and they were seeing it as purely professional. They were his colleagues – they were all macho guys – and they saw the situation differently from me. They would wait for him to set the tone.

Not me though. I found my way to the male locker room and was met with a guy on the door who tried to tell me I couldn't go in. 'Oh, yes I can,' I replied. 'There's only one person who can possibly be in there and he won't mind.' Sure enough, Andy was in there, slouched on a chair with a towel round his waist. He looked so defeated.

'I'm so sorry, Mum,' he said, as he looked up at me through watery eyes. 'I've let everybody down. I'm just so sorry.'

I couldn't believe it – how could he even be thinking like this? I didn't know whether to shake him or hug him. He had just played Roger Bloody Federer in a Grand Slam final!

'Oh, Andy,' I said, putting my arms round him. 'You haven't let anybody down. Do you have any idea what it is like for me to sit there and see you play in the final of a Grand Slam? Against the greatest player ever. It's unbelievable how well you've done and you've got so much to be proud of. You'll learn from this; you'll come back stronger, and you'll get there one day. You mustn't ever, ever believe you are letting anyone down. Never.'

It was as if all the progress he had made had been forgotten, and it took someone who had seen every step to remind him how many there had been. The closer he got to a Grand Slam, the steeper the fall in his and the public's eyes if he didn't make it. And that year more than almost any other, it reminded me of the importance of unconditional emotional support and I felt my responsibility to him as a parent rather than as part of any 'team' he had behind him.

The tone was somewhat different at the next year's Australian Open, as Andy had a special request from a fan who wanted to watch him play: Billy Connolly. He had specifically asked if he could come and see one of Andy's matches, so I set it all up for the beginning of the second week. I'd arranged to meet him in the player's restaurant and as I sat there I was ridiculously nervous. He was someone I had so often watched on TV since I was a teenager. He is a Scottish hero and someone I would never have dreamed I'd have the chance to meet, let alone have asking to meet my son.

When I found myself walking towards him, I started laughing. In any other circumstance it would have been rude, but I somehow couldn't help myself. Maybe it was nerves. He hadn't done a thing and I was giggling like a schoolgirl at the sight of him sitting there, at a white Formica table, facing me.

'It's so nice to see you smiling,' he said, with a familiar twinkle in his eyes.

'What do you mean?' I replied. 'I'm always smiling!'

Very slowly he replied. 'Oooooh nooooo you're noooooot.'

Oh here we go, I thought. Someone else who thinks I'm a nightmare. And I tried to be annoyed, but I couldn't stop grinning, and on top of that, all I could hear was my own voice bellowing internally: 'You've having tea and a doughnut with Billy Bloody Connolly!'

Part of me was frustrated that yet another person thought I was the Grinch who never smiles, but, honestly, it is hard to be anything other than amused in Connolly's presence. I was pretty much crying with laughter for the entire match. Absolutely unheard of for me. His commentary, peppered with some very colourful language, was so much more entertaining than anything I'd heard on TV. Interestingly, once the match was over, Billy just slipped away. He refused all requests for interviews saying he was just there for the tennis, and the day was all about Andy.

In the spring of 2011 my role in Andy's team was questioned in the most horrible way possible. By now I was used to seeing – and ignoring – articles and opinion pieces about Andy every time he lost a big match. They would often analyse my involvement and question my role in his career. It hurt, but they were journalists who I'd never met, who didn't know anything about us or our journey – what did they know? Then the *Express* printed an article with the headline 'Time to Cut the Apron Strings, Andy Murray', quoting Boris Becker saying Andy would never win a Grand Slam with me around. 'I don't know why Andy prefers Judy close by . . . He needs to ditch her.' It stung. A lot. I'd been able to dismiss the journalists and their reams of copy, but the opinion of a Wimbledon champion, commentator and coach was a lot harder to disregard. Even just popping out for a loaf of bread to the local shops was tough when every Scottish tabloid had his words plastered over their front pages. Happily I had a chance to face Boris two years later after Andy had won the US Open and Wimbledon.

By now, I had been unofficially coordinating both of the boys' teams for about five or six years, keeping a careful eye over their transition into adulthood and professional life, while trying to give them space and maintain a mother–son relationship. It had been quite a juggling act, as teams got bigger and Andy in particular had moved on from coaches with relative frequency, switching when he felt he had learned all that he could from someone, keen to move onwards and upwards. After Brad, he worked with Miles Maclagan for a while, then Àlex Corretja, specifically to help his clay court game, and then Danny Vallverdu, his old pal from his Barcelona days, who started as a hitting partner and ended up being on his coaching team for some time.

On top of that, there was the matter of finding a tennis-specific fitness trainer – someone who could turn Andy from a gangly teen-ager to a player who had the physical strength to match his emotional doggedness over a five-set match. The minute that a young player starts to have some success, they are offered spaces and appearance fees at major events. The more you win, the better the opponents, the higher the standard of tennis, and the greater the demands on the body. Left unattended, this can lead to injury fast, but of course the great advantage is that with bigger earnings you can pay for the physical trainers, nutritionists and physiotherapists. Then there are the luxury extras such as signing up to a restringing team – a company who will collect your rackets from your hotel each evening, and string them for you overnight, so that they're ready the next morning at the right tension for the conditions and court surface. And that was just the tennis side. There was a whole business team to be recruited and organised as well, and of course the input of sports psychologists at key times.

Over time, as Andy in particular grew more confident around all these people, and more able to pay for what he wanted without needing to panic, I was able to step back. And it was at this point that my old friend and protegé Leon Smith popped up with an offer that presented a whole new career opportunity for me, which proved far too interesting to turn down.

13

Girl up, or how to create opportunities for women

In which I make a choice to work with the women in the game,
having noticed how male-dominated the culture can be.
Shocked by the prejudice and encouraged by the talent,
I find both a new voice and a new vocation.

Leon Smith, whom I had known since he was a junior player, was now captain of the GB Davis Cup team. I had mentored him all of his adult life, having brought him to work with me when I was the Scotland coach at a time when he had dropped out of college in order to pursue a coaching career. Back then he had bleached blond hair, with a centre parting and a diamond in each ear. He was truly Beckham-esque and all the juniors thought he was 'the bomb', Jamie and Andy included.

He had been brimming with enthusiasm for that Davis Cup role, and sought my advice when he applied for the captaincy a year or so earlier. It had looked like it would be a choice between him and Greg Rusedski, and of course the smart money would have said Greg stood a better chance, having been a world-class player and GB Davis Cup stalwart. I wasn't so sure though, and pointed out to Leon that it wasn't necessarily all about playing level or experience, but also about his rapport with the players, the team-building and management, and that he could surround himself with others who could provide that playing expertise or any other gaps in his knowledge or experience. I had been around long enough to know that you don't need to be an expert in absolutely everything. You need to understand what's required and find the right people to help you deliver it.

I explained that if asked in the interview about his comparative lack of experience, he simply had to make a strategic effort to explain who he would employ around him to plug any of those gaps. He got the job and I was thrilled for him. I loved that he asked me to help him with his very first Davis Cup match in Eastbourne. He wanted me to do the video analysis of the opposition. He had taken me at my word regarding team building. I did the analysis of the Turkish team, put it on a DVD, went through it step by step, clip by clip, presented it to him and his team of coaches and left him to share it with the GB players.

Nevertheless, I promised to head down to Eastbourne for the match – even though neither Andy nor Jamie were on the team – for moral support. The Davis Cup was not just a huge deal to Leon that year, it holds an enormous emotional sway among British tennis players and fans. It's a long-standing and prestigious event, like Wimbledon, despite not being as much of a money-spinner as the Grand Slams. But it's the team aspect that really seems to tug at the heartstrings and capture the fans' imagination. Its industry nickname, the World Cup of Tennis, is certainly appropriate: after the bulk of the year competing as individuals, the Davis Cup brings players together as teams, rooting for each other instead of working out how to beat each other, and enjoying a sense of comradeship that is often absent from the Tour.

Similar psychologically and emotionally to the Olympics, it's an event the players relish for the love of their sport and national pride, rather than because they need to do it for points, rankings or cash.

Mindful of all of this, I sat on my own in the stand behind the baseline for three days and texted Leon's coaching team anything interesting that I picked up. It's easier to analyse a match from behind the baseline rather than on the team bench at the side of the court. After that tie, Leon proved to himself that he could do the job, and before long he was flying.

A year or so later, in his role as Head of Men's and Women's Tennis, he asked me if I would be interested in taking on the captain's role with the Fed Cup team, the women's equivalent of the Davis Cup. It was the first time in forever that someone had approached me about coaching in my own right, rather than as someone related to one of the boys. At first, I wasn't sure about heading back into that world because of all the travel, the commitment and the hours. Yet I didn't mind the challenge of going back to the coaching life. And there was something else that tugged at my curiosity: this would be my first opportunity to do something specifically for the women's game. It might be a chance to develop the female coaching workforce, to build the profile of the female players, to even up the playing field a little bit. That way, perhaps future female coaches and players might not have to go through some of the loneliness, the frustrations or the downright prejudice that I had endured over the last twenty-odd years.

I decided to take Leon up on his offer, and this idea only grew stronger when I spent much of December 2011 and January 2012 travelling with the squad to their various WTA tournaments. I wanted to spend as much time as possible with the squad and their coaches, in the knowledge that the better you get to know them as people, the more chance you have of influencing their performance and finding the right way – or the right words – to do it. I was also getting my first proper look at how the women's Tour works. I was in Auckland at New Year and then Hobart and Melbourne for the Australian Open. Former British number one Jeremy Bates was in Auckland, and I headed to one of the player parties with him and Fed Cup team member Anne Keothavong, whom he was coaching at the time. I knew one or two of the players who were a similar age to Jamie and Andy and had been juniors with them, but I hadn't been following the women's game in the same way that I had the men's over the years, so they were mostly unfamiliar faces. But one thing struck me that evening, and was reinforced the next day as I sat in the players' lounge early on waiting to see the girls: there were very, very few female coaches.

Throughout my career, from my decision not to head to train in the US because I couldn't find anyone who had done it before, through years of watching my boys believe in their own abilities because of what they had seen their own heroes achieve, I have been aware of what an enormous impact positive role models can have. These people don't have to be saints, but they have to be visible. For young boys and girls to truly believe that something is within their grasp, they have to be able to see it. And the convention in all sport, but particularly tennis at this time, was that the men's game was the more important. The women's game was still dominated by male coaches, male pundits and male leaders in governing bodies. Sure, I had an instinctive sense of this as a result of thirty years in tennis, but I had never seen it laid out before me quite as explicitly as I did that week.

That trip was a huge eye-opener for me – I had never stopped to actively consider the dynamics in the women's game before. But as I sat there and watched player after player greet or arrive with her coach, I realised that of course there are more male coaches than female: it's a job which is hugely incompatible with many women's lives. It demands being on the road for at least thirty weeks of the year, a near impossible feat when women are most often the ones taking care of the family. It had never been too much of a struggle for me, because being on the road had meant seeing more of my kids, not less. But my family was not the norm.

Then there is the simple fact that being a coach is the kind of job which is very badly suited to career breaks. To be a top-level coach, you have to be prepared to submit to the demands of top-level players, and that doesn't lend itself to pragmatic considerations such as getting pregnant, taking maternity leave, or having a steady income. Most coaches are self-employed, living contract to contract, sometimes with little more than a verbal contract, so there's nothing like maternity pay, let alone severance pay, pensions or other benefits. Again, these were never concerns for me.

On top of these factors, I also started to notice that most of the women players on the Tour preferred not to warm up or hit with each other in practice. They liked to work with men as hitting partners, so they were often inclined to hire coaches who could double up as both. In the men's game, you'll get male players playing practice sets with each other, even though they might be huge rivals on the Tour. Women don't seem to like hitting with other women. In this way, they protect themselves by avoiding comparisons to other women. A great deal of this comes down to the complicated female psychology of competition. In the long term though, it's actually keeping men in a position of power in the women's game, simply by a matter of economics.

This had fostered an atmosphere where, on scanning the players' lounge or the practice courts, it looked as if men were in charge. Just a glance around the room showed a lot of women being told what to do by men. The WTA Tour even allows on court coaching. Once a set, the players can call their coach onto court at an end change – to tell them what to do. This doesn't exist on the men's Tour. So the women's Tour was as much of a male-orientated culture as the men's tour. This in turn created some uncomfortable dynamics, for the younger players especially.

If you're away from home for weeks on end with a man with whom your relationship is merely professional, who do you talk to about your fears and worries? Where do you get your comfort, your personal advice, your solace in tough times? With whom do you comfortably discuss the changes in your body? Or even what's going on in your head? At best, you might be lucky enough to find a sympathetic coach or one who might have daughters, and has dealt with these sorts of situations at home. At worst, you could find someone who sees coaching as merely a matter of delivering technical and tactical advice, rather than providing emotional support as well. It perhaps also explains why so many parents coach their daughters.

On my return from that trip, I started to research why there were so few female coaches in the UK and why most got stuck at the lower levels. A large part of the problem seemed to be the coaches pathway for women. Or lack of it. There weren't enough opportunities for women to develop their skills or progress. I immediately made it part of my mission at the Fed Cup to take a number of female coaches with me on trips, wherever I could. As far as I was concerned, Leon may have taken me on as the Fed Cup captain and coach, but I was going to expand that role as I saw fit, and look at the bigger picture; it was time to build the image of the Fed Cup, to create a workforce round it and to look to the future. And to do that, we would need a bit of old-fashioned team building. I was almost tempted to start buying puzzle books again!

Run by the International Tennis Federation, like the Davis Cup, the Fed Cup does not require players or coaches to be on hand year-round. The top sixteen countries are divided into two world groups, while all the other nations are divided into regional 'zones'. At the beginning of February each year, the two teams who come top of each sixteen-team zone go into a play-off with one of the teams relegated from the higher-up 'world groups'. This is the chance for countries to move up to the top tier world groups and to get home-and-away ties.

Despite being what I called the 'big sister' of the Davis Cup, the Fed Cup is generally much less well known than its male counterpart, although it does have the curious accolade of consistently having slightly higher viewing figures than the Davis Cup for the actual final. In fact, research has shown that tennis is one of the few sports regularly watched by more women than men, which is far from represented by the timings of games (prime-time slots go to the men), the prize money (women have had to fight for their prize money to be equal), and so much else (don't even get me started on sponsorship!).

None of this was helping the Fed Cup's image in Britain though, where very few people even knew what it is. The zonal matches in February usually attract very little press attention because they take place just after the Australian Open, and most UK media have headed home for a rest. If you don't break out of those zones in February, you don't play in the Fed Cup again for another year, making it all but impossible to build any sort of momentum in the press or within the team itself. I had my work cut out.

In preparation for our first trip in February 2012, I set about creating something of a media and social media blitz. The team was on Facebook, Twitter, making fun video clips, writing blogs for places like the BBC Sport website, and trying wherever possible to show that team tennis was something young women could engage with. I wanted us to be seen having fun and for readers to get to know our players – Laura Robson, Heather Watson or Johanna Konta, say – in places where young and not so young women go for their news and entertainment already: women's magazines, female sections of the newspaper, non-sporty places, as well as sporty blogs, rather than trying to drag them over to the more overtly male domain of sports pages with a sense of duty or worthiness.

It is always going to be largely women who will watch and support women's sport, so if you're trying to connect with women, I believe it's important to do it on their terms instead of trying to change them to suit what you're already doing. I understood the value of engaging with the image and fashion side of things, too. I wanted to show that sport can be glamorous, as well as exciting. If young women and girls are already reading about what their icons are wearing, let them hear about our team tracksuit too. Or let's get the team into a photo shoot wearing fantastic team dresses with great make-up. After all, it's not as if footballers aren't posing with ever more adventurous hairstyles and in new outfits day in, day out.

What I didn't want was to bombard young women with stats about matches, scores or training plans, or anything to do with weight loss. Personally, I would much rather read about a sportswoman's actual life if I came across them in a magazine. I am always fascinated to hear stories about people like Jo Pavey, the athlete who is coached by her husband, or Catriona Matthew, the professional golfer whose husband is her caddy and who travels with her mum as the nanny to keep the family unit together.

Women face all sorts of challenges every day. When you hear about someone who has stepped out of her role and become the breadwinner, it's always an interesting, often inspiring story. I would love to see more of these stories in women's magazines alongside the day-to-day travails of reality TV stars I have never heard of – I was determined to try and get my girls into the pages of the magazines, getting their personalities and their sport out there.

That first year, the team was largely split in two, by age and experience. The old guard were Elena Baltacha and Anne Keothavong, who were both around twenty-nine years old and had played in plenty of Fed Cup matches in their time. If I had been able to choose two people to lead my team, hand on heart I would have chosen those two every single time. Both of them had made the top 50 in the world, yet although they had achieved a lot, they weren't quite household names in the UK. But in terms of passion, dedication, commitment and experience, they were perfect role models for the two younger girls, Laura Robson and Heather Watson, both still teenagers then.

I joined the Fed Cup full of ideas about team building and plans for the future, but to my shock I discovered that the two older girls did not speak to each other. Even more shocking was that this had been going on for years. It was a classic example of how two female players born in the same year, who had come up through the same very narrow British tennis system, came to see each other as enemies. I had never seen a division like this – based on little more than sheer competitiveness nurtured by a toxic system – anywhere on the men's Tour. These girls had barely spoken to each other since they were teenagers, because they thought that to be competitive and ambitious ruled out any potential not just for friendship, but for respect. I was determined to change this. If the same had happened to me, I would have been half the woman, with half the career. The friendships I had made as a young player had sustained and supported me all my life, sometimes proving the only thing keeping me sane at all!

Our first fixture was in Eilat in Israel, and I was so excited to get there. But when we arrived there wasn't much of a fuss; the venue was more of a community sports centre really. I had been expecting something a little more grand, and I'd expected a bit more support too. Leon had come out, and a couple of others, but basically it felt more like a club match, rather than a global competition on the scale of the Davis Cup.

Still, the lack of ceremony did leave us more time for team bonding. I had brought a load of games with me, and had asked all of the others to do the same. We had the lot: table games, Pictionary, charades, as well as darts for the team room. The only game that almost didn't make it, unsurprisingly, was Laura's game of Pass the Bomb (the timer was shaped like a hand grenade!), which had been confiscated in the ferociously tight security at Tel Aviv airport! We had been briefed to expect heavy security, and had even gone as far as to engage a private security company to take us from the international to the domestic terminal.

In the evenings, I wanted to build the same trust and camaraderie in the team as I had wanted to foster in the kids I drove around the country back in the day: to keep everyone together, so that individual competitiveness, anxieties about matches or simply isolation and self-reflection could all be kept at bay. And by then we were also fighting a battle against the dominance of mobile phones and iPads, as well as social media anxieties. I combatted that with a host of girls versus boys competitive games. Our team was all female and our back-room staff were all male. Perfect for team-building.

I'm proud to say that not only did we qualify and get the chance to go to Sweden for the World Group play-off, but by the time we headed home, Annie and Bally, as they had become known and who had ignored each other for most of their lives, were now sitting together on the bus to the airport, as well as on the flight home, and, crucially, had also agreed to team up to play doubles together. They went on to become great friends. Result. Annie is married and has a daughter now but Bally passed away, cruelly taken by liver cancer just a few months after she retired from tennis. She was only thirty, had just got married and had a whole new life to look forward to. Her death hit me and the boys very hard. Yet another reminder of how precious life is, how we never know what's round the corner and why we should make the most of every moment and every opportunity.

As always on these trips I had a back-room team of four and wherever possible I tried to give at least one place to a young LTA member of staff who showed potential. I knew that I had to invest in people to help us develop a stronger tennis workforce. The guy I had brought with me to do the video analysis was painfully shy, really quite inexperienced and unbelievably nervous when addressing an all-female team, but he was totally dedicated and by the end of the trip, and many team games and forfeits later, he was happily standing up and presenting his findings as if he'd been doing it for years.

When we headed to Sweden for the next round, I arranged for four female coaches to come with us. They were not directly attached to the team, but they came to learn, and I spent a lot of time explaining how everything was done and showing them the ropes for this sort of trip. They had no direct impact on the results we achieved that year, but they might do in years to come. I was busy building a workforce, creating opportunities for female coaches and trying to foster confidence wherever I could. Leon had given me a coaching role, but I was really doing people management, motivation and marketing.

It was out of these first experiences with the Fed Cup that the idea for my tennis programme for girls, Miss-Hits, emerged. With the Fed Cup, I was working with our best players, but what about the next generation, and the ones after that? So I started looking even further back at how many young girls we had coming into the game, and I realised this was where our problem lay. The numbers were tiny.

In the past the vogue had been for elaborate and expensive countrywide talent identification programmes, designed to discover the best seven- to ten-year-old kids. I had been involved in the LTA's new Talent Performance Programme in 2007 as a part-time consultant for Scotland, but though the grassroots vision had been admirable, the selection process and the training camps had been set up as if for professional players, not eight-year-old girls. They were, frankly, a load of bollocks. It's immaterial who the best seven- to ten-year-old kids are if you're only using this kind of physical selection test. Inevitably, they're all going to be kids whose parents can afford for them to play tennis from a young age and have private lessons. No wonder tennis seemed like a sport geared to the well-off.

Quite aside from the fact that it is actually somewhat dangerous to label a kid as 'nationally identified' at seven or eight years old (the risk of emotional damage if they ever fall from that pedestal is enormous), spending so much on a selection method which benefits so few, rather than simply getting as many kids as possible playing the game and having fun at that age is madness. There might be smart, well-coordinated, passionate kids out there who haven't been privately trained by an expensive or experienced coach to pass a special eight-year-old's test, but who might be stars of the future. If we invest in growing the game at the grass roots, more players will emerge further down the line.

There weren't many girls going into this system, and very few being identified. Research was showing that the numbers of girls playing tennis aged ten and under were decreasing and even fewer were competing regularly, which was leading to tournaments being cancelled. Instead of looking at the reasons why girls weren't competing and changing the format to make it more fun – more team-based, for example – the powers that be took the easy way out and lumped the competing girls in with the boys. There will always be some little girls who are happy competing with boys – those with brothers most probably – but to many others it will be intimidating and might well herald the end of their involvement in the game.

It wasn't the girls that were the problem. It was the system. And it was time to change it.

Once again, I looked at all of the research I could find. Tennis Australia had some great findings, and I studied what was going on with girls in other individual and team sports too. What was being done to attract them and encourage them, what was putting them off, what was keeping them in their game.

One of the key problems is the sheer volume of activities fighting for little girls' attention these days. Most of those things are fun, lively, musical, non-competitive and can be done with their friends. Things like dancing, gymnastics, cheerleading are always cited as favourites – where they can have fun with their bodies and take pride in them, but not be engaged in active competition, which they often deem as being the domain of boys. And it's no surprise that so many girls think that. Boys are repeatedly told it's their role in life to be competitive, and to win, from a really early age. At around five to eight years old, they often tend to be more noisy, more physical, more confident and more competitive. We give footballs, building kits and all sorts of 'doing' things to boys as gifts, while girls are often given either appearance-based games or quieter tasks such as colouring-in, sticker books or crafts. Even a pregnant woman with a kicky baby will be casually told she has 'a future footballer' in her if she knows it's a boy, but if it's a girl she'll simply be told her daughter 'must be feisty'. It's nonsense!

Then there is the problem of the cold, which research shows is a huge inhibiting factor for girls. This is a self-perpetuating problem, as the child who is less confident will move less, so they'll make contact with the ball less, so they will become less competent and more static ... making them even colder. No one knows more keenly than I do that playing sport in the dark and the cold is miserable in comparison to playing it in the warmth on a sunny day, unless the coach can make it active, engaging, stimulating and fun.

The prospect of a game like tennis being 'too difficult' is also a challenge. If you don't have the coordination skills, developed at home or in the playground, you will find tennis quite difficult. These days, kids are so often on electronic gadgets, only exercising their thumbs, that they can be really clumsy – they simply haven't had the chance to develop the motor skills that underpin most sports. So now I find we have to teach those core physical skills like throwing and catching before you can get them to hit the ball with a bat over a net.

The fifth major factor brings us full circle: the scarcity of female coaches. Primary school teachers tend to be female, so children get used to that dynamic. If their first tennis coach is male, it's quite possible that some girls will struggle with an unfamiliar man delivering the session, especially if that man is inexperienced in how to work with girls. Or you reach adolescence and just as your body starts to change and you feel increasingly awkward and uncomfortable about it, the coach is male and may not understand what you are going through. Girls tick differently to boys and that's why we need many more female PE teachers and sports coaches to help keep them in sport through the teenage years.

As you can imagine, once I had done my research, it no longer seemed surprising that girls were dropping out of the game as they reached adolescence. So many of the factors putting them off simply boiled down to 'It's not fun any more', 'My friends stopped playing, so I did, too' and 'I feel like it's all geared towards boys'. But what was the solution? Well, one thing I immediately agreed on when I discussed it with Laura Middleton, who has been one of my closest friends since we were both players and doubles partners back in the 1980s, was that it was time to stop talking about it and *do* something. And my attempt to address this problem has been Miss-Hits.

Miss-Hits is a tennis programme designed specifically to get girls aged five to eight into tennis, to help them to love it, and to provide a fun, stimulating, easy-to-deliver sessions that might attract more women into tennis coaching, too. We've incorporated what girls want to do wherever possible. For example, we have built a warm-up to music into the programme, but we call it the dance section. Job done.

Laura and I created it together and invested in it. I am so proud of what we've managed to do. And we have a lot of fun doing it! It's a twelve-week programme, divided into two six-week blocks, and we travel around the country and beyond, training coaches, in the hope of leaving a generation of new female tennis players and coaches in our wake.

I wanted it to feel like a tennis party. We created a gang of diverse animated characters – Selena Serve, Valentina Volley, Bella Backhand, and so on – to engage with the kids. There is a website, an app, teacher manuals, stickers of the characters, the lot. We don't even start the kids with tennis balls but with balloons and soft chiffon squares that fall slowly, are brightly coloured and are something the children can learn to track or catch at a much slower pace than an actual ball. At this stage, we don't even teach them how to hold a racket, we can just do the demonstration and set them off. There's no point bamboozling them with technique. The key is in the demonstration; children don't want to listen to you, they just want to play. I learnt that from my own kids. So we created games that do the teaching instead. We have our chiffon squares, balloons and little fluffy balls that tiny hands can grasp easily and aren't scared to see flying towards them.

We worked on it for two years, piloted it endlessly and eventually came up with a programme which I absolutely love. It launched in association with the LTA in 2013. We had so much fun choosing the activities and equipment: certificates of achievement, the hit mitts, the Chinese skip ropes and even a cuddly toy called Billie the Ball Dog, which one pupil gets to take home for a week if they've done something particularly well or something amusing. The programme is backed up by a website and a free app. The app is a game in itself and teaches the kids the rules of tennis in an unconventional way: you choose which character you want to be, you're swiping, understanding the simplest tactics of hitting the ball away from your opponent, and when the ball goes out of play, Billie the Ball Dog trots off and gets the ball for you. It's a great support for the coaches, as teaching a child how to keep the score in tennis can be a difficult and often thankless task. I invested a lot of money into it – I could have paid off my mortgage instead! – but I don't regret spending a penny because I know it's going to make a big difference.

For me the fun of sport is playing the game, feeling yourself improve, and engaging with your community, whether that's through schools or clubs. When I was coaching kids in Scotland twenty years ago, I tried to come at everything from the angle of actually playing the game, competing for enjoyment – even inventing games and competitions in the same way that the boys had done with that stepladder in their bedroom. You don't always have the facilities, and you will always have mixed abilities, but you can also always have fun. It was this very philosophy that actually led to the development of my very first sports programme in 2011, Set4Sport. I took every game the boys and I had played when they were little – cereal box table tennis, homemade obstacle courses, umpteen balloon games, garden 'crazy' golf, and so much more – and translated them into fun, easy-to-follow activities for parents to play with their children. The activities were created for three- to eight-year-olds but the programme was aimed at parents. Giving them lots of ideas for playing actively at home and helping their kids to develop those crucial core motor skills that underpin every sport, using everyday household items. The games do the teaching for you. They are simple and fun and, played regularly, will not only develop coordination skills, but family bonding, too. If kids learn to enjoy exercise and competition at a young age, it can become a way of life. And what better way to do both than as a family. Sport can become too serious too soon for many kids who have shown even the tiniest bit of potential these days; I see this as a real danger. It is hard on the few 'exceptional' kids and off-putting for those who just want to have fun with their friends. If I were to have a philosophy for long-term athlete development, it would be that the skilled kids be encouraged to cling to their sense of play for as long as possible.

These days I love my work with Miss-Hits, and with a project I launched the following year, Tennis on the Road, which is basically a van full of equipment that I drive around Scotland with another coach, taking tennis into areas you wouldn't normally find it – mainly rural or deprived. We build workforces in the local communities by showing parents, teachers, students, youth leaders and coaches how to deliver starter tennis. These projects, as well as my time with the Fed Cup, which ended in early 2016, have done wonders for my own confidence and my understanding of the tennis landscape in Britain. I just wish I could have done more for the Fed Cup while I was there, but we didn't manage to field a full team for the last three years due to illness and injury among the players. It was a fantastic experience, though, and was the first time in decades that I had been recognised as a good coach in my own right rather than Jamie and Andy's 'pushy mum'. Whatever I do in my career, I want to be effective and I had come to realise that role models are important for stimulating interest and excitement in sport, but that any sport is only as good as its grass roots. And our grass roots are weak so I reckoned I could have far greater long-term effect on tennis in Scotland if I shared my twenty-five years of coaching experience by building a bigger and stronger workforce.

I had spent nearly ten years trying to improve tennis in Scotland during my time as National Coach, and my role there was totally subsumed by my new exposure on a bigger stage as the boys' mum. The opportunities and respect that Leon Smith, the Fed Cup and Miss-Hits afforded me, allowed me to keep my own identity at a time when I was slipping back towards becoming tabloid fodder again, and prepared me to step into the spotlight – in a capacity of my own choosing – to a greater degree than ever before.

In the summer of 2012, the year that Andy and Jamie both played as part of Team GB in the London 2012 Olympics, I was asked if I would speak at a women's event as the parent of Olympic athletes. I had never dipped a toe into the waters of public speaking, still shuddering at the memory of being humiliated onstage at the Scottish Sports Awards only a few years before. But the organiser was an inspirational Scot named Frank Dick, who had been the GB athletics coach during the glory years of Sebastian Coe and Daley Thompson, and who had taught me so much about his Athlete Centred Approach when I was a rookie Scottish National Coach. I learned loads from him. So whenever he asks a favour, I'm there, no matter how daunting.

I took a group of four female coaches with me to this event, keen to provide another learning experience for them. I steadied my nerves and did my bit up onstage, taking part in a Q&A as well as I could. The final speaker was a woman called Caroline McHugh, who gave a talk on The Art of Being Yourself, which struck such a strong chord with me. Her belief was that you don't have to wait for someone else to give you permission to be yourself; you already are yourself and you shouldn't waste time on 'trying to be as good as' anyone else, as you are already the best at being you. It felt like a radical readjustment to see myself in these terms.

I had for some time been regularly asked to appear as a public speaker, but had always said no. As far as I was concerned, my place was on the court. I wasn't even that welcome in the offices of certain tennis or sports bodies as I was always, apparently, rocking the boat. But something clicked that day when I heard Caroline speak for the first time. I *did* have experience that I *could* be sharing with a wider audience. Perhaps what I had to say no longer needed to be restricted to coaching groups or tennis alone. She made me realise that I had a voice and I should use it.

Within a few months, a chance to put this little nugget of new-found confidence to the test presented itself when Women in Sport – a government-funded charity in the UK, then known as the Women's Sport and Fitness Foundation – asked me to be the spokes-person for some research that they had recently commissioned. My first instinct was to shrink back to my previous self. 'I only know about tennis,' I told them. 'I can't speak for all of sport!'

But then they showed me the statistics. They were gobsmacking.

Their research had discovered that only 3 per cent of all sports journalists in the UK are women, that only 5 per cent of all sports coverage in newspapers is about women athletes, and that half a per cent of all sponsorship money, across all sport, goes to women. Sud-denly all of those times I had been seen as a curiosity rather than a hard worker, a menace rather than a go-getter, made sense. Those rooms full of male coaches, those young female players encouraged to ignore rather than support each other, those pictures of me pumping my fists taken by banks of faceless male photographers . . . it all slipped into a different context when I saw that report. I had never been that bad; I had just been different. The inequality really hit me and prompted me into action. It was time to speak up. And so I did. A full day and a half of media engagement raising awareness of gender imbalance in sport.

Not long after that research gig, I was invited to take part in an eighteen-month project to deliver a strategy for the government on womens sport, and I loved being part of a group of influential women from the world of business, politics and sport. It was both fascinating and empowering. These days, projects like that are among my greatest professional pleasures, and I even have a new project, She Rallies, which launched in 2017. Not only do these projects help me feel that I am creating something of worth beyond the boys' trophies, but the process of accepting that I have something of value to say has played an immeasurable part in helping me keep my head above water, most notably when the boys encountered their biggest professional challenges yet.

14

The right partner, or how to find the perfect match

In which I see the value of trust, teamwork and relationships
as more important than ever as the stakes get higher,
the money gets bigger and the crowds get louder.
The training, the technology, the titles can only get you
so far: the people are everything.

The push and pull of the boys' careers and the accompanying emotional ramifications continued unabated while I was busy with the Fed Cup, Miss-Hits, Tennis on the Road and Women in Sport. It felt as if the minute one of them hit their stride, the other hit a roadblock, and before long they would swap roles for another bumpy few months.

Since his success at Wimbledon in 2007, Jamie had been doing well, but not brilliantly. He was ranked between 30 to 60 in the world, had picked up a few ATP titles and had reached the final stages of several Grand Slam mixed doubles events, though mixed doubles carry no ranking points. The key to a successful career for him was men's doubles, but things were a little unsettled, and some of that was caused by him.

After working with Louis Cayer for about fifteen months, he had a lot of success very quickly. As I now know is very common – especially with male players that age – Jamie began to think that he knew it all, that he could do better with a different partner, and that he could manage without a coach. Like a student who has just graduated and feels that they know everything about everything, Jamie wanted to prove that he knew best and that he could do it on his own. I was pretty shocked to see him shift so quickly from the self-doubt that had been dogging him only a couple of years previously to this new level of conviction and self-belief, but the briefest of research showed that this development was far from rare.

All of a sudden, his attitude was: I don't need anyone. I know what I'm doing and I can manage it on my own. In some ways this was quite upsetting after so many people had invested so much time, money and care into helping him. I thought he was making a big mistake, but I've always tried to look at both sides of an argument and I could see he was growing up, wanting to stand on his own two feet. You give them wings so they can fly. And Jamie had decided to fly.

But the most philosophical of all of us was Louis himself. 'Don't worry,' he told me, with a measured calmness. 'We just need to let him go. He'll come back. I've seen this with several players at this age and stage. Let him go. He will make his own mistakes and he will come back in his own time.' And he was absolutely right. The break lasted about four years, but things were far from calm in the meantime.

For many years, Jamie was obsessed with hitting the ball hard and with perfect technique, like a classic twenty-first century singles player. But with doubles, that's not the skill you need; it's about being clever. You need a whole arsenal of shots: the lobs and the dinks, the changes of pace, depth, spin and height. It's not about hitting it hard and deep to the baseline like it is in singles. I remember travelling to Italy to watch him in a challenger event with Jamie Delgado, his then doubles partner, and it was clear to me that by hitting all of those 'perfect' shots they were playing into their opponents' hands. They were hitting the ball beautifully, but they weren't playing the game smartly. The best doubles players put the ball where their opponents neither want nor expect it, and if they can do that well, it is almost immaterial how powerful the shots are.

I think Jamie wanted to look like the other top players at the time – able to hit constantly hard from the back of the court – and had lost focus on where his actual strengths lay, and how to use them to his advantage in doubles. He had no coach these days – he couldn't afford one because he was living hand to mouth on the Challenger circuit where doubles prize money is tiny (and shared with a partner) but living costs are huge. I was mildly self-conscious when I tried to explain to them what I thought they needed to do – after all, I was Jamie's mum and he was more than a grown man by now, so I didn't want either of them to feel patronised or uncomfortable. But I knew I was right so I went ahead and suggested it anyway . . . and then got out some soft sponge balls. Yes, they look as if they are designed for kids, and yes, they are really. But it's impossible to hit them hard and fast, so they make you think more carefully about touch, feel and placement.

'You have to cause trouble for your opponents,' I told them. 'You're both skilful enough, so focus on that, not mere power.'

What he really needed was a good solid partnership – with someone who was also focused solely on doubles. He had played with fellow Scot Colin Fleming for a while, but, while they still remain close friends, the playing partnership fizzled out after a year or so. The trouble was that singles players often enter doubles events just to get a bit of practice on the court surface and a bit of extra prize money rather than being properly committed to winning doubles matches, or they just want to head off to the next tournament when they're knocked out of the singles. This does not make for a long-term partnership. You need both players to be committed to forming a team.

This was demonstrated in the harshest way when Andy – who was by now climbing the ranks of the Tour at a steady pace – was offered a £20,000 appearance fee at an ATP tournament in Nottingham in 2006. Keen to help his brother, to give him the chance to gain some extra points for his ranking at a prestigious tournament, Andy asked to trade the fee for a wild-card entry for Jamie in the doubles event. The organisers agreed and Jamie was set to play, but suddenly Colin was offered a spot in the Wimbledon singles qualifying event the same week and prioritised that as a singles player. He pulled out of the doubles. No big match for Jamie, and no appearance fee for Andy. It was a tough blow for both of them, and a harsh learning experience for Jamie in particular, who then realised the absolute necessity of finding a partner who was committed to doubles for the long term.

The reality of finding the right partner was far tougher than we anticipated though. By the end of 2012, things were looking pretty bleak. Obviously, we'll all remember 2012 for the sheer joy of the boys playing doubles together at the Olympic Games in London, and the happiness and unadulterated sense of team spirit that this brought us all. But that aside, the year was unremittingly hard for Jamie. Even then, only a few years ago, there were few players seriously committed to doubles, and finding a steady partner was an utterly thankless task.

Most players are singles players at heart who take part in doubles to get extra court time or to do a friend a favour. Doubles can have a fantastic impact on your singles play: for your serve, your returning, your net play and even working out the angles on court. Largely, potential partners were taking part in doubles matches as a means to an end rather than because they wanted to win or excel at doubles, and the insecurity was making Jamie's life a misery.

He had got married a couple of years earlier, in 2010, and his Colombian wife, Alejandra, was waiting for her UK passport to enable her to continue her career in London. Just at the point when he most wanted to be able to step up and provide, Jamie was struggling more than ever before. And the psychological implications were tough, too. Every week he had to check the entry lists for various tournaments, work out who was entering what and where, look at the deadlines for signing in as a team and then put out feelers for a partner. He was having to juggle the Tour schedules and rankings of countless potential players, working out who would be on the right side of the world and when, and who might have a high enough ranking to ensure they would be accepted into the draw as a team.

This was happening month after month. Having to put himself out there time after time, asking people, cajoling people, literally trekking around a tournament site to try and track someone down who might take on a match with him. It was time-consuming, emotionally draining and left Jamie in a really dark place. Sometimes, if they were at the same tournament and their schedules were aligned, Andy would play with him – as he often does with other British players if they need him to – but even then, no matter how strong the bond between them, they both knew that it was a favour; that Andy's main focus was singles and that Jamie was the one who needed the input.

Meanwhile, Andy's 2012 had a few rocky patches of its own. He had been working for most of the previous year with Danny Vall-verdu, as well as with Darren Cahill, a brilliant Australian coach attached to Adidas who were Andy's clothing sponsor at the time. Darren (a former coach to Andre Agassi) and Andy had got to know each other well during that time and Andy asked him if he would consider working full time with him. But Darren had two children at a critical time in their schooling, and he was reluctant to commit to all of the travel required of a full-time coach. However, he was very keen to help Andy find the right person for the next stage.

You see a lot of people coaching on the Tour, but it is never that easy to really get to know them or how they operate, as everyone's real work goes on outside of the tournaments, and the higher you climb up the world rankings, the tougher it is to find the right fit. Darren knew Andy well both as a player and a person by then, and he had a better overview of the entire Tour than any of us did, so he did some thinking and after a while he surprised us all by suggesting ex-pro Ivan Lendl.

My first response when Andy told me about Darren's idea was not particularly enthusiastic. I just thought of Ivan the player in his heyday: never smiling, totally robotic, hard as nails. 'Oh God, no, that'll never work,' I blurted out before I realised that perhaps that description had also been used to describe both Andy and me in the past.

Lendl was something of an enigma. He hadn't gone into coaching after he had retired, but moved to Florida to focus on his golf. He'd all but disappeared from the tennis scene for years, and now here he was again, looking to coach, coincidentally the same year that he had opened a tennis academy himself. I was suspicious that he might just be wanting a top player attached to the new academy to build its profile. But Darren was insistent, swearing that he actually thought it could be a good fit. And I really trusted Darren, as I knew Andy did. It was another instance where I stepped back, knowing that relationships and personal recommendations are everything in this game, and that in this situation I knew far less than Darren.

The two of them met up in the off-season at the end of 2011, at a restaurant close to Ivan's place in Florida for lunch. The great game of player–coach speed dating was on once again. Andy was wary, but Ivan was not going to jump into something he wasn't convinced about either, and nor should he. But it turned out that they got along brilliantly, and Ivan agreed to work with Andy for the three remaining weeks of the off-season to see how they got along.

From very early on, it was clear that they were kindred spirits, and similar in many ways: the drive, the work ethic, the absence of flamboyance or effervescence in interviews, the love of sarcasm. Neither of them was the type to willingly start sharing thoughts and emotions in newspaper columns, and they understood that in each other, too. Also, while both seeming like quite gruff, blokes' blokes, they are both very comfortable around women. Like Andy, Ivan's first coach was his mother, and both were used to having strong female influences on and off the court. Andy had me, my mum and Kim, while Ivan had his mother, his wife Samantha and no fewer than five daughters. He had also worked with a female psychologist to improve his game when he was a player, and was very keen for Andy to do work with her too. Even today, now that Andy and Lendl are working together again after a two-year break, a lot of the work that they do together is talking rather than playing – and it serves to remind me that what separates the best from the rest is what goes on between the ears.

The single greatest asset that Ivan brought to Andy was experience: he had been there himself, as a player, at that top level. Andy

had never had a coach who knew what it felt like to play – and lose –
Grand Slam after Grand Slam, under ever-increasing pressure from
the public and the media. There were by now a number of big
matches Andy had lost simply because he had let his emotional control of the match slip away. Ivan provided an enormous sense of
reassurance just by being able to say: 'I know, I've been there.'
Finally, Andy had a lead coach who knew what that desolation felt
like and how to combat it. Ivan, like Andy, had lost four Grand Slam
finals before he won one. When the off-season ended, Ivan committed to join Andy for the Australian Open in January 2012, where he
made the final against Novak Djokovic.

Soon they were working well together and had built up a good
relationship. Ivan was helping Andy enormously with setting and
resetting his focus. His mantra was that consistency of performance
is all about consistency of focus. Andy had a tendency to let himself
get distracted by all sorts of things – someone in the crowd, the
gamesmanship of his opponent or sometimes an issue with his clothing or his shoes. You simply can't afford to do that. If you lose your
focus for a few seconds, your serve could be broken and in men's tennis that can quickly cost you the set. Djokovic himself used to lose
focus a few years ago, but he seemed to have mastered it. He simply
didn't let up, so if Andy wanted to start beating him, he had to find a
strategy of his own, and this was where Ivan was invaluable.

But nothing could have prepared any of us for what that 2012
Wimbledon final against Federer did to Andy's spirit. For the third
time in a Grand Slam final, Roger Federer had got the better of him,
this time on home turf. Watching him at the trophy presentation
left me totally distraught. Seeing him struggling to get his words
out, knowing how hard he had worked, how close he has come and
how much he had wanted it, not knowing if he would ever get that

chance again . . . I knew how emotional he would be and how tough that speech was to make in front of a huge crowd and millions of TV viewers around the world. I just wanted it to be over for him. It was agony watching my child standing out there on his own, suffering in front of all of those people. I wanted to be able to jump down from the player box and give him a hug, to tell him that he was amazing, that he was loved, how proud I was of him and that he would do it next time.

And he did. In a way, that loss was the best thing that could have ever happened to his career. It unlocked something in his relationship with the public, who had never seen him visibly distressed, sad rather than angry or petulant. People seemed to appreciate that he wasn't the stereotype of the stroppy young man they had been building up all this time; he had a heart, and now he was vulnerable.

He came back stronger, but this time it took a bit longer. He went home, he spent time with Kim and the dogs, and he indulged in some fun, non-sporty activities to try and cheer himself up. The dogs are always great for that as they have no idea if he's won or lost; they are only ever interested in the smelly socks from the darkest corners of his kit bag.

He just wanted to sit on the sofa vegetating and feeling sorry for himself for a couple of days, but while that was perfectly understandable, none of us – Kim, Jamie, his mates – could let him do that, so we encouraged him to get active, get out of the house. The family and support group swung into action big time, making sure he was up off the sofa, keeping busy and moving on. He went go-karting with his mates, played golf, went to watch the live TV game show *Mock the Week* and visited Battersea Dogs Home with Kim. Fortunately for all of us, it was an Olympic year, so he had to get back in the saddle within a week. The Olympics were in London, he was playing doubles with Jamie as well as playing singles, and before he knew it he was back on the grass courts at Wimbledon.

That Olympic summer in London was great fun. I was captaining the women's GB team, so I was busy looking after the girls. The LTA had rented a house in Wimbledon for the duration and it was a stone's throw from the venue. It was my kind of thing, with people coming and going all day for food, rest or physio treatment. It felt like a proper team unit. Both of the boys loved being part of Team GB. After years of feeling the weight of the nation's expectations on his shoulders alone, Andy was now part of something bigger, and Jamie was just as delighted to be back in an environment like the one they had known as children: travelling as a pack, working as a squad, and playing for your country. The only disappointment was that they missed the opening ceremony because they were playing the next morning and couldn't afford to spend four hours on their feet in the Olympic stadium.

The boys lost their opening match in the men's doubles against an Austrian pair. I watched them win the first set and then had to leave to watch one of our women playing singles. I was so torn. I so wanted to watch the boys but my job dictated I be with the girls. The Olympics gave Wimbledon a whole new vibe. There were advertising hoardings, burger bars, sports fans as opposed to tennis fans . . . and coloured clothing. It felt quite different. And so did Andy. A week later he got to have the experience that Jamie had had five years earlier: winning at the All England Club. And it was made all the sweeter by taking place on the same court, against the same opponent who had shattered his dreams only a few weeks earlier.

Perhaps it was because he had finally stood on Centre Court as a winner, perhaps it was having had Ivan's counsel for another year, or perhaps it was simply that he was ready, but a few weeks later he won his first Grand Slam title at the US Open. Mirroring Ivan Lendl's career trajectory yet again, he succeeded on what was his fifth attempt at taking on a Grand Slam, and like his new mentor, he did it in a match that was gruelling to say the very least. He was barely able to stand by the end of the epic five sets, and nearly five hours, against Novak Djokovic.

When I finally got home a couple of days later, I didn't leave the house for nearly three days. In fact, I barely left the sofa, staying in to watch mind-numbing crap on telly and eating rubbish. I was totally and utterly drained. And I didn't want to speak to anyone, I just wanted peace and quiet. Everything had changed, and it was going to take a little time for that to fully sink in. Britain's seventy-seven year wait for another Grand Slam winner was over, and at least some of the monumental pressure he had been under was off. But not entirely . . . because there was still the small matter of Wimbledon.

No one could have predicted that 2013 would be a golden year for any of us, as it certainly didn't start off that way. Andy lost again in the Australian Open final, and Jamie was still without a regular doubles partner. He had played in Melbourne with Colin Fleming whose current partner was injured, but neither of them played well and they lost in the first round. Jamie was very down and contemplating his future, and Andy was frustrated at another missed opportunity. Meanwhile I was away in Israel with the Fed Cup team so was unable to do much to help either of them.

However, it was at this point that Jamie came across John Peers, an Australian player who was working his way through the Challenger circuit, the level below the ATP Tour. He had been doing very well and although his ranking was a bit lower than Jamie's he was committed to doubles and plays on the left side of the court. Jamie plays on the right so they decided to give it a go, and this was the start of three very successful years together. They committed to doubles, to each other, and to training with Louis Cayer again, and they just got better and better.

Louis was delighted to be working with Jamie again. He was now employed by the LTA as a specialist doubles coach and as a performance coach educator. He had been helping Jamie on and off during Davis Cup matches and the Olympics, but until Jamie found a settled partner Louis simply wouldn't have the same impact working with a solo player, so there would have been little point in contracting him. But because Jamie and John were now fully devoted to making it work, it was as if the die were cast. And Louis is such a good man – the best coach I've ever met, and dedicated, caring and professional. He loves Jamie like his own son. So the turnaround was relatively quick in comparison to the doldrums Jamie had been in for so long.

Louis was a leader, someone who had a long-term vision for Jamie, and in response Jamie soon started to mature, to invest in himself by employing hitting partners on the road and a psychologist to help him manage his emotions better. He was the sort of player who would get horribly down on himself, which meant that over the years he could be terribly difficult to coach. He could hit a hundred balls, and even if there were ninety-nine good ones, he would only dwell on the one bad one. If you end up investing time on that one bad shot, you can lose sight of what you *can* do and disrupt your entire focus, and this was the road I had seen him starting to take. It's as true in other parts of life as it is in tennis – regret, looking back, it can be so paralyzing. Sport teaches you to keep looking forward, keep moving, keep hoping. However, investing in himself instead, working on his emotional control, and trusting Louis once again were enormously positive steps, and before long things began to slip into place for Jamie. As ever, knowing that one son was having a more settled time, my attention quickly turned to the other.

By now, I had found Wimbledon stressful for many years, and was almost dreading it in 2013. You never go in thinking, This is going to be the year! Because you can't let yourself think that far ahead. But I knew it was possible.

I'm sure that Andy remembers it differently, but for me, Wimbledon 2013 was all about the lemon iced doughnut. In the players' lounge before Andy's first match, I sat and ate a radioactive lemon iced doughnut with a cup of tea. Comfort eating. It was so good, and Andy won so confidently that I decided to do the same thing before his next match. And the next. Before I knew it, I was doing something I had never done before in my life – following a superstitious little routine that I was too scared to stop in case it jinxed the result. Every time he played, I had to have a lemon iced doughnut. That each and every one was absolutely delicious and enormously calorific, was of course irrelevant; *I was doing it for Andy*. And my habit wasn't even a secret – on one of the match days, the BBC drone footage caught me shovelling it into my mouth. I was completely unaware until someone texted me later that day to say they'd seen me on the BBC stuffing my face with cake.

Doughnuts aside, there is very little that I can actually remember about that Wimbledon final, which is highly unusual for me. Normally I will come away with a total handle on the ebb and flow of the match, a clear visual memory of the key points, and how Jamie or Andy seemed emotionally. But on this occasion, I was just in some other place. It was as if I had zoned out until the very end. Later that same day, Andy mentioned something to me about a problem he'd had with one of his shoes and I had no idea what he was talking about. One of his friends, Rob, had left the match, driven to Andy's house in Oxshott – twenty-five minutes away! – to get a fresh pair and driven back with them, all during the match. But I don't remember a thing about it.

I do know that I didn't sit in the players' box, which was also quite unusual for me. Ever since Andy was a small boy, I have known how off-putting he finds it when he looks up and sees those close to him are chatting or laughing or generally not paying attention to the match. We don't ever know when he's going to look up and need that encouraging glance, which perhaps explains why I sit with my eyes trained on him all the time. Consequently, I don't really care what I wear when I'm watching his matches, as long as I'm comfortable. I'm there for the tennis. End of. Loose fitting tops, jeans and no heels are my staples. I am often sitting there for hours, after all!

Andy and his coaching team decide who sits where in the players' box for matches, and they keep the same format throughout an event. It's important to have continuity, as Andy only likes to have people in the box who are part of his team or are family or friends. It's easy to be distracted by strange faces in the box such as celebs or sponsors you don't know well. He needs to know that when he looks to the box, he will get positive reinforcement every time from familiar faces.

But the players' box on Centre Court at Wimbledon is unlike that at any other Grand Slam. It is mixed, with eighteen seats for the guests of each player, all lumped together, only semi-divided by a bit of staircase. I always used to sit on the inside of the front row, then I moved to the outside of the row behind. I always sit on an end. It means I only have one person to sit beside. Believe me, I don't want to sit beside anyone when I'm watching the boys. And nobody wants to sit beside me!

This time I moved back to the row behind the player box and sat at the end of the aisle. There's truly nothing worse than having an opponent's supporters shouting in your ear for the duration of the match. Across the aisle from me were the Serbian camp and an absolute Buster Bloodvessel kind of guy: bald head, tattoos, built like a brick shithouse. I could see him out of the corner of my eye and it seemed like he was trying to wind me up the whole way through the match. Every time there was a big point or a great shot from Novak, he would stand up, turn towards me and give a massive fist pump and tribal roar. I never flinched. Not once. But I knew what he was doing.

As if that wasn't bad enough, my brother started passing round a tin of my mum's shortbread when Andy was two sets ahead. I threw my brother my best death stare. It's not a picnic. The match is not over yet. You can't relax until it's done. I was furious! I don't relax for a moment when I'm watching my boys. Tennis is so unpredictable, you never know what's going to happen. I never relax until the last point is won. I watched the shortbread work its way around the box and returned immediately to gargoyle mode, silently vowing to kill my brother afterwards.

I might not remember much about the match as a whole, but I can remember those first three match points, and I will remember them for the rest of my life. He lost them all. I could hear my heart thumping. I could hardly breathe. Then he saved a break point. More torture. Then he had a fourth match point. It was if the sun had come out after a long, hard winter when he finally dropped his racket and lifted his arms to accept the crowd's cheers. He clambered up through the crowd to the player box and hugged everyone in the front row. I was three rows back. I was longing to go and give him a big hug, but I stayed put as he celebrated, knowing that I couldn't face getting nailed in the press again for being a pushy mother, trying to take credit for him or whatever their latest angle might be. But as he started to climb back down, the crowd started to shout 'What about your mum?' He turned back and I walked down to the front row to get my hug.

As soon as the trophy presentation ended, Andy was committed to hours of media. Meanwhile, I was in the players' lounge trying to organise some champagne so that Andy's team, friends and family could celebrate, as well as trying to arrange for any friends of the family whom Andy would want there to have access passes. I was running around in a frenzy trying to sort all of this out, when someone from the All England Club appeared and said to me, 'Would you like to come and pick out your dress for the Champions' Ball?'

I wasn't the type of person to turn up to a Grand Slam final with a 'just in case' ballgown in tow. But apparently the folk at Wimbledon had it all covered. They have an incredible system for novices like me. Together with my best friend Laura, and Anne Keothavong, I was led down to the ladies' dressing room, which had been transformed into an Aladdin's Cave of gowns.

These were my pre-*Strictly Come Dancing* days, when sequins and sparkles were still alien to me. I didn't really want to be down there looking at dresses, because I knew that all of the fun and excitement was happening elsewhere. I wanted to be cheering and hugging my family and my mates, and congratulating Andy's team. But before I knew it, the lady in charge said, 'Please, come in. We have some Jenny Packham dresses for you to try. They are only for the Murray family.'

With that, and once I had clapped eyes on the beautiful silver sequinned dress in front of me, it was hard to say no. I simply asked if it was a size ten, and when she said yes, I said 'That's fine. I'll wear that', but she insisted I try it on. I just bunged it on over my jeans, with my ballet pumps still on underneath, but she encouraged me to actually take my jeans off to see the proper fit of the gown, and tried to offer me a pair of strappy sandals with skyscraper heels. The last thing I wanted was to be heading off to a ball in a pair of shoes that were new to me; I was bad enough in heels at the best of times. So I politely declined, but accepted the loan of a pashmina and a clutch bag, and let them set about doing my hair and make-up before I headed back upstairs for some more fizz with the gang.

I arrived at the ball with Kim's mum and dad. I got out of the car first at the InterContinental hotel in Hyde Park, where there was a classic red carpet extending out in front of me. I had no idea where we were meant to be going, so I just headed for the enormous sign that said 'Ballroom'. People and cameras were following me, and I had no clue what to do. Stop? Smile? Wave? It just seemed a bit inappropriate to do nothing, but equally daft to start acting up for them, particularly as I was terrified of tripping in my heels and painfully aware that my phone charger was hanging out of the dainty little bag I had been loaned. Finally, I got to the top of the red carpet only to be told, 'I'm terribly sorry, Mrs Murray, but you've come in the wrong way. You need to be over there.' So I headed back down the red carpet, hoping that somehow no one else had noticed.

Once inside the InterContinental we were ushered to a small private room to wait for Andy and Kim to arrive. Ivan and the rest of Andy's team were there in their dinner suits and dicky bows. As was women's champ Marion Bartoli and her dad. It was already pretty late and everyone was starving. Yes, there was fizz and nibbles and a whole load of photos to be taken before going through to the dinner.

I remember joking with Dr Bartoli that we would have to get together for the first dance. He looked totally horrified at the prospect and was probably delighted to discover that the age-old tradition of a first dance between men's and ladies champions was no longer relevant: it wasn't a ball, it was just a dinner. I wasn't so thrilled. All those years of reading about the Champions' Ball and now it was a thing of the past. Suddenly my sparkly ballgown seemed a little OTT.

It was a wonderful evening, and it made me incredibly proud to see the spirit of optimism that night from everyone connected to British tennis. Seventy-seven years after Fred Perry's win, we had a Wimbledon men's champion again. And – most of all, perhaps – I had the most enormous sense of relief. Nobody would ask that damn question again: 'When's he going to win Wimbledon?' And I found myself thinking . . . if he never wins any title ever again, I'll be happy. He's done it. That's it. Enough.

Except that feeling didn't last long. As with everything. The success only lasts a short while and then you are on to the next event, the next challenge. We never let the grass grow under our feet. Always driven, always moving forward, always looking ahead.

15

Do what you want,
or how to live a little

*In which I make a decision based on joy and pleasure alone,
and take a chance on* Strictly Come Dancing. *Where I
thought I would learn about dancing and show business,
I learn the pleasure of not being brilliant and doing it
anyway – and don't regret a second.*

With Wimbledon conquered, Andy was in the spotlight more than ever before. But at least he was *doing* something to be there – he was a Grand Slam champion! The attention that had always come my way when he was commanding an audience continued to grow with his success, but in my case it was usually just images of me *watching*, passive rather than active. And of course, if I wasn't *doing* anything when the focus was on me, the focus would be on my appearance, which continued to be the case as much as it ever had been. Despite my recent foray into occasional public speaking, I wasn't reaching audiences the size of breakfast TV or tabloid newspapers, thankfully.

Something had shifted, though. The talk started to be not that I was too much of a scruff, or somehow inappropriate or unladylike. Instead, it started to be about whether I had taken on a 'style guru'. Yes, instead of the previous sneer about my lack of glamour, the perception seemed to be that these days perhaps I had a little too much. I had changed two things about my appearance around that time: my hair and my teeth. People had picked up on this, but the overall perception was now that I had a 'team', a 'guru', or even a 'glam squad'. I even read that I had taken on Andy's ex-manager Simon Fuller to create a new image for me.

It was a strange mixture of confusing, amusing and insulting. People were so quick to scuttle past the fact that I had a career of my own, that I loved my career, and that all things considered I had done pretty well at it. I was still seen as a mother, at times an inappropriate mother, and a professional tennis watcher, little more, little less – and because my image was all that people knew of me, it was all they discussed of me. During the 2013 Wimbledon Championships, I was staying at Andy and Kim's house during the tournament. One morning, I came downstairs for breakfast and Kim was already up. As I walked into the room, she was curled up on the sofa chuckling away to herself.

'What's so funny?' I asked her, as I started to sort myself a drink.

'I'm just watching breakfast TV, they're having a whole debate about your hair,' she explained, turning to grin at me.

'What do you mean, a debate about my hair?' I asked.

'Well, some people are saying it's wonderful that you've let yourself go grey naturally and others are claiming you've paid for it.'

'Ha!' Of course I had paid for it: I couldn't believe anyone would think that my 'white hot blonde' look was natural!

Earlier that year, I had been in Melbourne for the Australian Open and had been doing a bit of shopping between matches. For the first time in years, I had started to feel a bit more confident about my appearance. Not just how I looked, but what I wanted to project about myself. I had been in a shop in the city centre, and the owner had fabulous whitish hair – shorter and funkier than mine is now, but a similar colour. And she had charcoal grey at the edges. It was a bit Cruella de Vil but it was seriously cool. She had bold, quite wacky clothes on, and despite being a bit older than me, I thought she looked absolutely amazing. At the time, my hair was coppery brown (but greying), with blonde highlights in – and after a couple of weeks in the Australian sun, those highlights were starting to look decidedly brassy.

Perhaps it was new-found confidence, perhaps it was just return-ing to Scotland in the February cold or perhaps I just really loved that lady's hair, but when I returned home, I headed to my own hairdresser and described her look as best as I could.

'Well, that's, um, quite bold,' was her sheepish response. But I had made my mind up. There was a lot that I couldn't change about how I was perceived around that time, but I could take control of my own hair colour, and I did, and I love it. Still. I didn't grow grey gracefully: I chose it.

If only sorting my teeth out could have been as painless a pro-cess. I had always hated my teeth, as long as I'd been an adult: I was terrified of going to the dentist, so I didn't go, so I needed to go more, but didn't, so it became ever more terrifying. I was able to talk the talk and walk the walk where exercise, fitness and diet were concerned, but my teeth were a disaster area. Then, as the camera's gaze turned to me, and I saw photographs of myself smiling, I was appalled. So I smiled less. So the press said I was too serious, always scowling. Here was a new vicious circle, perpetuating the idea that I never smiled. Misery! I was often smiling. Just not in the player box and never on camera. Eventually, enough was enough, and I decided to deal with my teeth or regret it for ever. I was not exactly prepared for it to take eighteen long months though. But, as with the hair, I don't regret a single moment of it, and I am now so much more relaxed about smiling and laughing anywhere near cameras – as well as being proud of having made choices about what I wanted to change, and being brave enough to follow them through.

It felt as if things were coming together that summer, and it was a good job that my confidence about life in the public eye was feeling less fragile, because within a few weeks, an opportunity came up that was beyond my willpower to turn down: I was approached to take part in the BBC's prime-time show *Strictly Come Dancing*.

I had been offered a couple of similar things in the past, including ITV's *The Jump*, but I had always found it very easy to say no to them as they simply weren't activities or shows that I enjoyed watching. *Strictly* was a very different matter though; it was a show that I had loved since it had first started, from the music to the costumes, and the thrill of watching others learn a brand new skill and executing it in front of millions. I watched it religiously, looking forward to it every week and recording it whenever I was out of the country. I had never dreamed that there would one day be a space for me in the line-up.

It wasn't an offer at this stage, but rather a chat to see if I understood what it might involve, to gauge my interest and whether I was prepared for the level of commitment. They were very clear: it really does involve parking your life for a good four months or so. And the more they told me about it, the more I realised that it wasn't just being part of the show that appealed, but the thought of doing something so completely different: tennis had been my life since childhood, and my career for twenty-odd years. The prospect of removing myself entirely from the tennis world for a while, and dumping myself in someone else's universe was intriguing. I told them I would be up for it, and told no one else about the meeting. I knew from experience that the bigger and more exciting the deal, the more likely it was that if you didn't keep quiet, it could be gone before you'd ever got it . . .

When they offered me a spot, the first thing I did before saying yes was to ask the boys what they thought, and if they would mind me taking part. I was well aware that no matter how long I lasted in the competition, I would be putting myself in the public eye in a completely different context than ever before, and that could have repercussions for them. The two, almost opposite, responses spoke volumes about their approach to life, even though neither of them tried for a second to stop me.

Jamie said, 'Oh, Mum, you'll love that, how fantastic!'

Andy put his head in his hands, laughing, saying, 'Oh my God, Mum, you'll be terrible!' They were both correct and their only real concern was whether I would be okay with such a radically different type of attention. It was Andy who asked me if I really understood what a huge audience the show had, and what a world of potential new criticism it might open up. Perhaps it was because he had taken his fair share of public drubbing over the years, or perhaps he felt responsible for what I had learned to cope with, or perhaps he really was afraid I'd be awful! But while I appreciated his concern, it didn't put me off.

In my heart, I had known from the first mention that I wanted to do the show. It had been a very long time since I had made a decision to do something that was just for me and just about me, pure and simple. Up until this point, most of the attention I'd attracted had not been by choice: I had been pictured unwittingly by drones, snapped collecting early morning bagels, and had my every facial expression and change of outfit at the boys' matches analysed by magazine and newspaper columnists. I had been the subject of opinion pieces but rarely interviews, where I might be given a chance to speak for myself. The attention I had received had never, ever been under my control, but always as a by-product of another, larger situation. This was a chance to do something entirely different, to let myself be swept up in a world beyond my control through choice. The tennis world is a relatively small one, especially once you have been a part of it for a quarter of a century. I was ready to enter a new world. After all, what was the worst that could happen? People might criticise me? That was nothing new. So, with an enormous grin, I accepted the offer and committed to *Strictly*.

Within days of saying yes, producers from the show start sending you dates for costume fittings, photoshoots, interviews and initial rehearsal times. I could feel the whirlwind gathering pace and while I was nervous, I was also ridiculously excited. One of the first meetings coincided with the 2014 US Open and for the first time in my life it felt wonderful to say, 'No, not this year. I won't be there,' to those asking if they would see me at Flushing Meadows. I had somewhere else to be now.

In a period of exciting firsts, my first day at *Strictly* was one that will shine for ever in my memory. All of the contestants for that year were gathered together at a huge house near Roehampton University to be introduced to each other for the first time, and to learn the opening group dance which we would perform together on the launch show. I was dizzy with excitement and found it almost impossible to concentrate. Where I can draw a tennis court on the back of a napkin, divide it into areas, and explain a strategy or pattern of play to almost anyone, Karen, our choreographer, seemed to be able to do something very similar with a ballroom floor and fifteen pro dancers and their celebrity partners. It seemed unimaginably complicated that she was able to see and plot how each of us would move and pass each other in a relatively small space, in the same way that I could predict and discuss the movement of a tennis ball across a court. And she was dealing with thirty people, where I usually concerned myself with two!

It was really overwhelming. I was like a child in a sweet shop, unable to believe that I was actually included in this line-up – or in the show at all – particularly as I was the only contestant who did not come from the entertainment world in some form or other. Thom Evans was the only other contestant whose background was in sport, but even he was now involved in acting and modelling and was used to the idea of 'performing'. Most of the rest of the gang seemed to know what Karen was talking about when she described the various moves we would be doing in this inaugural jive: the 'mashed potato', the 'alligator', 'just jacks'. I had no idea what she was talking about and busied myself with staring around the room, trying to work out whom I could possibly copy.

Perhaps we were all doing the same thing – I suspect we were. Scanning the other contestants, trying to establish in each case who was, if not actual competition, then at least someone we could ask what we were meant to be doing, without being horribly embarrassed, someone to bond with to ease the 'first day at school' nerves that were crippling all of us. We were learning a whole new social dynamic, who we all were, why we recognised each other, and whether we were going to be the same in person as our public image would suggest. I was fighting my own battles on that front, just hoping that people would see me grinning and goofing things up on the dance floor, and know that I wasn't the fist-pumping tiger mother that the tabloids might have had them believe.

In the end, all of the female contestants broke the ice enough to decide that we should film little segments of the dance on our mobile phones and start a WhatsApp group to share them with each other. That way, we would all have each others' numbers, and we would be able to re-watch the steps we didn't understand, or couldn't remember, and practise them in our own time. We got through that first dance in the end, despite it being the most complicated opening number the show had ever choreographed. (They didn't tell us that until later.) But the WhatsApp group has remained to this day: whenever one of us has a new project, or some big news, it will be reactivated amongst the same gang – close friends, messaging and chatting away, supporting each other from afar. There is a lot of talk on *Strictly* about how the group becomes like family, but in our case it really did create some solid and lasting friendships.

Once we were assigned our individual partners, the real test of the project was to come. Understandably, I never had any problem at all with the training or the hours of going over and over something until we had got it right. It was just that . . . I would so rarely get it right. It had been over thirty years since I learned a brand new skill and I just couldn't remember a thing from one day to the next. I loved the physical aspect of the dancing, learning how to move my body in new ways and trying out all the different steps.

I would give almost any of that a go. But it was the acting, the poised gracefulness, the 'taking on a character' that I really struggled with week after week. That and the heels. I wanted to be fabulous at it, I really did, but every time I tried the 'acting' element, I just felt like an absolute pillock.

For our dance the first week, we did a waltz to 'Mull of Kintyre'. At one point I had to dance backwards slowly and elegantly into Anton's arms, all so very 'floaty-floaty'. But that sort of self-display simply isn't in my nature. I would giggle, I would tense up, I would forget my steps. I desperately wanted to be good – but I couldn't let myself go.

'You need to relax your arms,' Anton encouraged me in rehearsal.

'Relax my arms? They've been tense all of my life! My livelihood has depended on it!' I yelped back, laughing at how ridiculous the situation was. 'Is that it?' I would ask, my arms as floppy and loose as I could possibly make them.

'No,' he would reply. 'You look like you're swatting a fly.'

What I loved about working with Anton – apart from his sense of humour – was watching someone from a completely different discipline trying to teach a self-conscious rookie like me. Analysing his techniques, how he taught, how he tried to win me over was eternally fascinating to watch – to the point where sometimes I tuned out and stopped listening to what he was actually trying to teach me, focusing instead on how he was going about teaching it.

Whenever we were training somewhere where there were tennis courts, we also tried to play tennis if we had the time. It gave me a chance to teach him how to play, and for him to see that I was actually good at something involving complex physical coordination! It was fascinating how comparable our coaching styles were. He was always hitting balls into the net with his forehand. 'When you hit,

243

you need to keep your elbow up, take it up with you and keep it high,' I'd say to him.

'Ah, that's exactly what I've been saying to you about the waltz all morning . . .' he'd reply.

Anton's greatest attribute was that he did it all with so much humour. He needed to with me. And he was very kind, taking the time to explain something in a different way if it hadn't really sunk in the first time round. Taking on a new skill at fifty-five was a tall order, but he never judged me for not being as good as some of his previous partners or other contestants on the show. He displayed the same egalitarian desire to teach that I have always aimed for, and I found it a real pleasure to watch him working. That was, of course, until I was required to actually come up with the goods and dance.

On top of the more understandable practicalities relating to my inexperience or discomfort with the performance angle, I also developed a head like a sieve, completely unable to remember a whole routine in the time it took us to go for lunch. We would work hard all morning, congratulate ourselves over lunch and then as we returned to the dance studio, I would realise I simply couldn't remember a thing. I don't think it was all ineptitude though; a lot of it was that I was too excited most of the time. As if the transition from before to after lunch wasn't bad enough, the shift from empty dance studio to Elstree Studio at the BBC each week was even more overwhelming. By Friday, I would usually have just about mastered our routine – but that would have taken place in a very specific, confined environment. Me, Anton and a CD player. I would have a certain door, radiator or mirror that I would be aiming for as I trotted out the steps. Then, just as my nerves kicked in, I would have to replicate the same routine on the studio floor, with elaborate lighting, a live band instead of the familiar CD, and cameramen on the actual dance floor following your every move for the close-ups. And then there were the props to negotiate. Jeez. It turned my brain to absolute mush.

Once we had performed that first waltz, I received a glimpse of how enormous the *Strictly* audience is, and how much people loved the show. I flew home to Scotland the day after the show as it was the final day of the Ryder Cup at Gleneagles and I had a formal invitation to go and watch. The hospitality tent I was invited to was fabulous, but I wanted to head out onto the course to see the action close up. I must have got about ten or fifteen steps along the grass of the main thoroughfare before people who had seen me on last night's TV started to stop and surround me.

I was mortified, as I couldn't really move, backwards or forwards, and it was starting to cause a bit of a blockage on the road. I felt very exposed, and rather embarrassed as everyone was asking for pictures and selfies – from me? Who had done one below-average waltz? I tried to be polite, but also tried to get to an area where I could quietly watch the golf, but it wasn't really happening, so in the end I sheepishly returned to the hospitality tent, slowly letting it sink in how enormously I had underestimated the reach of the show.

The second week was the first time I would be able to be voted off the show, and that was the one I really cared about, as I knew that all the boys wanted for me was not to be the first contestant eliminated from the competition. One of the best pieces of advice that Anton gave me was that for the first two or three weeks, the audience voting at home didn't really care how good we were as dancers, they just wanted to see a bit of personality and to figure out who they actually wanted to watch on TV every week. It made sense, as that was exactly the way I approached the show as a viewer, and it was a huge release to be able to laugh and enjoy myself rather than getting upset about being at the bottom of the leader board.

It was just as well that Anton was right, as the cha-cha-cha we performed that week was one we only just got away with. The show beamed a tennis court onto the dance floor, as well as a net, and we performed to Tom Jones' 'She's a Lady'. My moves were far from ladylike though. The props I was given were an old wooden racket with a warped head and a broken string, and a tennis ball covered in glitter and sequins. I could hardly move I was shaking so much as the music began and it was time to act out our little tennis flirtation. I threw the glitter ball high into the hair and nearly missed it completely with my duff racket. Instead, I hit it straight at the cameraman directly in front of me, where it bounced off the lens. I looked to Anton for help, but he was so distracted by me firing tennis balls at the camera that he had mistimed his knee slide towards me, had to grab me behind both thighs to stop himself from skidding into the audience, and headbutted me directly in the groin. It was impossible for me to regain my composure after that, and I literally robot-walked my way through. It was awful. The judges were less than impressed, but their opinions never bothered me because, as a long-term viewer, I understood that they each had their own personas to maintain and besides, I knew I was terrible, I didn't need anyone else to tell me. People asked me for months afterwards how on earth I coped with the criticism on the show, but I would just laugh. 'It's nothing compared to what I've dealt with over the last twenty years!'

To my delight, the votes for me rolled in, week after week. People either enjoyed watching me messing things up every Saturday, or they liked to see someone having a go at something totally new, or maybe they could see that I wasn't an overbearing ogre after all and that I was loving every minute. As time passed, I could sense people's response to me changing, even on the street, when I was buying a coffee, or at the petrol station. People love to watch a transformation – just as I always had – and in me that is what they were getting. Or at least, it is what they felt they were getting. I had known all along that the desire to dance, to have a laugh, to work as a team was always part of me, and so had close friends and family – but for too long it had been buried by the one-dimensional sporting clichés and lazy stereotyping of certain media.

Free from any anxieties about either leaving first or having to win, I made the most of every week I was allowed to stay on the show. I loved the costumes and the make-up, I loved the sense of camaraderie and I loved the challenge. I never got used to wearing the heels though, and spent every single moment in them convinced that I was about to fall. My favourite dance was the week that we did the Charleston, where I was able to wear a flat pair of pumps and let myself go to the jaunty 'Varsity Drag'.

We made it through eight weeks all the way to Blackpool where our Mary Poppins routine to 'Let's Go Fly a Kite' saw me disappear into the Tower Ballroom roof in a cloud of balloons. Anton had told the technician 'if she messes this up, don't let her down!' Hilarious. I was finally voted off that week – and quite rightly too, as the rest of the dancers were becoming really skilful by now. The release, the laughter, the sheer sense of fun that *Strictly* gave me is something I shall never forget. I reconciled myself with whatever public profile I now had, made my peace with it and decided to enjoy what it brought me instead of worrying about how an unknown public saw me. Most importantly, I made good friends, not just with the dancers and other contestants, but also with myself.

16

Love, better than victory

In which I see my boys reach the very top, and each of us realise that what got them there was the love of playing: without the passion, the hard work would have been meaningless.

I t was easy to slip back into the world of tennis once the excitement of *Strictly* ebbed away. Three days after Blackpool I was back in my Tennis on the Road van at a primary school in East Lothian. The Fed Cup kicked off in January 2015 and the year was bookended by the boys' participation in the Davis Cup. On the whole, it felt like a period of consolidation for all of us, with Jamie finally reaping the rewards of the extraordinarily hard emotional and physical work that he had put in over the last few years, and Andy edging his way up those final few slots in the rankings.

Jamie's turnaround was particularly joyful to watch at this point. It had been a big fight for him to keep on top of things emotionally over the years, and now he seemed to have cracked it. Injuries aside, Andy's rise to the top five had been relatively smooth, largely an unstoppable upward spiral, but Jamie had been up and down like a yoyo, facing many more challenges. I had always said to him: 'You have the skills to get there, you just have to match it with the set-up, the resilience and a little bit of luck.' And when I had said it more times than he could bear, his wife would be just as supportive, telling him at every juncture to go for it, to believe in himself, to chase what we all knew he was capable of.

Once you have been working with a world-class coach, investing in your fitness training and physiotherapy, these things slip into your daily routine. But when you have had a rough couple of years, when every single penny counts, it is a huge mental shift to say to yourself – and of course to your new wife! – yes, I deserve this, I *am* worth the investment, I *do* deserve special treatment. And this was the mental leap that he'd had to take. He needed to *believe* that investing in himself financially, physically and (crucially) psychologically was worth it. For as long as he still doubted that, the investment was pointless – but watching Andy and the amount he invested in himself became the inspiration. He would see all of these different experts helping Andy with everything from nutrition to physiotherapy and slowly he started to think, 'Actually, I need to do a bit more of this, to do whatever it takes, add whoever is needed, to get to the very top'. It was a huge financial leap of faith.

The legacy of his years of self-doubt and hawkishly watching his budget is that Jamie is now the most extraordinary travel-booker. Honestly, he could set up his own travel agency now – he knows which route goes via where, which airline has the best prices, and which flights will get you in at the most convenient time with the most sleep possible. This is the result of years of not having the luxury of being able to afford the flight which left him least exhausted, because he still needed to save those few hundred pounds. In the end though, he did it. He turned things round; he chose to believe in his worth and to put in the work – and the people – to make it come to fruition, and yes, eventually it paid off as he and John Peers made it to two Grand Slam finals in 2015.

By the end of the year though, things had run their course with the partnership. Three years was an extraordinarily good innings to have with one partner, and he was even luckier when, just as it looked as if he and John would be going their separate ways, he discovered that the Brazilian player Bruno Soares was looking for a new partner. For the first time, he managed a relatively seamless transition, and started with Bruno at the beginning of 2016.

Andy had endured a bit of back and forth of his own around this period, having to take a lot of time off after the US Open in 2013 to have an operation on his back. It was a worrying time. The operation in itself was quite straightforward, but the prospect of messing with his back at all had been daunting as the risk is huge. But it had to be done – the pain had restricted him for too long, and in so many ways. To counteract the weakness, he had spent hours with his physiotherapy team and working in the gym, and had to opt out of all sorts of recreational fun which usually kept his mind off the stress of the Tour. He couldn't play golf or football, he'd had to stop go-karting (one of his favourite pastimes), the cumulative effect of which further curtailed his already limited social life. But the operation was a success, though it took him some time to get back to full strength. By the end of 2014, he was cramming in as many tournaments as he possibly could, to keep his rankings up and make the end of year Tour finals.

While this had been going on, he had made another switch of coaches, this time to the French ex-player Amélie Mauresmo. Ivan had not felt able to commit to the number of weeks per year that

Andy wanted for a coach, so after two very successful years together, they had decided to go their separate ways. As ever, the combination of personality-fit and tennis experience had been hard to find. After all, there are a limited number of ex-players who want to remain on the road, following the Tour around the world. And within that small group not all will be compatible with you. The better you do as a pro player, the fewer coaches there are who match your needs and make a real difference.

Amélie was suggested by Darren Cahill, the same guy who had suggested Ivan to Andy. He had made such a good call in suggesting Ivan, and he knew Andy so well as a person that his advice was immediately followed up. Andy and Amélie had a couple of meetings and played a bit of tennis together, and it all seemed pretty simple. Andy really enjoyed her company, and felt positive about the move.

Just as my dad never saw me 'as a girl' on the court, Andy didn't judge Amélie by her gender on court either. The example that I had been set, I set for Andy. The relationship was all about the skill set and the personality fit, and in this case they just clicked. After all, you can have all the technical expertise in the world, but if you can't sit down and have dinner together to discuss ideas and strategy, it's never going to work. That aspect is just as important – if not more so – as your feel for the game and technical know-how. Perhaps the greatest gift that Amélie had as a coach was that she listened to Andy, rather than just talking to him. There comes a point in your career where you want to feel like you're operating in more of a partnership, to feel a bit more in charge of your own destiny, and that was certainly something she provided for Andy after his recent spell with someone who had been more of a mentor.

Amélie was great to have around, and fitted well into the team, but the reaction to Andy hiring her was staggering. Some of the off-the-record comments and text messages that Andy received from male players in reaction to his decision to work with Amélie were quite mind blowing. Some players were bolder, saying what they thought directly to the media, but some kept their comments behind closed doors, and those were the most shocking.

Most people seemed to see the move as unusual or as some sort of statement. A female coach being hired by one of the very best male players had never happened before, so it caused endless column inches and opinion pieces. Neither Andy nor Amélie had any idea that their partnership would create so much interest, and in some ways that caused unnecessary added stress because it was going to be endlessly examined. Amélie was judged not just by whether she could move him from a top 4 player to a top 3, 2 or number 1 player but by what she could add to his game, but as a woman working in a man's world.

The flip side of the situation could be found in the wonderful example it set for other female coaches. It brought female coaches onto the back pages and TV screens and led to quite a few of the top female players hooking up with ex-top female players. Before long, Aga Radwańska had taken on Martina Navratilova in a coaching or advisory capacity, and then Madison Keys took on Lindsay Davenport. And there were others, too. There was a bit of a sea change in the industry, and despite the hubbub that surrounded them, Andy and Amélie had a very successful couple of years together. I was enormously proud of the choice my son made, and the way he handled the ensuing media maelstrom. Those early battles with the press felt like a very long time ago indeed. He knew what he wanted in a coach. He knew what he needed. And it had nothing whatsoever to do with gender.

As 2016 began and we headed to Australia again for the Open, I was full of optimism for the year ahead. Being on the team that won the Davis Cup for GB had given both boys huge delight and lots of confidence. It had been an incredible experience. When GB beat France in July 2015 to reach the Davis Cup semi-final, I kept everything crossed that the home tie would be in Scotland. We have no major tennis tournaments north of the border so the boys have no other chance to compete on their own patch. Glasgow's Emirates Arena got the nod and when the teams were announced on the opening day of the match against Australia, I looked around the venue as the players walked on to the court and marvelled at 8,000 fans in the east end of Glasgow going absolutely crazy for Scottish tennis players and a Scottish coach. I remembered the days when tennis struggled to get one line in the results section of the Scottish papers and one man and his dog watching our biggest tournaments. I felt the most enormous sense of pride. A Davis Cup semi-final in my country with my kids and one of my coaching protégés as captain. Wow.

Needless to say, the final in Ghent was a big deal, too. There was a lot of speculation around the tie and whether it would go ahead amid terrorist alerts in Brussels. It added an extra level of tension to the event: longer queues at security check-ins, increased bag searches, massive police presence everywhere. The GB team was facing Belgium and I knew we were favourites to win. It was incredible seeing the boys playing together again. They played doubles in both the Olympics in 2012 and 2016, but there was an added sweetness here because of the importance of the Davis Cup for the tennis community.

I had a feeling that 2016 was going to be a special year. But I just wanted everyone to stay happy, healthy and focused and was, to be honest, a bit preoccupied by the prospect of Andy and Kim having a baby, as well as my own Fed Cup work, which always peaked in February.

But Jamie, who was very happy in his new partnership with Bruno Soares, still working with Louis Cayer, won a title in Sydney and off the back of that, stormed his way to the final and came away with the Australian Open Doubles trophy. His first Grand Slam. Andy meanwhile made it to another singles final and was pipped to the post by Djokovic. I missed all of the action, though, as I was en route to the Fed Cup in Israel, and I was on my way home from there when Kim and Andy had their baby, Sophia, in February.

With his traditional stealth, graft, and sense of surprise, by early April 2016, Jamie had become the number 1 doubles player in the world. As ever, it came just at the right time to give Andy a bit of a nudge. It's impossible to play for eleven months of the year and be great every week, and by March 2016, Andy was struggling a little on court. He was also reaching the end of his time with Amélie, who by now had a baby of her own and was finding the travelling increasingly difficult. So, seeing that Jamie had reached number 1 and – as with so much in their careers, up to and including Wimbledon – that he had done it first, gave Andy the spur he needed to pull out absolutely all of the stops. It was the old 'if my big brother can do it, so can I' swinging back into play . . .

I resigned from my position as Fed Cup captain that spring. It was time to reduce the travel, to pick and choose the tournaments I wanted to attend, and to spend a little more time with my family. It may seem as if I'm always there, but with Andy and Jamie on the Tour for more than thirty-five weeks of the year, if I want to see them, I usually have to go to them – they rarely have the time to come home.

The second half of 2016 was one of the most extraordinary

periods of my life, starting with Andy winning Wimbledon a second time, then seeing Jamie win the US Open Doubles – making it two Grand Slams in a year for him. The year ended with the boys' joint triumphs at the ATP Tour World Finals, and both of them finishing the year ranked at World number 1. I am very good at praising the boys, or any students that I am teaching, but I find it quite hard to bask in their glory for fear of taking it for granted.

Perhaps it is a result of having seen the impact of the Dunblane tragedy on my home town, first hand. Life is precious but it is also fickle: you never know what is round the corner, so I find it hard to suppress the instinct to keep on moving to the next thing, whatever it might be. There is so little time to celebrate in tennis as the schedule is so full. If you win a Formula 1 event, you spend hours spraying champagne everywhere and then don't have another race for weeks. At the top end of tennis, particularly if you are playing until the end of the week, you often leave for the next tournament directly from the previous one. Football only has big finals two or three times a year, maybe more in a World Cup or Euro year, but tennis affords its players no such luxuries. Perhaps that is why our tough Scottish mindsets find it so satisfying. But it is a joy – and extremely important! – to stop from time to time and appreciate what you have achieved.

Last year I tried. I tried hard for all of us. To stop a little, to look around and think about what we had achieved, and maybe even to relax and enjoy it. When Andy won Wimbledon for the second time, he had three hours of media while I was whisked off to what I now refer to as the Sparkle Room. Sparkles aside, the most treasured moment of the day was when I received a text from Andy telling me to come down to where the ice bath was as he was in there and had ten minutes to kill. So, amidst all the hubbub and mayhem of those few hours, I made my way to him, and managed to snatch a quick chat, just the two of us, and of course a photo with the trophy, which he refused to put down for even a minute.

When we finally left the All England Club, it was after 9 p.m. and we were in a convoy of cars heading to the Champions' Dinner which was at the Guildhall in the City of London this time. As we headed east across London, our driver started to tut, wondering what the car in front was up to.

'I have no idea why he's heading this way,' he said. 'I'd never go this way to the Guildhall.'

My mum and I looked at each other and shrugged in the back seat. We had no idea either.

'Where's he off to now?' said the driver, exasperated. Then it hit me. I knew exactly where he was going: the McDonald's drive-through.

Andy had mentioned that he was starving when I'd seen him a couple of hours earlier in the ice bath, and I knew better than anyone his normal routine after tournaments – and this dated back to his Under 12s days. We are all a product of our environment and our past, and in Andy's case this meant a McDonald's on the way home . . . even after a Wimbledon final.

We pulled into the drive-through behind Andy's car, and I saw him – in his dinner jacket – sticking his head out of the car window to the left. The next thing we heard was shrieking from the order booth. The guy was freaking out! My mum and I laughed and laughed as we saw Andy's grinning face. The shrieks continued as the guy called his colleague over, and then we saw Andy being passed an enormous order of food. A moment's treat to congratulate yourself can come in all kinds of ways.

Within days it was on to the next tournament, and the pace did not let up for either Andy or Jamie for the rest of the year. If anything, the pace picked up considerably. By the end of November,

Jamie and Bruno together had ascended to the position of World number 1 doubles team, and the same month, Andy became the World number 1 singles player.

That December, I tried to impress upon both of my boys how far they had come and how well they had done. Even simple things, such as the fact that after their Olympic success, Dunblane was awarded one of the Team GB gold post boxes on the high street, meaning that tourist buses now stop to see it, instead of taking the ring road and avoiding the small businesses. This makes a huge difference to the quality of so many people's lives.

It makes all of us so proud, my parents especially. My dad doesn't go out that much any more, but he still loves to watch the matches. My mum, however, finds every moment delicious. The boys' success is the greatest pleasure in her life. She will get her hair done on the Saturday if one of them is in a big final on the Sunday . . . just in case any of her friends, or of course any journalists, come to the house to congratulate her or discuss the victory. She likes to be doorstep ready. And if either of them wins something, she'll head out at the first available opportunity, saying something spurious like, 'I've got to pop out for some rolls.' We know what she's up to though, it's not just the bakery she heads to – she's up and down the high street for hours talking to absolutely everyone, or 'doing her laps', as we like to call it. 'I just could NOT get out of there!' she'll claim in faux-exasperation when she finally gets home and settles down with a cup of tea.

She often tells people that their success is all down to her, and she genuinely seems to believe it! Her logic is that if her parents hadn't sent her to boarding school in Bridge of Allan, she would never have met my dad, and they would never have had me, and I wouldn't have had the boys. My dad is just happy with his conviction that he invented topspin.

258

Epilogue

I t has taken me a long time to want to tell my story, because for years I did not feel that it was entirely my story to tell: Jamie and Andy were still climbing the ladder of the tennis world, and I was trying to stay out of their limelight, to let them shine on their own terms, without a mum with her own story to tell.

These days, with them both settled and successful, having reached the top of their respective careers, the biggest challenges are working out when to seize those moments to just stop and enjoy things. Having a child who excels in something is the 'dream problem' for a parent, but it can also be overwhelming, isolating and challenging. People have said about me: 'Oh, it's okay for her, she's a coach.' But I wasn't a coach when this all began. I was just a mum who liked playing tennis with her friends: it was my source of community, of solace, of fun, not my career. There have been many times when it has been a hard, lonely journey for me.

But the underlying critical factor, for all of us, has been that we love what we do. You simply could not do this job, in any capacity, if you didn't. And such a huge part of loving your sport is the positive associations you make as a child, which is why I am so passionate now about getting young kids, especially girls, into the game. It's mostly a solo sport, but all sport is really about people and relationships. You have to enjoy spending time with the people you train with, and who work and travel with you day in, day out. Winning alone is never enough.

What most people see when they watch a top player on the court is the performance. Nobody sees what goes into making that performance. It's like seeing a finished film: the casting decisions, the script rewrites, the rehearsals, the green screen effects, they miss all of that. Just as you need a good director no matter how huge your budget, you need the emotional resilience to survive in tennis, because big shots alone will never be enough.

When I look at Jamie and Andy and their careers now, or when I look back at my own, I think of the story of the old Scottish king Robert the Bruce, and the spider. Defeated in battle so many times by the English in the fourteenth century that he has all but given up hope, Robert the Bruce lies down in his cave and sees a spider above him, trying to weave her web. Over and over, the spider tries to throw her thread from one edge of the cave wall to the other, but it's just not working. Just as Robert the Bruce starts to feel a sense of kinship with the spider, she throws the thread again, and this time has success. Galvanised, Bruce tries again, too, and soon his battle – the Battle of Bannockburn – is won.

There are few competitors who embody the spirit of trying and trying again until they work out the route to success more than Jamie and Andy. At times, it was an almost impossible slog for all of us. But we are far more likely to keep trying if we enjoy the challenge. If there were any legacy I could leave beyond those boys, it would be to foster a love of tennis, sport and activity in as many of us as possible. Because we can all be the spider, if we are all given the opportunity to discover what we truly love, and believe it is worth fighting for.

INDEX

John Menzies, 23
Junior Dunlop Maxply, 5–6
Junior Player of the Year, 142–6

K
Kensington, London, 10, 16, 17
Keothavong, Anne, 200, 205, 206, 232
Keys, Madison, 253
Klitschko, Wladimir, 186
Konta, Johanna, 203

L
Lampard, Frank, 184
Lapentti, Nicolás, 187
Largs, North Ayrshire, 10
Lawn Tennis Association (LTA), 51
    Baron's Court HQ, 105
    Coach Education Programme, 102
    Draper, Roger, 184
    and Enfants de la Terre tournament
        (1996), 69–72
    and Fed Cup, 207
    and French Open, 102–3
    and GB Under 14s team, 66
    girl's squad, 16
    and Miss-Hits, 212
    and Murray, Andy, 106–10, 184, 186
    and Murray, Jamie, 88–93, 104, 106
    National Tennis Centre, Bisham
        Abbey, 70, 83–8
    and Olympic Games, 226
    Performance Coach Award, 52–60
    Petchey, Mark, 154
    Under 10s, talent spotting of, 59, 61
    and US Open Juniors (2004),
        135, 137
    and Wimbledon, 160
Leicester City F.C., 42
lemon iced doughnuts, 229
Lendl, Ivan, 222–4, 226–7, 233, 251–2
Lendl, Samantha, 223
'Let's Go Fly a Kite', 247

Lightbody, Ellinore, 33, 66
lingerie, 26
Lloyd, Scott, 96
lob shots, 219
London, England
    Baron's Court, 105
    Battersea Dogs Home, 225
    Guildhall, 257
    Hyde Park, 233
    King's Cross, 10, 17
    Olympic Games (2012), 214, 220,
        225–6
    Queen's Club, Kensington,
        10, 16, 17
    Southfields, 172

M
MacDonald, Alan, 73, 132, 136
Maclagan, Miles, 189, 194
Majorca, Spain, 102
Manchester United F.C., 48
Marks & Spencer, 143
Mary Poppins, 104, 247
Matthew, Catriona, 204
Mauresmo, Amélie, 251–3, 255
McDonald's, 257
McHugh, Caroline, 214–5
McKellen, Ian, 161
media
    and Andy, 137–8, 153, 156, 163–70,
        194–5, 239, 256
    and Jamie, 167–8
    and Judy, 157–63, 168–70, 194–5,
        214, 229, 235–40
Melbourne, Victoria, 200,
    227, 237; see also Australian
    Open
Members enclosure, Wimbledon, 161
Miami, Florida, 78–81, 98–101, 128
Middleton, Laura, 210, 211, 232
Midland Bank primary school
    championship, 39